D1472781

To aid you in developing your membership plan,
all worksheets in this book are available FREE on-line.

If you would like to download electronic versions
of the worksheets, please visit

www.josseybass.com/go/ellisrobinson

Thank you,
Ellis Robinson

THE NONPROFIT
MEMBERSHIP
TOOLKIT

THE NONPROFIT MEMBERSHIP TOOLKIT

ELLIS M. M. ROBINSON

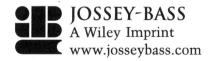

JOSSEY-BASS
A Wiley Imprint
www.josseybass.com

Copyright © 2003 by John Wiley & Sons, Inc.

Published by Jossey-Bass
A Wiley Imprint
989 Market Street, San Francisco, CA 94103-1741 www.josseybass.com

The worksheets that appear in this book may be freely reproduced for educational/training activities. There is no requirement to obtain special permission for such uses. We do, however, ask that the following statement appear on all reproductions:

The Nonprofit Membership Toolkit by Ellis M. M. Robinson.
Copyright © 2003 by John Wiley & Sons, Inc.

This free permission is limited to the reproduction of material for internal organizational use. Systematic or large-scale reproduction or distribution (more than one hundred copies per year)—or inclusion of items in publications for sale—may be done only with prior written permission. Also, reproduction on computer disk or by any other electronic means requires prior written permission. Requests to the publisher for permission should be addressed to the Permissions Department, John Wiley & Sons, Inc., 111 River Street, Hoboken, NJ 07030, (201) 748-6011, fax (201) 748-6008, e-mail: permcoordinator@wiley.com.

Jossey-Bass books and products are available through most bookstores. To contact Jossey-Bass directly, call our Customer Care Department within the U.S. at (800) 956-7739, outside the U.S. at (317) 572-3993 or fax (317) 572-4002.

Jossey-Bass also publishes its books in a variety of electronic formats. Some content that appears in print may not be available in electronic books.

Library of Congress Cataloging-in-Publication Data
Robinson, Ellis M. M., 1952–
   The nonprofit membership toolkit / Ellis M. M. Robinson.
     p. cm.—(Chardon Press series)
Includes index.
  ISBN 0-7879-6506-5 (pbk.)
  1. Nonprofit organizations—Management. 2. Membership campaigns.
I. Title. II. Series.
  HD62.6.R63 2003
  658'.048—dc21   2003012154

Printed in the United States of America
FIRST EDITION
PB Printing   10 9 8 7 6 5 4 3 2 1

THE CHARDON PRESS SERIES

Fundamental social change happens when people come together to organize, advocate, and create solutions to injustice. Chardon Press recognizes that communities working for social justice need tools to create and sustain healthy organizations. In an effort to support these organizations, Chardon Press produces materials on fundraising, community organizing, and organizational development. These resources are specifically designed to meet the needs of grassroots nonprofits—organizations that face the unique challenge of promoting change with limited staff, funding, and other resources. We at Chardon Press have adapted traditional techniques to the circumstances of grassroots nonprofits. Chardon Press and Jossey-Bass hope these works help people committed to social justice to build mission-driven organizations that are strong, financially secure, and effective.

Kim Klein, Series Editor

For Willow, Olivia, and Allyson,

Robbie and Chris,

and future generations of activists and fundraisers

Contents

List of Worksheets and Exhibits

Worksheets

Exhibits

Preface

What this book can do for you

If you are like most people working for nonprofit organizations, you have way too much work to do and far too little time to do it. So why would you want to give some of that precious time to leaf through and perhaps even read the material that's in this book?

The most important reason to read this book is to make your life easier. Whether you are a board member of an all-volunteer organization, a harried executive director of a one- or two-person office, a development director who is trying to juggle all aspects of funding your organization, or the person whose responsibility is focused solely on membership, this book will help you learn from colleagues' experiences, incorporate time- and money-savings systems into your membership program, and avoid expensive mistakes.

This manual presents easy, practical ways to make the most of your time and resources in building your membership. The *Toolkit's* recommendations are based on the experiences hundreds of colleagues around the country have generously shared with me, as well as my own experience for more than twenty-five years as staff, board member, and consultant to local, regional, state, and national nonprofits.

The second reason to read this book is that members are your very best source of energy, expertise, influence, and financial support. In this manual you will find countless proven ideas for how to make the members you already have happier and more engaged in all aspects of your work. You'll also find ways to recruit new members and to build your group's influence, effectiveness, and constituency.

The third reason you need this book is because of two sobering statistics. As reported in *The New York Times* (June 9, 2002), the years of ever-increasing money from foundations and corporate giving programs are behind us. According to *Giving USA 2002: The Annual Report on Philanthropy for the Year 2001,* foundation grant-making increased 18.2 percent in 2000 over the amount given in 1999; following the precipitous downturn of the stock market in 2000, foundation giving increased only 5 percent in 2001—the smallest gain since 1994.

Similarly, the increase in giving by corporate foundations from 1998 to 1999 was 15 percent, reflecting the large profits seen during the dot-com boom; the following year, giving by corporate foundations increased only 2.6 percent, actually *less* than inflation.

Fortunately, no nonprofit needs to rely exclusively on foundation and corporate giving programs to fund their work. As *Giving USA* also reveals, year in and year out, individuals have been the strongest and most reliable supporters of nonprofit organizations. In 2001, individuals accounted for 83.5 percent of all funds donated to nonprofit organizations—and the record shows that they have held that predominance for many years.

This book will help you identify ways to make up losses of foundation or corporate funding and build the long-term, reliable, immediate source of funds, time, energy, and expertise that you need to make your group's work possible.

How to get the most out of this *Toolkit*

This manual is designed to help new groups begin a membership program and existing groups improve and upgrade their membership efforts. The *Toolkit* provides issues to think about as you launch and formalize your membership program, along with a step-by-step guide to implementation, appropriate for organizations at various stages of development—for example,

- Your organization is just starting up

- You are planning to initiate a membership program

- You are searching for better ways to organize the membership program you have

- You are hiring your first membership director or development director

Each chapter walks you through the theories and practice of managing your membership program. Narrative, checklists, worksheets, and exercises help you prioritize, schedule, and manage the many projects and activities that are involved in running an effective membership program. The *Toolkit* also serves as a useful "checkup" for existing membership programs to make sure your fundamentals are well established before incorporating more features.

After you've covered the basics in the earlier chapters, you may want to further build your effectiveness by incorporating one or more of the advanced techniques suggested in Chapter Twelve.

From zero to twenty thousand: this book is for you

The Nonprofit Membership Toolkit is written especially for small- to medium-sized social-change organizations, from those just starting up to groups with as many as (or hoping to have as many as) twenty thousand members.

Whether your group provides social services to your local community, promotes alternative transportation throughout your county, advocates for clean water and air at the state level, or promotes equal rights at the national level, this manual will help you retain the members you have and attract more. If yours is a local or regional organization, your ability to be in regular, personal contact with your members and prospects—along with your access to volunteers—allows you to take advantage of hands-on techniques that build on the trust and credibility that comes from being "neighbors" to your members and prospects.

Larger statewide advocacy groups and organizations seeking to influence national and international policies will find the *Toolkit's* systems-building recommendations, Chapter Ten's direct mail strategies, and Chapter Twelve's advanced techniques especially useful. Your access to staff, along with your ability to recruit from a relatively sizeable population, allow your organization to put the best mass communication techniques to work for its cause.

This *Toolkit* is directed primarily at advocacy groups: organizations that are seeking to convince elected and appointed policymakers to make changes for the public good. In my view, virtually every nonprofit has some role in advocacy, even if it is limited to convincing the county commissioners to approve the health clinic's capital budget. In the United States, every nonprofit group has a legal right to lobby and advocate for change; Chapter Fourteen discusses the limits and opportunities for lobbying inherent in your tax status. Whether your group is structured as a 501(c)(3), 501(c)(4), or has other nonprofit designation, you will find the procedures and examples highlighted in this *Toolkit* helpful.

Worksheets, checklists, and calendars

Throughout this book, you'll find a variety of aids designed to help you work through the strategic, management, and administrative questions that present themselves as you put together the best membership program for your organization.

Access these worksheets on-line. All of the worksheets in the *Toolkit* are available as blank Excel spreadsheets, complete with formulae, on the Jossey-Bass Web site, at http://www.josseybass.com/go/ellisrobinson. Feel free to customize these electronic versions to make them easier to use for your own specific situation.

Tell me what you like and what you don't like. I have developed these worksheets and checklists over the past fifteen years of membership work and ten years of teaching. Most of them I use at least monthly, many weekly, and some nearly every day. They have been improved over the years by suggestions and reworking by clients and class participants. And I'm sure they could be even better. If you have suggestions for how to improve them, or if you've created an even better worksheet, send me a note at EllisRobs@aol.com. Thank you.

Case studies and samples

One of the benefits of this book is an abundant collection of real-life examples of how membership professionals in your situation, or one similar to yours, have solved the problems that are presented to you every day. I am indebted to the many colleagues, friends, and their hosting organizations throughout North America who have allowed me to reproduce their success stories (and a couple of non-success stories) in this manual. These case studies and materials provide examples of how to put in place the theories and practices discussed in this book. I have learned much from these shared experiences, and I hope you will, too.

In that spirit, I encourage you to be generous with what you learn as well. Your competition for members is not your fellow nonprofit organization. Rather, it is the endless distractions of today's marketplace, the workplace, and life in general. The goal of this *Toolkit* is to help you work smarter and more effectively. Each of us can do that best by learning from each other, sharing our success stories, and avoiding the need to re-invent the wheel. As comedian Henny Youngman said, "There are no old jokes, just old audiences." This truism works to our advantage when it comes to membership. Find a buddy, find a colleague, get on the mailing list of organizations you admire, do what you can to learn from others, and apply what you learn to your program. Thanks to the generosity of hundreds of talented colleagues throughout North America, this book will give you a start.

What you'll find in each part of the *Toolkit*

Part One discusses the membership partnership and helps you explore how members can help your group achieve its program goals more effectively. It covers what motivates people to join organizations, how to develop benefit-focused messages, who is considered a member and for how long, and what members you need to attract to retain credibility and assure long-term success.

Part Two builds on the decisions you made in the previous section and helps you apply them—consistently and systematically—to managing the members you already have. *I highly recommend completing this section before you move to the recruitment section.* Even a group that is just initiating a membership program is likely to have some existing supporters who could qualify as members (and who probably already consider themselves members). Before you jump into adding new members—all of whom will need additional time and attention from you—be sure that your in-house programs for serving and communicating with your members are solid.

This part includes chapters on renewals, special appeals, acknowledgments, and integrating your membership message and partnership into all your organization's communications. Once you put this section's recommendations in place, you will be ready to incorporate membership growth into your organization. Better yet, this growth can now happen without alienating your current members, short-shrifting your new members, or burying you and your colleagues in unmanageable amounts of work.

Part Three discusses and compares the variety of tools that can be used by both all-volunteer groups and staffed organizations for attracting new members to your organization. It also provides detailed worksheets, checklists, and examples to help you decide which techniques will work best for which audiences and how and when to integrate them into your membership program. A number of success stories provide examples of how to plan, implement, and evaluate recruitment options.

Part Four includes specific examples of how to integrate the systems you have developed in the first three parts into a comprehensive, doable membership plan tailored specifically to the needs of your organization. It also suggests ways to encourage your members to increase their investment in your organization by becoming monthly givers, major donors, or remembering you in their will.

The resources that conclude this book offer more details on several of the recommended protocols and systems discussed in the *Toolkit.* These include listings of services and vendors I have found especially helpful; recommended books and other sources for more information; tools for managing membership records and finances, source codes, activities, and tracking forms; and copywriting tips for fundraising letters.

Don't try to do it all at once

One of the challenges for you, the reader, is how to choose among the many ideas in this book. Please keep in mind that no group has the perfect membership program and no one can put in place more than a couple of significant membership changes each year—and I'd limit that to just one, if it is a really big change.

I suggest reading this book to broaden your perspective on membership, identify some tips that can help you make your work easier and more productive, highlight some important next steps, provide a source for new ideas when you are ready to take the next step forward and, most important, give you a chance to congratulate yourself on steps you already have in place. As tennis champion Arthur Ashe has said, "To achieve greatness, start where you are, use what you have, do what you can."

You are your organization's most valuable membership asset

The goal of this *Toolkit* is to help you combine what you already know from experience about your membership program and what you can find out about your existing members with the strategic needs of your organization's programs in order to come up with a dynamite way to bring your organization the strength in numbers, savvy, expertise, influence, and in fundraising to make your community a better place.

Being a great membership manager does not require an advanced degree or any special scientific training, although a good grasp of numbers sure helps. What it does take is a clear understanding of who your members are, why they like your organization, a passion for details and "customer service," a personal enthusiasm about the importance of your organization's work, and a dedication to making change for the better.

As the person working most closely with your group's membership program, you are the one who will set the tone for how members are treated by your organization. You will determine, to a great extent, how clearly each member can make the connection between their participation and the mission of the organization. You will create the procedures for communicating with members to spread your message. Inherent in each of those activities are the values and respect your organization will transmit to each member and prospect.

This book is designed to help you create the most effective framework for managing, maintaining, and attracting members to your organization. Here you will find countless examples and the fundamentals to help you with your decisions. But ultimately, you're in charge. Let's get started.

Sanibel, Florida   Ellis M. M. Robinson
May 2003

Acknowledgments

This *Toolkit* would not have been possible without the generosity, experience, and encouragement of hundreds of individuals. Although I can never thank every contributor personally—each client and workshop participant over the past fifteen years has had a hand in the learning included here—there are several people who deserve special recognition and appreciation.

This book began with the commitment and confidence of those colleagues who shared the vision for an Intensive Membership Development Program. Many thanks to Ann Krumboltz and the Brainerd Foundation, Tim Greyhavens and Wilburforce Foundation, Dyan Oldenburg and TREC (Training Resources for the Environmental Community), and Kathleen Beamer and David Jayo of REI (Recreational Equipment Inc.).

REI also provided a generous grant that made it possible for me to take time off to write this *Toolkit*. Thank you to the Environmental Support Center for serving as fiscal agent. And thank you to my clients for their patience during my writing retreats.

My hat goes off to mentors Horace "Huffy" Huffman Jr., Don Trantow, and David Burwell, who trusted me in new, exciting jobs that helped me learn and grow more than I thought possible.

Talented professional colleagues-as-friends have taught me much, allowed me to benefit from their expertise, and encouraged me throughout this process: Sal Canino, Karen Curr, Dan Drais, Pat Frayne, Mary Humphries, Kevin Kasowski, Kirsten Lee, Becky Long, Gary MacFadden, Harvey McKinnon, Bob Moore, Jo Moore, Amy O'Connor, Chuck Pettis, Natalie Reeves, Lynn Robinson, Angel Rodriguez, Arlie Schardt, Steve Sullivan, Norm Swent, and others.

My clients have been generous with their time, trust, and support. It has been a joy to have the privilege to work with many of the groups featured in this *Toolkit* and with dedicated fundraisers Brad Aaron, Jodi Broughton, Barbara Culp, Andrew Davis, John Dendy, Liz Edrich, Susan Elderkin, Megan Graham, Susy Levin, Tracy Walczak-Lohman, Mark Redsten, Patty Renaud, David Wilkins, and others.

This *Toolkit* is filled with dozens of examples of great membership work. I am grateful to all those who shared their experiences, tracked down the statistics, and provided fresh samples—those included in this book, as well as the hundreds there was not room for.

I am especially honored to include examples by Susie Stephens, bicycling advocate extraordinaire and consultant to the Methow Conservancy, and Sarah Forslund, outreach director for Green Corps. Both of these energetic and dedicated women died tragically during the past year. The examples of their work here provide a small glimpse of the light they brought to the causes they championed and the friends and family they loved. They are missed.

The experts at Jossey-Bass and Chardon Press deserve the credit for making this book and the accompanying Web site readable and usable. My appreciation goes to Kim Klein, Stephanie Roth, Nancy Adess, Carolyn Uno, Johanna Vondeling, Allyson Brunner, and the others who pushed, prodded, wordsmithed, and polished my just-in-time deliveries.

My friends have been an inspiration and source of constant encouragement throughout the learning and writing process, especially Lisa Black, Susan Eder, Elaine Schaeffer, my fellow island Zontians, and Northwest tea ladies Arlene, Barbara, and Gayle.

To my family—Nancy, Susan and Rob, Donna and Gerry, Ben and Laura, Eli and Amanda—thank you for keeping me smiling.

Finally, my heartfelt thanks go to the three people to whom I owe the most. My mother, Mary V. Robinson, taught me everything I know about organizing, beginning with backyard fairs at age five. My father, Ellis F. Robinson, taught me to love language, learning, and figuring things out. My husband and business partner, Dick Mark, gave me the confidence to tackle this project and the support (and ample supplies of chocolate) to complete it. Thank you now and always for your strategic insights, your political acumen, our inspired rants, your unending encouragement, and the chance to live and work together in paradise. What a wonderful life!

E.M.M.R.

About the Author

Ellis M. M. Robinson has more than twenty-five years' experience in membership development, fundraising, and nonprofit management. Her experiences range from executive director of a small, local nonprofit to director of administration and development of a national organization. She has helped found more than a dozen groups and businesses, and has volunteered on boards of directors of local, state, and national organizations. Highlights include increasing the membership of Northwest Ecosystem Alliance from 1,500 to 6,000, of Alaska Wilderness League from 600 to 12,000, and of Rails-to-Trails Conservancy from 400 to 60,000.

Ellis is now president of The Buttonwood Partnership, a consulting firm working with nonprofit groups nationwide to develop and strengthen membership programs and assure long-term strategic and funding success. The Buttonwood Partnership, founded as Access Marketing in 1990, has provided services to more than five hundred local, state, and national organizations.

A talented trainer, Ellis's presentations and training sessions have been sponsored by Alaska Conservation Foundation, the Environmental Support Center, Land Trust Alliance, Training Resources for the Environmental Community (TREC), Seattle Direct Marketing Association, Island Institute, Non-Profit Direct Marketing Association, Island Press, and others.

THE NONPROFIT
MEMBERSHIP
TOOLKIT

PART ONE

Integrating Membership into Your Organization

The most successful membership organizations are those that acknowledge and embrace members as an integral part of their operation and purpose. Such a partnership builds a sustainable bond between your organization and your members, creating the loyalty and mutual respect that lead your members to contribute time, expertise, and funding critical to your group's continued success. Whether your nonprofit is just beginning to explore the notion of recruiting members or already has a membership program in place, the chapters in this section will help you affirm and formalize the importance of members to achieving your organization's mission.

Chapter One introduces the concept of a membership partnership and outlines how to integrate membership into your organization in ways that enhance both your group and the members' experience.

Chapter Two recommends several organization-wide exercises for reaching consensus on your membership priorities and message.

Chapter Three covers who is considered a member, for how long, and what members you need to attract to retain credibility and assure long-term success. These exercises help you create a logical, program-based system for managing your members. This chapter also helps you and your leadership develop consistent, resonant membership messages.

The fundamental decisions and systems described in these three chapters create the basis for actions in the rest of this *Toolkit*.

CHAPTER 1

Introduction: The Membership Partnership

In the best membership programs, the member and the organization share a clear, mutually beneficial understanding of the benefits of membership to both parties. Practically speaking, this means that everyone on your team—your board members, staff, and key volunteers—can explain why members are fundamental to the success of your organization. Members, too, can identify how their involvement contributes to your group's success and, just as important, how that support makes a difference.

This chapter will help you create a culture within your organization that will ensure that these definitions agree, are complementary, and are embraced by all parties. By clarifying the role of members within your organization, along with your expectations of them and your promises to them, you can build member loyalty and involvement and receive greater financial stability from their increased support.

Better still, by developing an intentional membership program like the one outlined in this book, your organization will be more effective in the pursuit of its mission. A thoughtful, integrated membership program helps your group create a dedicated, engaged cadre of constituents who are willing to speak out and invest time and energy to help make the changes your organization is working for.

Why call them members?

As you've probably noticed, I am partial to the term *member* to refer to individuals who are givers, joiners, supporters, or donors to your organization. There are two reasons for this bias.

First, I think the term *member* connotes a personal connection with your organization, a shared ownership. In some cases, in fact, this is the legal meaning of the word. In Canada, for example, and with some organizations in the United States, there are specific distinctions between members of an organization and donors to an organization, wherein only members have voting privileges. In the United States, the voting members of the organization are also the legal governing members of that organization. (In most nonprofit organizations in the United States, the legal members—the voting members—are the board of directors only.)

In my experience, this kind of legal voting power is not necessary when building a loyal cadre of members. What is important is creating a culture within your group that treats your supporters respectfully and engages them in your programs, activities, and decision making. Most members aren't looking for a vote; instead, they're looking for a way to create community and to have an impact on the very real issues that affect them and their loved ones. When you create this atmosphere within your organization, your members will reward you with loyalty, involvement, and donations.

The second reason I prefer the term *member,* especially instead of the term *donor,* is that most organizations desire member participation beyond simply a checkbook relationship. If you are looking for involvement from your supporters in ways that include volunteering, political activity, expertise, and influence, acknowledge their role with the honor and privilege of the term *member* rather than *donor.*

Define why you need members

Here are some possible reasons that you need members to fulfill your organization's mission, goals, and activities:

• *Credibility.* The number of members, as well as their characteristics, can reinforce the validity of your group. For example, a group seeking to improve the quality of life for coastal fishing communities may count among its members people who work there, people who vacation there, and even people who have moved away but still feel a connection to the place. However, if the group is to be credible in its work, its membership *must* include a significant number of current residents of those coastal communities, as well as fisherfolk.

• *Political influence.* An advocacy group that is seeking to influence government decisions needs to include among its members representative constituents of the local, state, or national officials who must act if your work is to be successful. Effective influence can be gained by recruiting specific politically influential individuals or sheer numbers of people (critical mass) in a given electoral district.

• *Expertise.* Members can provide important knowledge and skills that could cost thousands of dollars for your group to purchase. Examples of such members include educators, scientists, lawyers, or accountants who may volunteer their talents for your group. Important expertise can also be place-based. For example, when the Rails-to-Trails Conservancy was founded, this nationwide trails organization depended upon its members to evaluate proposed railroad abandonments in their local communities and advise the Conservancy on the route's appropriateness as a future trail. In this case, members were asked to be where the organization staff could not be, serving as the initial researchers of possible projects for the group.

• *Outreach and validation.* Despite the ability of communications technologies to spread information wide and fast, word-of-mouth endorsements are still the most powerful builders of credibility and positive reputation. Perhaps the most powerful and effective affirmation—and membership recruitment tool—available is when a friend, colleague, or relative tells a prospect, "I'm familiar with that group, I trust them, and I joined because they are working on issues that make a difference in my life."

• *Volunteer time.* Members are often an invaluable source of person-power to help you accomplish your work. While members provide you with donated hours, volunteering provides members with the chance to meet people who share their values, learn more about an issue they care about, give back to the community, and have fun!

• *Financial stability.* Once convinced of the worthiness of your group, members can be counted on to give financial donations consistently, often increasing the size and frequency of their gifts over time. Moreover, members are far more likely to give you money than are foundations or corporations. According to the annual sourcebook *Giving USA 2002,* individual giving is the largest source of support of nonprofits, accounting for 83.5 percent of all funds donated in 2001. In addition, unlike corporate or foundation grants, gifts from individuals can usually be given quickly and repeatedly. Members are also your best source of major donations and bequests. Existing members are much more likely to give a sizable gift or to remember your group in their will than are unfamiliar, "cold" prospects. (See Chapter Twelve for more on upgrading member donations.)

Why people join organizations

There is a reason that I put "financial stability" last in the preceding list. Consider your personal checkbook for a moment. Are you at a loss for what to spend your hard-earned money on? Do you carry a large balance at the end of every month because you just don't have anything rewarding to buy?

If you are like most of us, the answer is an emphatic "No!" Instead, you are probably juggling too many required payments with too little income—and a long list of things you would like to spend money on when you end up with a little left over at the end of the paycheck.

The reality is that few folks are contributing to your organization now, or might be inspired to contribute to it in the future, just because they are looking for someplace to donate. Rather, your most loyal and generous supporters are investing in you because your organization offers them a way to fulfill a specific need or goal in their life. Your goal is to figure out why they care about your work.

What makes membership in your organization compelling and rewarding? Here's a simple exercise to help you better understand your members' motivations.

First, take a moment to write down each organization that you belong to. Your list might include your daughter's PTA, your church, your alumni association, the local rape crisis center, your state environmental organization, or your community political club, as well as national nonprofits.

Looking at this list, identify exactly why you joined each of these groups. Just jot down the first reasons that come to mind. This exercise helps illustrate that you understand why people join organizations, because you have made the decision to join at least as many times as there are organizations on your list.

Ask your group's board and staff members to make these lists as well. Then, count up the total number of organizations joined by your participants and compile the reasons people gave for why they joined. What patterns do you see?

When I do this exercise with my classes, we find that the reasons for joining are pretty consistent. Here are the top reasons people usually give for joining an organization:

- ***The mission of the organization.*** This isn't much of a surprise. However, when we look at where we spend much of our energy in our membership programs, selling the mission does not often figure. How many times, for example, have you talked about other ways to beef up membership services—what kind of premiums you should offer, how long your newsletter should be, whether you should be giving membership cards? Though these are valid questions, when you think about the most important reason people join your organization, it is invariably because of *why* you do what you do. It is because you are helping your members make a difference on an issue that matters to them and their family. When you focus your membership work and your messages on your mission, the rest becomes secondary.

- ***To have a sense of community.*** As the world's population moves towards seven billion people, the Internet, CNN, and newspapers and magazines on every topic imaginable bring that world to our front door. Most of us feel a need to find a personal place where we can connect safely with others who share our values, where we can build trust and be comfortable. This is about people's desire to be with people who are like them, and it's about finding a realm in which you as an individual can make a difference. Your organization has the opportunity to create that safe place for your members, and if you do, they will become more loyal and more connected—and your organization will be more successful.

• *Representation.* Today, our lives and livelihoods are governed by decisions made locally, county-wide, regionally, statewide or provincially, nationally, and even internationally. It is virtually impossible for one individual to affect all of the agencies and elected officials that have some power over one's life. That's why your organization's ability to represent your members' interests before elected and appointed decision makers is such a benefit to the individual. Many of your members may think to themselves, "Sure, I know I should go testify at that public hearing next week, or I should write a letter to my state legislator, or I should make a phone call to the local councilperson about this issue that I care about. But the reality is that I'm working, I have children to care for, the dog is sick, or the car broke down, I have rent payments to make, and my life is already too full and getting more so. It's also downright intimidating to talk to government officials. I really don't want to embarrass myself." These are just some of the reasons that many of your members probably value your work as their spokesperson and find their membership worth the investment.

• *Information and education.* Ten years ago, our lives were already filled with more information than we could possibly process. And that was before the Internet. Author David Shenk estimates that "one weekday edition of today's *New York Times* contains more information than the average person in 17th-century England was likely to come across in an entire lifetime" (David Shenk, *Data Smog: Surviving the Information Glut.* New York: HarperCollins, 1997). With so much information out there, it's just not possible for most of us to keep on top of all the issues we care about. That's another reason that people come to your organization. Your organization's job is to help your members better understand the issues that affect their life and livelihood. You help your members to be knowledgeable and responsible through your newsletter, special reports, special appeals, e-mail updates, and other kinds of information services.

• *Empowerment.* Most members value their nonprofit organization because it is bringing about social change on issues they care about. In addition to representation and information, your members want to be part of a successful effort that is larger than themselves. When you offer volunteer opportunities for members to help deliver program services, when you provide tips on how and when to write a letter to the editor or attend a public meeting, when you coordinate a lobby day to the state capital, your organization empowers your members to make a difference beyond what they could do alone.

- *Other direct services.* Members also join because of services you provide to them or to people they care about. This is especially true for health and human service organizations. The parents of an asthmatic child, for example, may join the American Lung Association to receive medical advice, discounts on treatments, and camp privileges for their son; new immigrants may join a local community center to enroll in English-as-a-second-language classes; young families may join the nearby zoo or nature center for inexpensive entertainment for their preschoolers.

- *I was asked.* In the grand scheme of things, this is arguably the most important of all of the reasons for joining. Your organization can have all the other benefits—a compelling mission, a great community, understandable information, valuable direct services, and capable, talented representation. However, if you don't ask them—and make it easy to respond—people won't join.

Thinking like a member

Throughout this *Toolkit,* I will ask you to return to these lists of why you and others join organizations and to remember what motivated your decisions to join. The more often you can put yourself in the position of acting and thinking like a member, the more you will be able to assure the success, continuity, and continuation of your membership program.

Moving from prospect to member

Let's look at how a prospect—someone who is not yet a member of your organization, but who you think should be—makes the decision to become a member (see Exhibit 1.1).

- *Perceived need.* Your prospect must first identify a need in their life that your group can fulfill. This is pretty basic. For example, the most likely people to join the local animal welfare league are those who agree that cats, dogs, and other animals being healthy and safe is valuable and will provide a worthwhile benefit to their life.

Even more important, the prospect must agree that meeting this need is probably not something she or he can accomplish alone. Part of advancing from the first step of identifying the need to the action of joining a group is acknowledging that this life goal can best be achieved by being part of a group. This is one reason that the most likely future members of your group are folks who are already members of at least one other group. They already have made the decision at least once that more effective change can be made by working together than by operating alone.

- *Familiarity.* Your prospect must know who you are. Though this sounds relatively simple, the competition is stiff for your prospect's attention. In his book

7. Opportunity

I have a convenient way to join now.

6. Perceived Urgency

I must take action now!

5. Believability

I understand and share your organization's objectives
and agree that they can be accomplished.

4. Credibility

I perceive that your organization has the history, leadership,
and other credentials needed to be accountable.
I trust you to do good work.

3. Common Values

Your organization is made up of or otherwise relates to "people like me."
I feel we are on the same wavelength;
we have enough common ground to consider a relationship.

2. Familiarity

I've heard of your organization before.

1. Perceived Need

This issue affects my life.
My world will be a better place if this issue is acted upon.

EXHIBIT 1.1.
Moving from Prospect to Member: A Decision Ladder

This decision ladder illustrates the steps a prospect usually goes through before making the decision to join an organization. Actions start with the most basic actions at the bottom of the ladder and progress to the top.

Data Smog, author David Shenk estimates that the average American is subjected to more than three thousand marketing messages a day. For yours to come through, make sure that your messages are clear, concise, and consistent. If your organization has a name that is confusing, is known by several different names, or otherwise is not clear in its identification, now is the time to choose one strong way to refer to your group and use it consistently. Chapter Two provides tools for creating the most powerful messages for your members and other constituencies.

- **Common values.** Because one of the strengths of membership is its offer of community, your prospect must be made to feel like "one of the gang." Before making the decision to join, your prospect must be convinced that she is among people who share her values, and that she is going to fit in. You can accomplish this in many ways. If you embrace people of all ages, make sure your promotional materials include pictures of young, old, and in-between. If you are trying to develop statewide appeal, make sure you highlight activities in several communities. If you anticipate a barrier, address it right up front. For example, the Bicycle Alliance of Washington didn't want prospects to think that only experienced cyclists qualified as members. So they listed their board members down the left side of their new-member appeal letter and identified them by their biking habits ("Weekend Rider," "Daily Commuter," "Recreational Rider," "New Parent, Riding Less"). Just about anyone who enjoyed any kind of bicycling could find a compatriot in this group and see that the group has fun, too.

- **Credibility.** You must be a trustworthy organization. You are asking your prospect to invest money, time, and trust in your organization. You owe it to him to demonstrate that you are accountable and reliable. Ways to do this include listing past accomplishments, documenting your history ("Founded in 1976"), using a street address instead of a post office box, underscoring that you use donations efficiently and responsibly, and referring folks to your Web site for more information, including financial data. Your board or advisory committee list can be helpful in establishing credibility as well, especially if your list includes known and trusted leaders of your community.

- **Believability.** Your goals must be realistic. This is sometimes a tricky balance. The excitement and energy that is created around a BHAG (Big Hairy Audacious Goal) can often be attractive but, frankly, not very believable if your prospect doesn't know much about your group. How to climb past this step in the ladder? Cite past successes. Or break your big goal down into manageable steps; show you have a strategy that will work. Also, be forthright about factors that might make a prospect nervous. For example, when Northwest Ecosystem Alliance proposed to raise $14 million to protect lynx habitat in Washington's Loomis State Forest, they had never raised a budget of even $500,000! So, they broke the goal into bite-sized pieces ($50 protects one-tenth of an acre) and got a commitment from the landowner up front that they could protect as much land as they could raise money for, even if they didn't reach their entire goal. (They reached their goal and more by attracting more than five thousand new members to support the campaign.) You and your team know what aspects of your work keep you up nights. Your prospects (and members) are savvy, too. Let them know that you have thought about the potential stumbling blocks and have a way to address them.

- *Perceived urgency.* Tell the prospect why action is needed now! With those three thousand or more marketing messages spinning past your prospect every day, you want to make sure that, when you *do* get his attention, he is compelled to act now and not put your request in the pile of things to do later. Perhaps the state legislature is going to be considering a key bill soon and his voice will count. A food bank or homeless shelter might be stocking up for the holidays. The PTA or Friends of the Library is preparing for the new school year. Tell the prospect why his membership now will make a difference—and, better yet, invite him to become more involved and take an additional action to aid that deadline (sign a petition, volunteer as a mentor, come for a hike along a threatened river) as well as sending a gift.

- *Opportunity.* Make it easy for the prospect to respond. The more ways you can make it possible for the prospect to join, the more likely it is to happen. Here are the basic steps: (1) Provide a return envelope in your mailing. (2) Always list your Web site and e-mail address. (3) Make sure there is a way for people to leave phone and e-mail messages anytime—and create a reliable system for responding to them daily! Here are some advanced techniques: (1) Consider using a toll-free phone number. (2) Take credit cards and invite faxed-back responses. (3) Insert a remit envelope into your newsletters (see samples in Chapter Six) so that, when the word-of-mouth "advertisement" happens—when a friend stops by a member's house to pick up the kids for soccer and leafs through your newsletter—the prospect can respond easily.

Define why your organization needs members

How you define your group's membership partnership is a two-way street: it must be compelling and worthwhile to both your group's mission and to the individual from whom you are seeking support. Consider scheduling a discussion on the partnership aspect of membership at an upcoming board meeting. Involve staff (if you have them) in the discussion. As an alternative, make this an agenda item for your development or membership committee or your membership and program staff.

First, divide into groups of four to six people. Start your small-group discussion by asking participants to share their own rewarding membership experiences. Designate someone in each group to take notes and report back to the larger group. Ask each participant to identify one membership organization they belong to, then explain what attracted them to that organization. They should talk about what made this such a rewarding membership experience, whether they were involved in any way other than supporting the group financially, and how they were treated by the organization. They should also describe the benefits of this membership involvement to them personally. After each person has

Membership Strategy = Program Strategy

This worksheet is designed to help your organization document how members help accomplish your mission, what your needs and expectations of members are, and ways to create an organizational culture that attracts and retains these members.

Complete this form independently, then share it with your staff and board colleagues to develop a common understanding and commitment to members.

List upcoming program milestones and anticipated accomplishment dates:

Year _____: _____

Year _____: _____

Year _____: _____

Year _____: _____

Year _____: _____

How could members help you successfully accomplish these milestones?

What characteristics, talents, or skills will be most valuable for these members to have?

Location? _____

Knowledge? _____

Skills? _____

Other? _____

What specific tasks and activities would you like members to perform and when? Define the value and benefit of each contribution to both your group and the member.

Time: _____ Task: _____

Value: _____

_____

Time: _____ Task: _____

Value: _____

_____

Time: _____ Task: _____

Value: _____

_____

Considering the culture of your organization, list the values and attitudes that your organization will extend to members in recognition of their involvement.

Our Membership Partnership: Draft a statement that links the success of your organization's mission with your hoped-for role, responsibilities, and involvement of members. Share these among your colleagues and develop an organization-wide promise to guide your recruitment of and treatment of members within your group.

spoken, the small group should identify common themes and share them with the larger meeting.

Building on this discussion, move to the specifics of your organization. Who does your group need as members to help achieve success, and when do you need them? Worksheet 1.1 may help you grapple with these issues. (Blank versions of all worksheets are available on-line at www.josseybass.com/go/ellisrobinson.)

Ask each participant (board or staff member or key volunteer) to complete Worksheet 1.1. Then, discuss responses with the rest of the group. If your group is sizeable, you might want to do this step back in your small groups. Finally, develop a consensus statement that all your stakeholders can agree with. Use this to guide the way your organization communicates and responds to prospects and members.

The next chapter will help you confirm these decisions with your existing members.

CHAPTER 2

The Benefits of Membership

In Chapter One you specified why your organization wants members and learned what steps a prospect takes to make the decision to join your group. This chapter will help you discover those magic words that will motivate your prospects to join.

Here's great news: All you have to do is ask the folks who have already made that decision (your existing members) to tell you what motivated them to join. If you don't already have members, you can use the techniques given here to gather this information from the people already involved with your organization—founders, board members, supporters—who are most likely to become members.

Finding out what really matters: conducting a membership survey

If you have not already conducted a membership survey, put one in your work plan now. If your last membership survey was more than three years ago, it's time to do an update. Your membership survey can be as complicated as mailing a questionnaire to each of your existing and past members, or as simple as calling twenty-five of your members and asking them three or four questions. The primary purpose of this survey is to understand the "whys" around your members' commitment to your organization.

There are lots of good resources to help you develop and analyze your membership survey. Rather than cover this topic in great detail here, I offer the following tips, some samples, and a planning worksheet.

My thanks to Chuck Pettis, President of Brand Solutions, for his extensive help with this chapter.

Tips for membership surveys

Here are some general tips on designing a membership survey, followed by some specific types of information you might like to collect.

- *Explain why respondents' answers will make a difference to your group's success.* You are asking your members to give up their valuable time. Explain to them that their responses will directly improve your organization's effectiveness by informing your planning process, helping you to prioritize future projects, or aiding your ability to build your numbers and visibility, for example. Note that membership survey responses are always advisory; they do not constitute a vote. Your members trust you to know best when it comes to issues; otherwise, they wouldn't support you. Survey responses give you the information you need to communicate about your work as effectively as possible.

- *Only ask for information you can truly put to good use.* For example, I recommend against asking about income; it's not necessarily a determinant of how much someone will give, and the question is often perceived as invasive.

- *Balance multiple-choice questions with fill-in-the-blank requests.* The former can provide comparable, objective data; the latter give you value-based statements written in the member's own words (subjective data).

- *Determine if there are comparable data elsewhere.* Comparable data (for example, from census or other government records or your or others' past surveys) will help you determine how your membership resembles and differs from that of other similar organizations or the population as a whole, or how it has changed over time.

- *Try to keep your questionnaire to two pages.* If you must make it longer, explain how long it will take to complete and, again, how valuable the responses will be.

- *Pledge to keep individual answers confidential—and keep that pledge.* This commitment does not prevent you from sharing compiled results of your survey or from quoting kudos (with permission).

Consider including the following questions in your survey. The first four questions provide invaluable verbatim responses that you may want to use in promotional materials later. If you are conducting your survey by e-mail or telephone and are limited by the number of questions, you can cover most of what you want to know with just these four.

1. Why do you support [name of organization]?
2. Please circle our three program areas that are most important to you. [Follow with a list of specific programs, as you refer to them in your newsletter and other communications.] Why are these most important to you?

3. What do you think is the greatest benefit of membership in [name of organization]?

4. Would you recommend membership in [name of organization] to a friend or neighbor? Please explain your answer.

The next three questions provide a glimpse of the member's lifestyle. Check comparable items such as age ranges elsewhere before you finalize this text. For example, if your county provides demographic information using the age range 20–29, use the same categories in your survey, to make sure you can easily compare the findings for your membership against findings for the general public.

5. How many adults live in your household? How many children under 18?

6. How long have you lived in [name of community or state]? [provide ranges]

7. Are you [provide categories such as the following] retired, working part time, working full time, looking for work, a full-time homemaker, a student?

The next four questions will help you find more people with characteristics that are similar to those of your members.

8. What magazines or periodicals do you subscribe to?

9. What other organizations do you belong to or support?

10. To which arts or sports events do you hold season tickets?

11. What is your postal code?

A word about anonymity

Give people the option at the end of the survey to tell you their name and contact information. Surprisingly, most people will give you this information because, if they support your organization with donations of time or money, they like the work you're doing and are happy to tell you the good things they're telling others about your group.

This willingness will turn out to be a great asset for you. You can then sift through the verbatim responses, go back to those who said glowing things about your organization and who gave their name, and ask for their permission to reprint those comments in your new-member prospecting piece, on your Web site, in your next brochure, or maybe in your annual report.

You should also ask your board and staff to take the survey. Their responses may be both different and instructive. Of course, your board and staff will likely have a greater knowledge of the organization than the membership as a whole.

More important, however, you may find that these insiders' priorities for the organization's work and the language they use to describe the organization—because they are so close to the issues and the day-to-day work of the group—are significantly different from the priorities noted and descriptive language used by your other members. By compiling board and staff responses as a separate subset from the membership as a whole, you may identify biases that may be influencing the effectiveness of your membership and communications effort. If you have a sizable staff, separate staff answers from those of the board.

How to learn the most from your membership survey

Worksheet 2.1 covers some of the other elements of designing a member survey, which include administrative issues and distribution and sampling issues. These last two issues will affect how many completed surveys you receive and from whom.

Two administrative issues need to be dealt with as you begin your survey project: who will be managing and analyzing the data, and who is on the survey production team.

• *Consider who will analyze the survey and how before you finalize the text.* Will it be interpreted by a board or staff member? A skilled volunteer? A statistics student looking for a class project?

• *Make sure you have the survey team in place.* One person may do more than one of the roles listed on the worksheet; for example, the project manager may also be the copywriter.

The "Distribution Method" section of the worksheet shows the typical response rates you can expect with different methods of getting your survey out to your members or supporters. The more personal the method, the higher the return.

Probably the most cost-effective method for distributing your survey is to use e-mail or a survey form based on the Web. Some groups have achieved response rates as high as 40 percent by distributing their survey through e-mail to their members. There are a few ways to do this. You can send a list of questions directly in an e-mail message and invite respondents to cut and paste their responses into a return message. You can e-mail an attachment or a hyperlink to your Web site or that of a service provider where readers can complete a survey on the Internet (see Resource A for a Web-based survey firm). An additional way of using e-mail is to send a reminder to folks to expect your survey in the mail, with a request to send it back.

The advantages of surveying by e-mail are speed, cost, and the fact that respondents will do their own data entry on subjective responses. The disadvantage of surveying by e-mail or through the Web is that most groups only have e-mail addresses for a small portion of their membership. This means that your responses risk being even more biased from the beginning. (Since the techniques suggested here all involve voluntary responses, your survey results will already be biased. However, since your most probable respondents are likely to be those most interested in your organization, this bias is not necessarily a drawback.)

Another disadvantage is that most people's e-mail address is at their workplace, where they may have limited time to respond to a survey. You may be able to counter their hesitation by noting early in your message that completing the survey will only take a few minutes.

To take advantage of the benefits of e-mail response rates and minimize the inherent biases, consider mailing your survey (by postal mail) to all your members and broadcasting an e-mail message to everyone you have an e-mail address for that the survey is on its way, their participation will make a difference, and that they can also complete the survey by e-mail (attached) or on-line.

At the other end of the response-rate spectrum is distributing your survey in a newsletter. Unfortunately, most organizations' newsletters are not action communications. If your household looks like mine, you have that pile of newsletters you're going to read sometime soon, and the pile just keeps getting bigger. If your membership survey is buried somewhere in that pile, it is easy to understand why response rates from newsletter-distributed surveys are so low. If you truly want to get a response to a survey and you're going to invest in a written one, also invest the money to mail it out separately.

Between these extremes of response rates are the various return rates you receive from stand-alone surveys. Depending on the audience you are most interested in hearing from and your ability and need to process data quickly, you may find that distributing a survey as a next-step involvement device for your members may be effective. For example, consider mailing your survey as a "Tell us more about you" device in your new- and renewing-member welcome packets. Although with this technique it will be a year before everyone has an opportunity to respond, your overall response rate will probably be higher than from a simple stand-alone survey, and you gain the added benefit of engaging your new and renewing members in an important task immediately.

If your focus is on collecting primarily qualitative information (those fill-in-the-blank questions), or if you need to obtain responses quickly and inexpensively, you may find that a volunteer phone-a-thon is a more effective and less biased method of collecting such information. This is a great task for members of your membership committee or even your board and staff. Recruit a group of colleagues, identify three or four questions you are interested in having answered, and start making phone calls. Ideally, the folks who are doing the interviewing can type responses and listen at the

Member Survey Worksheet

This worksheet is designed as a checklist and planning aid to help you and your colleagues conduct a successful membership survey.

Survey Production Team:

☐ Project manager: _____

☐ Copywriter: _____

☐ Editor: _____

☐ Reviewer(s): _____

☐ Designer: _____

☐ Other: _____

_____

Data Management & Analysis:

☐ In-house staff: _____

☐ Temporary hourly staff: _____

☐ Intern or volunteer(s): _____

☐ Other: _____

_____

Distribution Method: Date of Distribution: _____

☐ Stand-alone mailing (10—20% return)

☐ With special appeal (5—15% return)

☐ With renewal and new member welcome packet (20—35% return over a year)

☐ In newsletter (3—7% return)

☐ E-mail (5—40% return from limited audience)

☐ Phone interviews (10—20% overall return; 50% of connections)

☐ Other: _____

_____

Reminder/Follow Up?   ☐ No ☐ Yes: _____

Survey Segments:

☐ Geographic: _____

☐ Length of membership: _____

☐ Giving level or history: _____

☐ Activism/involvement: _____

☐ Other: _____

_____

Non-member Segments?

Notes:

same time. You want them to capture the exact phrasing that members use when they talk about your organization. This approach has the added advantage of allowing more than one person to be directly involved in the information gathering and in hearing the specific responses of your members. It also provides an opportunity for interaction with the respondent.

If you don't yet have members or have very few, this telephone technique is likely to be your best choice. Conducting a telephone survey can also be a great way to test a survey that you're going to be distributing to a larger group, as well as an effective way to collect reliable information in a hurry from a relatively small audience.

Similarly, a telephone survey can be a good way to engage a specific audience in decision making. Say, for example, you are interested in finding out how members in a specific neighborhood feel about one of your programs. A live, in-person survey allows the opportunity to engage these folks in your future planning and discussions about the program while also opening the door for a follow-up at the end of the conversation. For example, it would not be inappropriate to wrap up the interview with a close such as, "Thank you so much for your time and insights into this issue. Our group is in the process of putting together a task force to be involved in recruiting more people like you from your community to get involved in this program. Could we contact you in the future to help out on that project?"

You can even use a survey in a special appeal and cover some of the costs with the donations that come in. Here is an example:

For the past several years, Oregon Natural Resources Council (ONRC) has sent a holiday greeting from executive director Regna Merritt each December to their members. This mailing serves two functions. First, it provides a more personal format for ONRC to thank their members for their support during the previous year, in contrast to more formal appeals. Second, it provides a follow-up to their year-end special appeal, mailed each November.

In 2001, ONRC included a request in its December mailing for members to return an enclosed questionnaire "to help ONRC establish our priorities for the next five years." This approach turned out to be an effective way to meet two objectives simultaneously: collect member priorities and encourage contributions. In the survey, ONRC asked its members to select the top two benefits of the organization's work from among six options. The answers were used to inform ONRC's strategic planning process and guide priorities for the year ahead. Responses to other questions helped ONRC craft a strategy for more effective communication of its goals to members and non-members alike. The campaign also raised $12,118 ($9,279 net), from 137 responses (about an 8 percent return from regular members). This response was comparable to the return rates for this year-end campaign in 1999 and 1998 without the survey. The addition of the survey did not seem to reduce response to the special appeal.

Finally, consider identifying different segments of your membership in order to analyze their responses against each other. For example, do you wonder if your members differ in their priorities or motivations by length of membership, rural or urban location, east or west part of your region, level of activism, or giving levels? An easy way to segment written surveys is to print each segment on a different color paper. By asking for ZIP or postal code, you can identify geographic patterns.

Share and use your responses

Once your survey returns are received and analyzed, share a summary of the findings with your colleagues (board, staff, committees) and members. Include an article in your newsletter thanking members for returning the surveys and sharing what you learned.

The group Leave No Trace, an outdoor education organization based in Colorado, used survey responses to help shape their discussion of whether to revitalize their membership (which had been a low priority in the past) or to let it die a quiet death. In order to provide an opportunity for productive discussion on the merits of membership, they held a half-day workshop. In advance of the workshop, the membership manager asked each participant to review about thirty responses to Leave No Trace's recent membership survey and bring their impressions and conclusions to the workshop.

The resulting meeting was a major boost to Leave No Trace's membership program. Staff and board members were bowled over by the enthusiasm and insights of the members as shown in the survey responses. Some of the responses surprised them and challenged their assumptions about the value of membership. The fact that each colleague was involved in the evaluation and review of the survey assured collective ownership of the conclusions and recommendations that were based on the survey returns. As a result of this process, the organization decided to launch a major membership program.

Put your survey learnings to work

The responses you receive to your survey will help you and your colleagues understand, in your members' own words, why the work you do makes a difference in your supporters' lives. In addition to being a great morale booster to you and your colleagues, the answers you get will provide a treasure-trove of quotes and phrases that explain how your members talk about your work.

By adopting those same words and priorities in your communications, you reinforce the values and culture that your organization has already established (helping to keep the members you have) and make your group more credible and compelling to new prospects, helping them climb that ladder to joining.

Membership leads the message

In most organizations, the membership program is responsible for communication to perhaps your most important audience: your members. These are the people who are going to be supporting you financially, speaking of your group to their neighbors and friends, speaking on your behalf before government bodies, and otherwise sharing the work of achieving your program goals. It is imperative that the messages your members hear be compelling, consistent, and correct. The entire image of your group—your name, your message, your culture, and your values—is your organizational identity, what you might call your "brand."

The membership team or person is also responsible for membership recruitment and the messages and representation of your organization that go out to hundreds or thousands of prospects who should be interested in what you do but either don't know about you or haven't yet been convinced to join. If your group uses direct mail as a recruitment tool, it is likely that the membership program distributes more official communications (unfiltered by reporters or other go-betweens) to more members of your target audiences than any other part of your organization—and perhaps more than all the rest of your group combined. The tools outlined in the rest of this chapter will help you make sure that these communications are consistent and compelling as well.

However, developing these messages and finalizing other branding decisions are not tasks for the membership person or team alone. Rather, a successful branding campaign involves your board, staff, perhaps key volunteers, maybe some of your most loyal or generous members, and even other stakeholders. The reason so many branding campaigns are initiated by the membership person is that you often have the most immediate and tangible need for branding. But it will only work if everyone in your group participates in the process.

Emphasize the benefits, not the techniques

We spend a lot of time in the nonprofit business focusing on what are called the techniques. The techniques are *how* we do what we do—file lawsuits, attend public meetings, testify in front of elected officials or appointed bodies, comment on proposed government policies, respond to requests for information—rather than *why* we do what we do, which are the benefits of our work.

The *whys* usually relate directly to the purpose of your organization. For example, your benefit to current and potential members may be that you are working to protect the quality of life in your community or assuring a quality education for every child. The techniques you use to accomplish these goals include speaking out at public meetings, advocating for adequate budget levels, or training tutors.

Another nearly universally valued benefit of a nonprofit is action that directly improves the conditions of individuals' lives. The cancer camp that helps a child play normally for a week, the mentoring group that helps a first-generation immigrant learn to read, the international assistance organization that brings clean water to a refugee village—all these nonprofits provide a heartfelt and effective way for a member to make a difference in someone's life, which is the most powerful benefit of all.

As you read the verbatim responses to your survey, identify the themes. Chances are your members will tell, in their own passionate, powerful words, *why* they support what you do. Then, repeat these same themes (assuming they are accurate, of course) in your communications. Whenever you talk about what you do—that is, the techniques—remember to link those activities to the benefits that motivate your members.

Sticky stats

I use the term *sticky stats* to describe those statistics or comparisons that enhance your members' or prospects' ability to comprehend the magnitude of your issue and that reinforce the perceived need for action. Sticky stats are memorable pieces of information: they "stick" in the reader's or listener's mind. By citing a credible source for your sticky stat, you further reinforce its believability and power.

You can test the effectiveness of your sticky stats through your membership survey, focus groups, or the murmurs in the audience when your slide show presenters use them. If your example elicits a "Wow!" or "I didn't know that!" from your audience, you've probably found a sticky stat. Here are some examples of sticky stats:

• The U.S. Geological Survey estimates there is only enough oil beneath the Arctic National Wildlife Refuge to satisfy domestic energy needs for less than six months. Oil industry officials admit that it will take "in the range of ten years" before any oil from the refuge reaches U.S. markets. Are you willing to give up the natural treasures of the Arctic for maybe six months' worth of oil ten years from now? (*Source:* Alaska Wilderness League)

• The United States spends more money on weaponry than do the next nine countries combined, but it is the least generous of twenty-two advanced countries when it come to foreign aid dollars per capita. Just ten cents per person per year would double the U.S. investment in humanitarian foreign aid. (*Sources: New York Times,* Apr. 9, 2002, p. A31; Center for Global Development)

• If the U.S. Fish and Wildlife Service's proposal for sixteen manatee refuges and sanctuaries were adopted completely, without any changes, less than 1 percent of Florida's waters would come under these regulations. (*Source:* Save the Manatee Club)

Sticky stats can also be enhanced by your choice of measurements and metaphors. For example, one thousand square miles sounds like much less space than 640,000 acres. By using metaphors, you also enhance your audience's ability to visualize the problem you are outlining. Saying that a portion of the Antarctic ice shelf measuring 1,231 square miles broke off is impressive—but explaining that an iceberg the size of the state of Rhode Island broke away is definitely noteworthy and memorable.

Comparisons can also reinforce the power of your statistics, especially when they build on existing sources of pride or rivalries. For example, "Alabama and Georgia pay their teachers $6,000 more, on average, than does Florida."

Effectively modeled statistics can help your constituents understand the importance of your issues and give them easily remembered information to share with others. Plan to work with your team to draft, test, and adopt the most effective sticky stats for reinforcing your organization's goals and objectives—and attracting more members.

Create your elevator statement

Now that you know what motivates and inspires your members to invest in you, you have the tools to prepare a brief statement that everyone involved in your organization can use consistently to explain why your group is so great. Imagine you are in an elevator, heading for the eleventh floor. On the second floor, a local leader who is not yet a member of your group (but should be) gets on alone, also heading for the eleventh floor. You have the next twenty seconds—the time it takes to go from the second floor to the eleventh—to explain what your organization is and why she or he should care.

The purpose of your elevator statement is to provide a clear, compelling, concise, and consistent way for everyone related to your organization to talk about your group. By developing an elevator statement, you make sure that whoever is in that elevator—board member, staff employee, key volunteer—the message will be the same.

The elevator statement, also called a positioning statement, gives you a standard message to guide all your communications: your Web site home page, the final paragraph of news releases, your brochure and annual report framework, your public hearing introduction, and your other communications and membership materials. It is developed from what you learned from your membership survey, what's in your strategic plan, and other guiding documents.

As you can imagine, drafting a statement this fundamental and ultimately so powerful should involve all your leadership. One way to start is to hold a membership workshop, as Leave No Trace did, to discuss the future of membership for your group. One of the outcomes of Leave No Trace's session was a draft elevator statement and an agreement from participants on how the final version would be honed and approved.

Here are some samples to get you started on this important next step in enhancing and building your membership program:

- More than half a million abused and neglected children need homes each year. CASA volunteers work to find safe, permanent homes where these children can thrive.
- Washington Toxics Coalition protects you and your loved ones from pesticides and other toxic chemicals. Washington Toxics Coalition provides information on the least toxic solutions to everyday problems and advocates for stronger pollution standards. By joining the Washington Toxics Coalition, you will help protect our children's health, our water quality, and our ecosystems from pesticides, toxic waste in fertilizer, and other dangerous pollutants that accumulate in our bodies.
- For those who love super, natural British Columbia, its spectacular ancient forests, wild salmon, and wildlife, The Sierra Club of British Columbia is an organization committed to protecting B.C.'s wild lands and waters. As a champion for conservation, The Sierra Club of British Columbia provides responsible grassroots action and a voice backed by credible information, and serves as an environmental watchdog of industry and government.

Your elevator or positioning statement should become your organization's most repeated message. The positioning statement is your first answer in a media interview and your best answer to the question, "What does your organization do?" The choice and use of vocabulary here is very important. Choose your words carefully. Make your position as clear and straightforward as possible. We're in a sound bite world. People want short, concise, and clear statements that make sense and that they can remember.

Making your name work for you

Let's face it, nonprofit organizations have some of the worst names. Most are too long or sound like government agencies. Many use initials or nonsensical acronyms. Names are more memorable than initials. Furthermore, a recent study for a large corporation found that people are getting tired of initials and prefer names to be spelled out, not abbreviated. Therefore, avoid initials and meaningless acronyms. For example, don't be NPRC, be Northern Plains Resource Council, or Northern Plains for short.

If you have several different ways your organization is referred to, informally or formally, as well as initials that you use, you are asking your constituents to remember several names. One name is enough.

During your Membership Day workshop, list all the different ways your organization is referred to both formally and informally, internally and externally, including initials and acronyms. Come to consensus on the name that should always be used first (for example, Northern Plains Resource Council), and the name that should be used in the second and successive references (in this case, Northern Plains).

If you have a name that is confusing or too long, consider adopting a new name that is shorter and more memorable. A name change is also appropriate if your group's current (and future) program goals are not consistent with your name. For example, if you were founded as a local group and now operate statewide, your name may need to be updated to reflect your mission. Similarly, if your group was founded with programs for children but now serves all ages, it might be appropriate to reflect that family focus in your name.

Certainly, the decision to change your group's name should not be made lightly or without good, program-related reasons. However, my experience is that members and other constituents are much more open to a name change than are the staff and board. If you provide your members with a reasonable explanation of why a new name will help your group be more effective in delivering the benefits your members care about, the vast majority of them will support your new name. Just make sure you have a solid consensus among your board and staff before undertaking a re-naming project.

If you plan to conduct a major membership campaign, I strongly recommend you change your name before your launch, to minimize confusion among new recruits. Be sure to test alternative names and make sure the one you choose does not have negative or inappropriate connotations.

A final note: the findings of your membership survey and the other branding work described in this chapter are not intended to change your program activities or priorities. Rather, the results of your survey and branding decisions will help your group discover better ways to let your members and the public know that you are working on their behalf on issues they care about. Once your group is clear about who and what you are, you are more likely to attract the members, political influence, and other support you need to be most effective.

See Resource A for additional references on surveys, naming, positioning statements, and other organizational brand identity tips.

CHAPTER 3

Defining Membership in Your Organization

How many members do you have? In my workshops this simple question invariably elicits a variety of responses and no small amount of discussion. This chapter will help you establish systems and protocols for classifying membership and dealing with the details that complicate the process.

One of the wonderful things about membership development is that there are virtually no wrong answers. However, it is important to establish some protocols and agreed-upon understandings so that, as you move forward, you can measure progress, identify problems, and capitalize on opportunities as they present themselves. Finding an agreed-upon and consistent way for measuring your membership is a critical part of those protocols.

Once you have finalized these decisions, complete Worksheet 3.1, the Membership Benchmarks Worksheet, to document where your membership program stands today. By creating this snapshot of your membership and updating it regularly you can track your progress, target opportunities, identify any challenges or difficulties before they get out of hand, and provide a valuable myth-busting service for your group by clarifying the realities of your membership.

If you currently have no official members, understanding the specifics of membership now will enable you to set up a practical system before you begin.

What does it cost to be a member?

Most groups consider anyone a member who has joined by donating at a basic membership level or above. This will probably cover 80 to 90 percent of your supporters. The questions arise around those who fall outside the norm. For example, how do you classify people who send a donation, participate in a paid special event, or otherwise give you an amount equivalent to a membership donation in response to something other than a direct membership recruitment ask? In most cases, the donor perceives that she is supporting your organization whether she has responded to a new-membership appeal, given a gift through your Web site, attended an auction or dinner, or sent in a memorial gift. Honor each of these contributions with the benefits of membership in your organization.

You will also receive gifts that are below the threshold of your basic membership rate—gifts of five or ten dollars or even a dollar or two. How you handle these levels of contribution relates directly to why you have members. If your goal is to engage a broad, diverse, and representative portion of your community in your organization, then the amount someone is able to give shouldn't make too much difference in being designated a member. Rather, their willingness to invest something in your organization is more important than the amount that they invest.

You may be asking, "Why do we need to require payment at all for membership?" That's a good question. The first answer is simple: in addition to your members' personal energy and participation, your organization needs money to carry out its work and assure long-term success. The second answer is a little less simple: we live in a society that equates value—that is, measures worth—by the price one pays for something. For that reason, it's important for your members to take the step of investing in your organization. That investment could be $1, $10, $100, or $100,000. From a membership perspective, it's the act of investment that's important.

People often ask, "Well, it costs us more than a dollar or two to service our members." That may be true, if you allocate the cost of developing, printing, and distributing your newsletters and other benefits evenly across your membership. However, the incremental cost of adding one more member to your services is negligible.

It helps, too, to be aware that there are countless examples of donors whose initial contributions were at the low end who went on to become staunch supporters through their participation and later gifts. We know, for example, that many individuals will "check out" your organization with a small start-up gift. How they are treated, what they see as future benefits, and how effective you are at communicating the value and progress of your organization's work will often encourage those individuals to upgrade their gifts in the future and become involved as a volunteer, an advocate, or some other talented expert for your organization.

One of my favorite client stories is about a long-term, steady member who inexplicably reduced her contribution to $5 for three years. The organization continued to send her newsletters, action alerts, and other communications. After three years, the member called the membership director and asked to meet. She presented the following story:

> For the last three years my husband has been suffering with cancer. In order to cover our medical costs and the stress of dealing with his illness, we had to cut out just about everything. However, we were members of nearly twenty organizations and still wanted to be engaged as much as possible—my husband received so much value and joy from reading the organizations' materials. We cut each of those memberships to $5 apiece. Only three groups, one of which is yours, continued to stay in contact with us. My husband died a few months ago and I unexpectedly received a settlement on a life insurance policy that we'd forgotten we had. As a result, I've split that $75,000 life insurance policy three ways between you and the other two groups who continued to allow us to be involved in their organizations. Here's a check for $25,000.

Of course, there's no guarantee that your organization will have a similar experience with your below-entry-level donors. However, the downside of embracing those few individuals as full and welcome members is very small.

Another question that often comes up is, "Since these folks didn't say they wanted to be a member, maybe they don't want to be members and they would be offended by such involvement." If you are concerned that a donor may be offended by your presentation of membership, you can make it easy for them to opt out in the materials in your welcome packet. (See Chapter Four for a listing of materials to include in a welcome packet.) Let the contributor know that their action—attendance at a lecture series, donation at an auction, purchase of a publication, or payment of a registration fee for a conference—has entitled them to membership. Explain in your welcoming materials what they can expect from this membership. If an individual does not wish to be considered a member, you can be sure they will contact you and let you know. Meanwhile, people who you probably would not be able to reach any other way but who have had an encouraging and positive experience with your organization are now among your list of supporters and privy to your communications, updates, and other member services—as well as to further solicitations for donations.

Volunteers and activists should be members, too

Many organizations have a cadre of volunteers, activists, and other talented folks who give their time to help the organization reach its goals. Questions often arise as to whether these people should be required to be members as well. Again, there are no wrong answers.

Many organizations do require that volunteers be members in order to participate in their many activities. I am partial to this approach. It establishes volunteering as a membership benefit. It also makes sure that each of your volunteers is informed about the organization and has taken the very important action of investing money in your organization as well as time; should volunteers run across a prospective member while carrying out their volunteer duties, they will be more comfortable talking about the values of membership because they have made the decision to join themselves. (In terms of legal and liability issues, there may also be some value to requiring that your volunteers be members. Check with your insurance carrier to make sure that you have adequate coverage for volunteers and event participants.)

To further encourage connection to your organization, try to recruit your activists from among your members—and encourage non-member activists to join. Again, this assures that these individuals—who are often representing the organization before governing bodies—are also fully "invested" in your organization and its purposes. In addition, because they are members, you are assured they are receiving your newsletter and other critical communications, and are up to date on the positions of your organization and concerns of fellow members.

If your volunteers or activists are not members now and you want to bring them into the fold, one of the most effective ways of doing so is through a peer-to-peer ask. For example, invite one of your most active volunteers who is also a member to sign a letter to those volunteers who have not yet joined, encouraging them to join. Recruit one of your enthusiastic member-activists to make a recruitment pitch at the upcoming legislative planning or training session. Offer a special new-member rate for volunteers or activists. Follow up with phone calls, a personal e-mail, or a one-to-one invitation. The most important thing is to reinforce your appreciation for the individual's time and talents while communicating the value of membership and the importance of their investment.

How to define a current member

Often when an organization's leader is asked, "How many members do you have now?" the number they give is significantly more members than are currently active in the organization's database. Some of this may be wishful thinking, but a lot of it is based on remembrance of a past success that has not been sustained.

Our organizations are often blessed with a long-term memory among staff or board. This can help assure continuity for the organization, but it also can sometimes create unreal and unreasonable expectations of the membership person or team. That's why determining protocols for how to define a current member and regularly documenting how many current members you have becomes so important.

Again, there are no wrong answers to this question of how recently someone must have given to be considered a member. Consider your existing situation and protocols, the reasons your organization has members (see Chapter One), and determine what makes sense for your group.

Most groups determine membership status by joining date or by expiration date. This method seems straightforward; however, a percentage of people who are past their expiration date but can be expected to renew can also be counted as current members. As we'll discuss in Chapter Four, for most organizations, between 55 and 70 percent of members renew each year. For a variety of reasons, it takes some members longer than others to complete that renewal. But because you know that most of your members will renew, you certainly don't want to discontinue communicating with them or providing other privileges. And you don't want to stop counting them as members. So you need to find a balance, not cutting people off so early that you interrupt services to your most dedicated members but not continuing them so long that the forgetful ones never renew.

For most organizations, a four-month "grace period" following the membership expiration date is adequate to cover the period when most members are renewing. Therefore, when you consider how many "active" or "current" members your organization has, you may consider all those who have contributed to you within the last sixteen months.

Tracking membership specifics

Worksheet 3.1 offers a system for regularly documenting the realities of your membership program. The form shown here includes real numbers for a state-based nonprofit group, as an example. The Jossey-Bass Web site (www.josseybass.com/go/ellisrobinson) includes a blank Excel spreadsheet of Worksheet 3.1, complete with formulas, that you can customize to reflect your organization. Following is a description of how to use each section:

A. *Current Active Membership* is the total number of members you have at the time you are logging these benchmarks. This sample organization considers anyone who makes a donation a member. They also know that most of their members will renew, but it will take some of them a while to do so. For that reason, they consider their active membership as anyone who has made a contribution of any size in the last sixteen months; in this case, 5,295. Revise this definition as appropriate for your organization. The total membership dollars are then calculated by summing the new and renewing membership gifts for all of those 5,295 members. The total of $193,800 means that the average joining gift is $36.60.

B. *Joining Levels* should also be adjusted to reflect your group's membership dues levels. If you have names for your membership categories, include them here, along with the giving amount or range. These categories are especially important as indicators of how many major donors and major donor candidates you have. When you update your benchmarks in the future, you will be able to easily track the effectiveness of your upgrading efforts (see Chapter Twelve). To double-check the accuracy of these figures, make sure that line "B. Subtotal" equals "A. Current Active Membership."

C. Total Annual Member Giving summarizes all the donations contributed throughout the past sixteen months by all your members. These include renewals, special appeals, and other donations. To ensure an accurate picture of the level of giving, do not include special event registrations, publication purchases, and other "fee for service" monies in this figure. In this example, members donated more than $85,000—nearly 45 percent more revenue—in addition to their membership joining or renewing gifts.

D. Average Annual Giving divides the total member giving by the total number of members. In this example, each member gives, on average, $52.93 annually—about 45 percent more than their average joining gift. Note that, for ease of calculation, this number is an average. As you become more familiar with your membership and more proficient with reports like these, you might want to calculate this as a mean or eliminate higher-level donors from this calculation, to minimize the impact that a few very large gifts might have on this number.

E. Member Loyalty documents the length of time your members have been with you. This benchmark will become especially helpful when you adopt new recruitment campaigns. By tracking the "j. Newbies," "k. Converts," and "l. Friends" categories over time, you will be able to identify how effective your renewal efforts are at retaining new audiences.

F. Estimated Lifetime Value combines the relative number of years your members stick with you with the Average Annual Giving level. In this example, in great part because of the number of members who have been with the organization for twenty-five months to ten years (the Friends and Best Friends categories), the organization can expect that a new member will donate an average total of $316 to the group over the life of their membership. This number becomes an important consideration as you project the investment-per-member needed for your membership recruitment plans (see Chapters Nine and Ten). It is difficult to justify making a net investment of $10, $20, or even $40 to get a new member until you put that number in the context of a member's lifetime value. (Note that Estimated Lifetime Value will decrease as the number of Newbies increases. This is because first-year members usually renew at a much lower rate than multiyear members—sometimes as low as half your average renewal rate.)

G. Lapsed Members are those people who have not yet renewed their membership, even though they have been contacted multiple times through your standard renewal mailing cycle. As I will discuss in Chapter Four, these people are usually your best source of new members; however, their responsiveness diminishes as time passes. This section is divided into three categories, by recency. Adjust these ranges and definitions to fit your situation.

    H. *Prospects and Inquiries* are those people listed in your database who have not yet joined your organization but know who you are because they have requested information, attended an event, signed a petition, or otherwise connected with your program or personnel. This list is usually your second-best source of more members. (See Chapter Eight.)

    I. *Geographic Distribution* helps identify where your membership comes from. Feel free to revise this category to reflect your programmatic priorities. For example, a regional group might divide this section by zip code, focusing on rural or metropolitan members. This distribution can help you identify new potential audiences as well as audiences that need attention.

    J. *Source* summarizes which techniques or campaigns were used to attract your members. (See Chapter Seven for discussion of techniques and Resource C for a discussion of source codes.) This information can help guide your future communications (for example, are you losing members recruited by telemarketing because you are no longer calling them?), as well as provide a continuing snapshot of your membership mix over time.

    Worksheet 3.1 provides important baseline documentation of the realities of your membership. It may take you an hour or two to set up the queries to extract this information from your database, but once you have set up the reports, you can update this information every quarter or six months, to summarize how your membership is growing. Changes in the data can also highlight shifts and trends before they become difficulties.

Keeping track of your members

The best way to keep your membership data is on a computer, in a predesigned database program (as opposed to one created in-house). By using an electronic database to log and update your membership records, you enhance your ability to distribute written and e-mail communications, evaluate campaign successes, compare and analyze membership trends, share data among committee members and staff (as appropriate), upgrade your systems as your membership and programs expand, and raise more money from well-cared-for members.

    By a "predesigned database program" I mean one that has been developed especially for membership systems. Such a database has already been enhanced with the record fields, reports, search options, and other features that you will need to manage your members well. Most allow you to customize for any unique internal requirements, if necessary.

Membership Benchmarks

This form offers a system for regularly documenting the realities of your membership program. It may take a bit of time to retrieve the information from your membership database, but it is worth it for the useful information it provides about your members. Here is a sample completed form. Access the blank Excel version at www.josseybass.com/go/ellisrobinson.

Date: 11/21/02	Baseline: 11/21/02			Update:			Update:		
	Number	Total Dollars	Average Gift	Number	Total Dollars	Average Gift	Number	Total Dollars	Average Gift
A. Current Active Membership (number of people who have donated in the past 16 months)	5,295	$ 193,800	$36.60						
B. Joining Levels (sum of a–i below should = A above)									
a. Number of active members who joined as **Associate** at membership dues level of $20.00–$29.99	960	$21,361	$22.25						
b. Number of active members who joined as **Friend** at membership dues level of $30.00–$49.99	1,921	$59,815	$31.14						
c. Number of active members who joined as **Sponsor** at membership dues level of $50.00–$99.99	919	$47,551	$51.74						
d. Number of active members who joined as **Guardian** at membership dues level of $100.00–$249.99	203	$22,240	$109.56						
e. Number of active members who joined as **Partner** at membership dues level of $250.00–$499.99	20	$5,650	$282.50						

	Number	Amount	Each / Percentage
f. Number of active members who joined as **Steward** at membership dues level of $500.00–$999.99	5	$2,500	$500.00
g. Number of active members who joined as **Defender** at membership dues level of $1,000.00–$4,999.99	4	$8,520	$2,130.00
h. Number of active members who joined as **Champion** at membership dues level of $5,000.00 or more	2	$13,000	$6,500.00
i. Number of donors who donated less than $20.00	1,261	$13,163	$10.44
B. SUBTOTAL	5,295	$193,800	$36.60
C. Total Annual Member Giving (total monies—all gifts—donated during the year by all active members)		$280,271	
D. Average Annual Giving (total annual membership giving divided by number of active members)			$52.93

E. Member Loyalty	Number	Percentage
j. **Newbies:** number of members who joined in the past 12 months	317	5.99%
k. **Converts:** number of members who joined 13–24 months ago	203	3.83%
l. **Friends:** number of members who joined 25 months to 5 years ago	2,471	46.67%

	Baseline: 11/21/02		Update:		Update:	
	Number	Percentage	Number	Percentage	Number	Percentage
m. **Best Friends:** number of members who joined 6 to 10 years ago	1,596	30.14%				
n. **Angels:** number of members who joined 11 or more years ago	708	13.37%				
o. **Founders:** number of members who have been active since your organization's beginning	0	0.00%				
E. **SUBTOTAL** (number should = A; percentage should = 100)	5,295	100.00%				
F. **Estimated Lifetime Value**	$316.00					
G. **Lapsed Members**						
Recent Lapsed (number of members whose last donation was 17–28 months ago)	1,911					
Mature Lapsed (number of members whose last donation was 29–40 months ago)	2,078					
Ancient Lapsed (number of members whose last donation was 41–52 months ago)	5,438					
G. **LAPSED SUBTOTAL**	14,722					
H. **Prospects and Inquiries** (number of people on your database who have not made a donation but have requested information, participated in activities, or otherwise found you!)	643					

I. Geographic Distribution	Number	Percentage			Number	Percentage			Number	Percentage
Wisconsin	5,252	99.19%								
Southeast: AL, AR, FL, GA, KY, LA, MS, NC, SC, TN, TX	7	0.13%								
Northeast: CT, DC, DE, MA, MD, ME, NH, NJ, NY, RI, VA, VT, WV	5	0.09%								
Great Lakes: IA, IL, IN, MI, MN, MO, OH, PA	20	0.38%								
Southwest: AZ, CA, CO, KS, NM, NV, OK, UT	8	0.15%								
Northwest: AK, HI, ID, MT, ND, NE, OR, SD, WA, WY	3	0.06%								
Foreign	0	0.00%								
I. SUBTOTAL (should = A)	5,295	100.00%								

J. SOURCE (What inspired your members to join?)	Number	Percentage			Number	Percentage			Number	Percentage
p. Word-of-Mouth	4	0.08%								
q. Attended an Event	7	0.13%								
r. Direct Mail	536	10.12%								
s. Telemarketing	631	11.92%								
t. Field Canvassing	1,788	33.77%								
u. PSAs, Ads	0	0.00%								
v. Workplace	72	1.36%								
w. Other or Unknown	2,257	42.63%								
J. SUBTOTAL (should = A)	5,295	100.00%								

Notes:

The most frequent database horror stories I hear come from groups in which a well-meaning volunteer custom-built a database system and then moved out of town, had a baby, got a new job, or otherwise had a life change that made them unavailable for ongoing technical support. This left the organization with an undocumented system and no skills to amend or improve it—or even reliably retrieve the information already in it. If you receive such a generous offer, see if you can instead enlist this expertise to research existing predesigned systems and recommend the best option for your internal use.

Which database should you use? If you are just starting out, consider adopting an inexpensive system such as ebase (downloadable from www.ebase.org). At this writing, ebase is free to users; however, you will find it gains in flexibility and power if you invest in a copy of FileMaker Pro, the software platform on which ebase is built. (FileMaker and most other software companies also have generous donation or discount programs for nonprofit organizations, which can make a sys-.tem more affordable.)

Before selecting your database solution, talk to membership colleagues in your community. Database choices seem to cluster, and that can work to your advantage. If you find that several sister organizations are using the same system, that probably means that you will also find ready access to local technical support and data entry people who are familiar with the program's nuances—both benefits that money can't buy!

It is important to keep in mind that your database, like other office technologies, will require changes and updates over time. This will be frustrating and time-consuming, and will involve at least some cash. For evaluations of various predesigned database systems, check out the May–June 2002 issue of *Grassroots Fundraising Journal* or the archives of *Nonprofit Times*. The sooner you adopt a logical, consistent, documented system for keeping your membership records, the faster that system will become an asset to your work instead of a headache.

Counting members: people or households?

For ease and accuracy of recordkeeping, most membership programs keep their records on a household basis. This means that each record in your database represents a household, which may include one, two, or more people who are interested in and supportive of your organization. Although you may not know how many people are in that household, households are all you usually have available to count.

If you are asked to provide a membership count that represents accurately the total number of individuals your organization serves and represents, consider working with two different membership numbers. The first, the number of memberships, is the most easily quantifiable and one that you will want to track most completely. This is the number of households who have contributed to your organization within a given time period.

It can be safe to say, however, that you actually and legitimately represent more people than you have membership records for. In most households more than one person is likely to read your newsletter and take advantage of your programs and activities. For many two-adult households, more than one person may be deciding where contributions go and their size. You can also expect to be able to call on all members of those households when it comes to attending public hearings, volunteering, participating in research, or other involvement with your programs.

The easiest way to manage these differences is to agree upon a multiplier. For example, if the 2000 census shows that your community or region (whatever you consider your service area) has an average household size of 1.67 people, then it's legitimate to say that your organization represents the number of memberships times 1.67 people. This is an appropriate number to use in your media communications, agency presentations, or advocacy and other outreach. (Be sure to document for yourself how you derived it, so you can maintain consistency.) For your own internal tracking and analysis, however, use the household membership number, especially in staff and board reports.

Setting member rates

Most organizations have a range of membership categories (with names such as Basic, Family, Supporter, Angel, and so forth). How you establish that range—and how much you ask members to contribute for each level—reflects why you have members and whom you are trying to attract. Here are some examples of how organizations thought about their membership fees.

Changing to reflect the times

When the group 1000 Friends of Oregon was first established, the goal of its founders, former Governor Tom McCall and executive director Henry Richmond, was to recruit a thousand individuals who would contribute $100 each to support advocacy on land-use planning for the state. At the time, now more than twenty-five years ago, land-use planning was seen as a relatively esoteric and sophisticated issue involving a great deal of legal work and legislative maneuverings. The founders expected potential members of 1000 Friends to be well-educated, well-connected "insiders"; the group was definitely not for everybody. Although 1000 Friends of Oregon never attracted the full thousand $100 donors, they did at one time reach a peak of more than seven hundred, establishing a consistent and significant financial base for the organization.

Within seventeen years, the organization had achieved such success that it felt it needed much more support. The playing fields for their issue and the decision making that affected it had moved to the appeals boards of local and county land-use planning agencies. In a state the size of Oregon, with hundreds of municipalities in thirty-six counties, a thousand members simply would not be enough to assure a vocal and informed turnout at local planning board meetings.

As a result, the organization began actively recruiting a wider public by offering a $20 introductory membership and promoting the "products" (or benefits) of their work to date: public access to all of Oregon's beaches, easy access to farms and forestland close to urban areas, and the resulting higher quality of life throughout the state. The campaign worked, and the organization grew to more than five thousand members and continues to maintain those numbers and be effective in carrying out its mission of protecting and promoting sustainable land planning in Oregon.

Building constituency quickly

People for Puget Sound was created in response to the dissolution of a state agency dedicated to protecting water quality. The organization's founders were determined to establish quickly and conclusively that the public wanted to see Puget Sound's water quality protected and improved. They set a goal of enlisting twenty thousand members within two years. They accomplished this goal in part by virtually eliminating the financial barrier to becoming a member. Not only could a family join for $5, the sign-up form included a place to list every family member, all of whom were then tallied in the organization's membership count.

The organization also wanted to educate young people about the importance of protecting their water resources. To do so, People for Puget Sound initiated an aggressive school outreach program. Children were encouraged to join the organization for just a dollar, for which they received a special kids' newsletter. This effort helped the organization achieve its goal of twenty thousand members within two years, although the number of households listed on its database did not reach that number.

Special offers for priority audiences

The two preceding examples demonstrate the power of linking your membership program directly to your mission and goals. To help attract critical but elusive constituents, you can also develop special offers or programs. Here's an example: As you can imagine, Alaskan fishermen, who depend heavily on their own abilities and resources, are generally fiercely independent and unlikely to join an organization. However, because their participation and support are critical to the legitimacy and credibility of Alaska Marine Conservation Council, the group needed to find creative ways to overcome these potential members' reluctance to join.

Alaska Marine Conservation Council developed an outreach program in which full- and part-time staff in coastal fishing communities, along with board members from various communities, participated in fairs and other events around the state. At these gatherings, they invited fisherfolk and other coastal community residents to learn about the organization and, more important, about the issues the organization was addressing that would affect the fishers' future ability to fish or crab. At those events, coastal residents and fishermen were invited to join the organization for just a dollar. By giving individuals a chance to meet, talk with, and learn about the issues from the leadership of the organization, the organization was successful in recruiting a substantial number of coastal community residents and fisherfolk to support the Council's work.

As you review or update how much you ask someone to give to become a member, look at them in light of what you are trying to accomplish as an organization. Feel free to adjust the rate for special conditions—a hard-to-reach audience, an introductory rate, a special discount as part of purchase of a registration for a conference or some other activity, a one-year gift membership for new residents. Test rates to see which work best. In your membership sign-up materials, always offer an "other" category of donation. Consider a "living lightly" or "student or senior" rate at perhaps half of your normal basic membership rate.

If your goal is truly to embrace as many of your community members as possible (however you define community), be sure to do what you can to minimize the financial barriers to joining.

Offering premiums and other goods and services

As you probably found out from your membership survey, most members join your group and continue to support you because they agree with your mission and appreciate the great work you do. Beyond these connections, additional, more tangible, membership benefits can help reinforce your organization's value to your donors.

Probably the most commonly offered membership benefit is a subscription to a newsletter. Your newsletter is a great way to update your members on the work you are doing and the progress you are making on the issues they care about. It's also a wonderful vehicle for connecting your members with the people involved in your group, associating faces with what might otherwise be the invisible workers of your organization.

Other tangible membership benefits include educational materials (books, pamphlets, fact sheets, videos, access to member-only areas of your Web site), special events (lectures, annual meetings, potlucks, hikes or outings), free services (admission to zoo or art museum, energy audit, day care, classes), and commemorative premiums (decals, T-shirts, tote bags, water bottles). These kinds of benefits can also be used to recruit new members or encourage current members to upgrade.

Be sure to test a new benefit before implementing it membership-wide, keeping in mind that the more complex your benefits schedule becomes, the more time-consuming and expensive it is to manage.

 Remember to inform your members of the value of the "goods and services" they will be receiving. In the United States, a benefit that costs the organization $8 or less (in 2003; the Internal Revenue Service updates this number every year) is considered an "insubstantial benefit" and does not count against the tax-deductibility of any of the member's donation. If the cost to your organization is more than $8 or 2 percent of the contribution, whichever is greater, and the premium or service was used as an incentive to the donor making the contribution, the tax-deductibility of that contribution is reduced by the market value of the premium. Note that if you give a premium to a member unexpectedly—that is, not as an incentive for making a donation—the gift does not affect the deductibility of the member's earlier or later contributions.

Finally, always give your prospects and members a chance to turn down your premium offer. Include a check box on your response form that says, "Please don't send me [the premium]; I want 100 percent of my contribution to go to [name of group]'s important work."

Documenting your member benefits

The most important considerations in membership development are to be consistent in your treatment of your members, make sure your membership policies reflect your group's culture and program priorities, and always keep your members' perceptions of benefits at the forefront of your communications.

Keeping a record of the decisions you make regarding your member rates and benefits helps assure consistency across the various people caring for your members (for example, volunteers, administrative personnel, or your successor). Such documentation will also help save time and energy in the future; once a decision is made, it won't get lost and need to be made again.

Here's a list of actions to take to put in place the procedures discussed in this chapter. Use the Membership Partnership you developed in Chapter One as the basis for your decision making.

- [ ] Create a "Membership Policies" notebook or other central location in which to keep the instructions listed here.

- [ ] Establish a protocol for defining members: minimum amount of gift, qualification of volunteer time (or not), length of non-renewing "grace period," and anything else you want to add.

- [ ] Work with your data entry personnel or a programmer to make sure that the definitions in the preceding item are reflected in your data entry screens, standard reports, and common queries. (See Resource B for how to set up donor records in a database.)

- [ ] Review your membership categories and revise, if appropriate. Consider testing an introductory offer or other discount to help you attract key audiences.

- [ ] Document which goods and services members receive at different giving levels and whether they affect the tax-deductibility of a member's contribution.

- [ ] Complete Worksheet 3.1, to document where your membership is today. Update this Membership Benchmarks worksheet at least every six months.

- [ ] Review your lists of volunteers and activists and initiate a program to encourage any who are not already members to join. Enlist a volunteer and an activist leader to help.

- [ ] Develop a standard welcome letter for non-members who participate in paid special events and other non-membership experiences explaining their member status and describing the benefits (see Chapter Four for more discussion on welcome packets).

Alaska Marine Conservation Council developed a Membership Procedure Handbook to help assure consistency of their membership program and to provide guidelines for the person filling in while the membership director was on maternity leave. The following outline for their manual will give you a set of topics to consider as you prepare your own documentation.

Alaska Marine Conservation Council Membership Procedure Handbook

To encourage a smooth transition of her membership duties during her maternity leave, Council membership director Tracy Walczak-Lohman prepared a handbook of membership decisions and procedures for reference by her replacement. The following table of contents shows the topics Tracy included in the handbook.

Table of Contents

- Newsletter
  - Procedures/membership responsibility, authority
  - Things to include in every issue
  - Mailing list preparation
- Bulletins and Action Alerts
  - Mailing list preparation
  - Timing
  - E-mail actions

Record Keeping Protocols

- Data entry procedures
- Integration with accounting records
- Accuracy-checking procedures
- History of database (underlying program, programmer contact info, upgrade history, and so on)
- What records get kept and how

Source Code Log

- Membership types
- Mailing codes and use

Financial Procedures and Fulfillment

- Incoming mail processing
- Creating batches/deposit procedure
- Thank you fulfillment
- Membership funding history

List Exchange Policy (who gets exchanged, who doesn't)

Monthly Giving Protocol

Major Donor Procedures

- What makes a major donor
- Benefits and TLC
- Cultivation procedures
- Tracking and history

Privacy Policy   Dev. office?

PART TWO

Managing
Your Membership Program

Although members bring vast resources to the organizations they support, they also create real costs in terms of time, energy, and money. This section outlines specific systems for taking care of the members you have now and those you will be recruiting in the future.

Perhaps the most valuable asset each member provides your organization is their goodwill and endorsement of your reputation. This section helps you establish efficient, effective, and consistent procedures for managing your members respectfully while encouraging them to make additional investments of their time, expertise, and contributions.

Chapter Four covers the details of renewing members, including the various strategies for soliciting renewals: mailings, telephone requests, use of premiums, and more.

Chapter Five demystifies special appeals, including when and how to use them to encourage your members to learn more about your organization, take action, and reinvest.

In Chapter Six we discuss the most common membership benefit, newsletters, as well as other communications with members.

Please review this section now, before moving on to Part Three on recruitment, even if you do not yet have any members. By putting in place the systems outlined in these chapters before you launch a major recruitment campaign, you will make sure that any current members you have are well cared for and that each new member is treated to a warm, professional welcome—without overwhelming your internal operations.

CHAPTER 4

Building a Renewal Program

Renewals are communications or other efforts you use to entice members to sign up for another year of partnership with your organization. By building the most effective renewal program possible for your organization, you assure your group an ongoing source of unrestricted income as well as a dedicated cadre of volunteers, activists, and word-of-mouth supporters. It's almost always less costly—in time and money—to retain an existing member or attract anew a former member than it is to recruit a new one. A further benefit is that renewing members are already knowledgeable about your issues and programs. Since most organizations' renewal rate is greater than 50 percent, recruiting renewals is your most cost-effective fundraising activity.

The concept of renewals is especially important to membership organizations. Unlike in pure donor relationships, most membership organizations recognize a reciprocity with their members: members pay dues in return for a year of information and other membership benefits and services. The purpose of renewal notices is to convince your members to continue their involvement with your group for another year.

This chapter walks you through the specifics of establishing a manageable, productive, and consistent renewal program.

When to ask members to renew

Most groups renew their members on an annual basis. Organizations establish membership years in two basic ways: on a calendar year, in which all memberships begin on the same date (often the first of January) and continue until the same time next

Thanks to my colleague Amy O'Connor for suggesting the six-week renewal cycle discussed in this chapter.

year, or on a donation year, that is, from the date the organization deposits a new member's joining or renewing gift. The first approach is most common with smaller groups that want to avoid the paperwork of sending out renewal notices throughout the year. If you have a relatively small, dedicated membership with close personal ties to the organization, this once-a-year calendar can be very effective.

The second way of managing the membership year is to begin the membership from the date the organization receives a new member's donation. For example, if you receive a check for a membership on May 6 and deposit it that same day, that member's membership year begins on that date.

The second approach is more respectful of your members' needs and is better for your organization's year-round cash flow. You are recognizing and honoring your members' preferences for when they are able to join and support you. For example, requiring all members to join or renew on a specific date may be convenient for you as an organization, but it may not be convenient for your members. If your organization shares the understanding that membership is as much a benefit to the organization as it is to the individual, then being respectful of members' ability to give and their preferred timing becomes important. And by scheduling renewals throughout the year, you assure your organization a steady, continuous flow of income. You also avoid tricky situations, such as what the first renewal date would be for the person who joins in May or later when everyone's renewal date is January 1.

Pegging the new member's renewal date to the date you deposit their donation, rather than the date of the check or the date you received the donation, helps assure quality control and accuracy between your membership database and your accounting system, as the daily deposit amount should match the total membership amount logged for that date. If they don't, you know you have an error in data entry somewhere. (For more details on how to establish this integrated system for your membership and financial records, see Resource B.)

Setting expiration dates

Your membership database should include a field for an expiration date for each membership record. (See Resource B for how to set up a donor record.) Although you can get by without an expiration date and instead calculate renewal dates based on the date of the last joining gift, expiration dates make it much easier to measure your renewal rate and monitor your renewal progress. Following are some suggestions on how to calculate these dates:

• *First-time members.* For first-time members, the expiration date is one year in advance of the date of deposit of their initial gift, regardless of whether that initial gift came in response to a new-member recruitment campaign, a special event, or perhaps even a publication purchase (depending on the decisions you made in Chapter Two).

- *Renewing members.* For renewing members, setting expiration dates presents a different challenge, because renewing members don't always renew just when their membership expires. Although there are no wrong answers, it is important to establish protocols and be consistent in their application. Here are some suggestions for handling the variety of renewal situations.

- *Early renewers.* When someone renews before their expiration date, simply add a year to the current expiration date. For example, Allyson Mark renews her membership on March 13, 2004, even though her expiration date is April 12, 2004. Allyson's new expiration date would be April 12, 2005, rather than a year from the date of deposit of her gift (March 13, 2005). This system ensures you do not penalize your most loyal and dedicated members by trimming their membership by a month or two because they renewed early.

- *Timely renewers.* In this category are people who renew any time from their expiration date to perhaps as many as four months following the expiration date. Why so long? We know from surveys that the most common reason people don't renew their membership is that they think they are still a member. This often means you didn't remind them often enough and they simply forgot to renew. As explained later in this chapter, it will probably take three, four, or even five attempts to maintain your strongest renewal rate. Since we know that the majority of your current members are going to renew, you don't want to cut them off from services just because they miss their first renewal opportunity, as they are still valuable to you as activists, volunteers, event participants, and in other capacities. However, you don't want to reward them for being late, either.

To balance these choices, make sure each of your members has at least three opportunities to renew, beginning two months before their expiration date, before you consider them lapsed or inactive. In the meantime, continue to provide them with services (your newsletter, action alerts, admission to events, and whatever other benefits you identified in Chapter Two), while encouraging them to renew. When they do renew within the "timely" or "grace" window that you have established, advance their expiration date by one year from its current date. For example, Christopher Baldwin's expiration date is August 30, 2003. He responds to your third renewal notice and sends in his check on November 11, and you deposit it on November 13. His new renewal date becomes August 30, 2004. After all, you have been providing him with services for all that time; he just paid for them a little late.

- *Lapsed or expired members.* Eventually, some members will renew so late that it doesn't make sense simply to advance their expiration date by a year. For example, if Christopher had chosen to renew in January, in response to your fifth renewal notice, rather than in November, and you simply moved his renewal date up a year to August 30, 2004, you would then begin asking him to renew again in June of 2004 (two months before his expiration date), just five months after he sent his renewal. At the same time, you have provided Christopher with at least three or four months' worth

Montana Wilderness Association Renewal Procedure

Policy: Membership Renewal Procedure

Developed by: David Steinmuller and Karole Lee

Approved by: Bob Decker, Executive Director

Date Adopted: June 10, 2002

Date Revised: September 3, 2002, John Dendy

Purpose: The Montana Wilderness Association depends on its membership for support; retention of members is a vital part of the Association's existence.

Procedure: Membership renewal procedures will be conducted as follows:

1. A member's join date will be the first day of the month following the month in which they join. Their renewal date will be the first day of that month every year.

2. Two months prior to the renewal date, a personalized letter soliciting membership renewal will be sent to the members. The letter may refer to MWA's recent accomplishments, current challenges, and so on, and should not exceed one page. A membership renewal card indicating the various giving levels and payment options and a self-addressed return envelope will be included with the letter.

3. On the renewal date, members who have not renewed their membership will be sent a second personalized letter along with another renewal card and return envelope, again asking them to renew their membership. The letter will contain a statement such as, "If you already sent us your annual dues, please disregard this notice and thank you for continuing your support of the Montana Wilderness Association." The renewal date will begin a four-month grace period, and the member will be reclassified as "grace" in the database.

of "free" services, so he probably doesn't merit the same kind of consideration as a brand new member. In this situation, you should first determine when you will consider a member expired or lapsed (three months, four months, or five months after their expiration date?), then reset the lapsed member's expiration date to eleven months from the date of deposit of their renewing gift. You might want to initiate a "look back" function before you choose to lapse a member. If we use the four-month timely or grace period for receiving a renewal, in Christopher's case you would look back in December to see if he had given a special appeal or other gift in the last six months. If so, you could credit that donation as a renewal and advance his renewal date.

• *Miscellaneous contributors.* As you probably have already noticed, your members have an extraordinary ability to retain the paper that you send to them. Groups I've worked with have had solicitation response forms and return envelopes show

4. All "grace" members will be retained on the central and chapter mailing lists for four months from their renewal date and will receive all publications, alerts, announcements, appeals, and other mailings during this period.

5. One month after the renewal date, members who have not renewed their membership will be sent a third personalized letter along with another renewal card and return envelope, again encouraging them to renew their membership.

6. Two months after the renewal date, the names and contact information of the members who have still not renewed their membership will be forwarded to the appropriate chapter.

7. Within one month, the member will be contacted with a personal telephone call or other solicitation from a chapter representative. If the member is not assigned to a chapter, a staff member in the Helena office will make the telephone contact.

8. Those members who agree to rejoin will be sent another membership renewal form with a *stamped* self-addressed return envelope, along with a short cover letter. The cover letter will include a statement such as, "Thank you for talking with me the other evening and agreeing to renew your membership in the Montana Wilderness Association. Your continued support is greatly appreciated."

9. The original renewal date will be retained for all members who renew within their grace period. Members who do not renew within four months will be reclassified as "lapsed" in the database, and their records will be retained in the database indefinitely.

10. Lapsed members who renew after four months from their original renewal date will be considered "returning members" to distinguish them from brand new members and from members who renew within their grace period. They will be given a new renewal date.

11. Returning members will receive a postcard specific to returning members thanking them for returning to MWA.

up two or even three years after they mailed them out. Suppose you are actively renewing a member and she sends a gift in response to an earlier special appeal, or in an envelope that's in your newsletter, or some other device. Although most members understand the differences between a renewal contribution and special appeal or additional gift, some are less tuned in to those nuances—or maybe they just grabbed the envelope and form that they found handy. If you receive an unrelated gift during the time you are actively trying to renew a member, consider that gift a renewal response and advance the expiration date appropriately. For example, Carla Rodriguez's expiration date is July 10, 2004. You mail her first renewal ask in May and a second one in mid-June. On July 20, you receive a check for $35, accompanied by the response form from your February special appeal. In this case, I would credit the contribution as triggered by or motivated by the special appeal inquiry (so the source code would remain the same as that for the special appeal; see Resource C for more on source codes). But the contribution would be considered a renewal, advancing Carla's expiration date to July 10, 2005.

• *Advance gifts.* You may also wish to establish a policy that any gift given within a period of time prior to the renewal date also advances the expiration date. For example, had you received Carla Rodriguez's special appeal gift on April 29— less than three months prior to her expiration date of July 10 and just a couple of days before you planned to mail her first renewal notice—you might choose to advance her expiration date by a year.

This decision takes some further thought. Most of your members probably understand the difference between a renewal gift and a special appeal gift. If they wish to have their special appeal contribution considered as their renewal donation, they will probably let you know, either with that gift or when they receive your first renewal notice. In that case, of course you respond, "We'll be happy to consider your special appeal donation as your renewal and we appreciate your generosity."

While there are a lot of options to consider, remember that there are no wrong answers, just the need to establish a consistent renewal system. To do so, review the decisions you have already made about the culture of your organization and your membership partnership. Then determine complementary parameters and procedures you want to use for renewing your members and advancing their expiration date. An example of one group's policies appears on pages 54–55, thanks to the volunteers and staff at the Montana Wilderness Association.

Once you've made these renewal decisions and documented them as Montana Wilderness Association did, invest in some programming time to incorporate these policies into your database system. This is especially important if you have more than one person doing data entry. A capable programmer should be able to customize your system in just a few hours to allow you all of the functionality of your renewal procedures and none of the handwork. This one-time investment will assure you a consistent and rational system for setting expiration dates. It will also help you optimize your opportunity to recruit renewal gifts from your members, while minimizing the possibility of offending anyone during that process.

Renewal timing

Effective renewal programs can operate on a monthly, six-week, bimonthly, quarterly, or annual basis. If yours is a relatively small organization (fewer than five hundred members) with a track record of a high renewal rate, consider sending out renewals quarterly, using a system that combines renewals with special appeals (see Chapter Five). Worksheet 4.1 provides a quarterly renewal schedule.

Renewal Schedule: Quarterly Mailings

This worksheet shows a quarterly renewal schedule for renewal notices and follow-up contacts for 2003 through mid-2006, according to members' membership expiration date. It also includes places to record the procedure used for each contact. This schedule can easily be extended to later years. Date ranges indicate the expiration dates to be included in each mailing.

Mail Date	1st Notice	2nd Notice	3rd Notice	Follow-Up or Phone	Next Steps
Jan. 2003	2/03—4/03	11/02–1/03	8/02–10/02	11/98—1/02	
April 2003	5/03—7/03	2/03—4/03	11/02–1/03	2/02—4/02	
July 2003	8/03—10/03	5/03—7/03	2/03—4/03	5/02—7/02	
Oct. 2003	11/03—1/04	8/03–10/03	5/03–7/03	8/02—10/02	
Jan. 2004	2/04—4/04	11/03- 1/04	8/03–10/03	11/02–1/03	
April 2004	5/04—7/04	2/04—4/04	11/03–1/04	2/03—4/03	
July 2004	8/04—10/04	5/04—7/04	2/04—4/04	5/03—7/03	
Oct. 2004	11/04—1/05	8/04–10/04	5/04—7/04	8/03—10/03	
Jan. 2005	2/05—4/05	11/04–1/05	8/04–10/04	11/03—1/04	
April 2005	5/05—7/05	2/05—4/05	11/04–1/05	2/04—4/04	
July 2005	8/05—10/05	5/05—7/05	2/05—4/05	5/04—7/04	
Oct. 2005	11/05—1/06	8/05–10/05	5/05—7/05	8/04—10/04	
Jan. 2006	2/06—4/06	11/05–1/06	8/05–10/05	11/04—1/05	
April 2006	5/06—7/06	2/06—4/06	11/05–1/06	2/05—4/05	
July 2006	8/06—10/06	5/06—7/06	2/06—4/06	5/05—7/05	

First Notice Procedure:

Second Notice Procedure:

Third Notice Procedure:

Follow-Up or Phone Procedure:

Six-Week Renewal and Special Appeal Mailing Calendar

This calendar shows when to mail renewal notices if you are following a six-week schedule. Date ranges in each cell are members' expiration dates. Dates in bold are combined with special appeals. As with Worksheet 4.1, it is easy to extend the calendar beyond 2004.

Mail Date	1st Renewal Notice	2nd Renewal	3rd Renewal	4th Renewal	5th Renewal	Renewal as Special Appeal	Other
2003							
February 3	3/1/03–4/15/03	1/15/03–2/28/03	12/1/02–1/14/03	10/15/02–11/30/02	9/1/02–10/14/02	4/16/03+	
March 17	4/16/03–5/31/03	3/1/03–4/15/03	1/15/03–2/28/03	12/1/02–1/14/03	10/15/02–11/30/02		
May 1	**6/1/03–7/15/03**	**4/16/03–5/31/03**	**3/1/03–4/15/03**	**1/15/03–2/28/03**	**12/1/02–1/14/03**	7/16/03+	
June 13	7/16/03–8/31/03	6/1/03–7/15/03	4/16/03–5/31/03	3/1/03–4/15/03	1/15/03–2/28/03		
August 1	**9/1/03–10/15/03**	**7/16/03–8/31/03**	**6/1/03–7/15/03**	**4/16/03–5/31/03**	**3/1/03–4/15/03**	10/16/03+	
September 15	10/16/03–11/30/03	9/1/03–10/15/03	7/16/03–8/31/03	6/1/03–7/15/03	4/16/03–5/31/03		
November 5	**12/1/03–1/15/04**	**10/16/03–11/30/03**	**9/1/03–10/15/03**	**7/16/03–8/31/03**	**6/1/03–7/15/03**	1/16/04+	Lapsed: 2/02–3/03
December 15	1/16/04–2/28/04	12/1/03–1/15/04	10/16/03–11/30/03	9/1/03–10/15/03	7/16/03–8/31/03		

If you have a larger membership, or if your renewal rate (or your cash flow) could use a boost, consider adopting a six-week renewal-and-special appeal cycle. This means that you will be sending out either a renewal letter or a combination renewal/special appeal every six weeks, for a total of eight mailings a year. Worksheet 4.2 shows how this schedule works. Chapter Five discusses special appeals.

First, I suggest you borrow a technique from Audubon Society of Portland (Oregon) and consider developing a single renewal letter to be used for each mailing, regardless of whether it is the first or a later renewal notice. Rather than a col-

Mail Date	1st Renewal Notice	2nd Renewal	3rd Renewal	4th Renewal	5th Renewal	Renewal as Special Appeal	Other
2004							
February 1	3/1/04—4/15/04	1/16/04—2/28/04	12/1/03—1/15/04	10/16/03—11/30/03	9/1/03—10/15/03	4/16/04+	
March 15	4/16/04—5/31/04	3/1/04—4/15/04	1/16/04—2/28/04	12/1/03—1/15/04	10/16/03—11/30/03		
May 1	6/1/04—7/15/04	4/16/04—5/31/04	3/1/04—4/15/04	1/16/04—2/28/04	12/1/03—1/15/04	7/16/04+	
June 13	7/16/04—8/31/04	6/1/04—7/15/04	4/16/04—5/31/04	3/1/04—4/15/04	1/16/04—2/28/04		
August 1	9/1/04—10/15/04	7/16/04—8/31/04	6/1/04—7/15/04	4/16/04—5/31/04	3/1/04—4/15/04	10/16/04+	
September 18	10/16/04—11/30/04	9/1/04—10/15/04	7/16/04—8/31/04	6/1/04—7/15/04	4/16/04—5/31/04		
November 6	12/1/04—1/15/05	10/16/04—11/30/04	9/1/04—10/15/04	7/16/04—8/31/04	6/1/04—7/15/04	1/16/05+	Lapsed: 2/03–3/04
December 14	1/16/05—2/28/05	12/1/04—1/15/05	10/16/04—11/30/04	9/1/04—10/15/04	7/16/04—8/31/04		

lection of letters that say, "This is your first notice," "This is your second notice," "This is your third notice," you have one letter that says, "It's time to renew your membership." For example, the Audubon Society is well aware that its members are passionate about birds, especially in April, when spring brings migrants back to northern areas. Therefore, the spring renewal letter focuses on the return of migrating birds while inviting members to renew their membership. This same letter is mailed to every member up for renewal at that time, whether they are receiving their first, second, third, fourth, or fifth notice. In addition to the name and mailing address, the response form includes a source code that lets your office know, when it is returned, which renewal notice the individual is responding to. (See Resource C for more on source codes.)

There are several advantages to following this one-letter-fits-all strategy. First, you can process all of your outgoing renewals together, taking advantage of mailing discounts (if you have two hundred or more identical pieces to qualify for bulk mail). Second, you avoid having several different letters going to several subfiles all at the same time. Third, each letter is timely. Better yet, this letter on a seasonal theme can be used not only this spring, but again at the same time next year (perhaps with minor updating) and every year until your members seem to tire of it or your program priorities change.

Since the majority of your members are going to renew their membership, all you usually need to do is provide them with enough renewal reminders to move them to write that check. Most of your renewal letters do not have to be long; one page will do. However, you want to provide your members with enough information for them to know that their past investment in your organization has made a difference and that continued support is needed and will be put to good use.

When using a six-week schedule, half of your letters to members will be special appeals. Since you want to make sure that your renewing members don't miss out on the latest news about your organization, add "It's Time to Renew Your Membership!" in the upper-right corner of your special appeal to members due for a renewal mailing, and change the ask to "renew now" instead of "send a special gift." Now you have adapted your special appeal to do double duty as a renewal letter. (Special appeals are discussed fully in Chapter Five.)

How many asks?

The reality of renewal rates is this: the more frequently you ask, and the more difficult it is for your member to overlook that ask, the more likely they are to renew. For most organizations, that means sending a renewal series of at least three, and sometimes four or five letters, perhaps with a final telephone follow-up. You can send fewer renewal letters if you bolster your efforts with hand addressing, one-to-one contact, or other personalized follow-up.

Here's an example: One island-based group off the coast of Washington state enjoyed a greater than 80 percent renewal rate from only two annual asks. This group successfully raised all of its annual operating budget of approximately $200,000 from its year-end appeal and one February follow-up. This two-letter series also functioned as the group's annual renewal. The group succeeded by putting a tremendous amount of effort into this single campaign.

First, each letter was personalized with the member's name in the address block and salutation. Second, and perhaps more important, the names of the membership were distributed among the few staff and board members, who agreed to call or visit every member after the letters were mailed, to secure the year-end gift and renewal. Since the group's membership is a combination of island residents and generous city-based second-home owners, its relatively small size (fewer than 1,500) and the staff and board's familiarity with the members made this combination of year-end-renewal and annual major donor campaign a success.

While this approach has worked for this group, each group behaves differently; you are the expert on yours. Normally, combining a once-a-year renewal cycle with year-end giving (when your members are most generous) ends up reducing the amount of money your group can raise year-round. In this instance, however, this is clearly a case of "If it ain't broke, don't fix it." If you are experiencing a similar strong level of support through your one-time-a-year renewal system, there's no need to change.

For most organizations, however, a series of three to five renewal notices is necessary to maintain a healthy renewal rate—or make a strong renewal rate even better. If you are sending renewal notices every six weeks, alternate a one-page renewal with a longer, more informative and educational combination of renewal and special appeal, and you should be able to maximize your renewal rate without overburdening your writing schedule.

New members renew less

Every organization has a different renewal rate, ranging from as low as 15 percent to a high of 85 percent. The tools described here will help you understand what to expect from your members today. You can undoubtedly increase your current renewal rate by adopting some of the techniques discussed in this chapter. However, you should also expect a significant slump in your overall renewal rate about fourteen months after a major recruitment campaign. This is because new members usually renew at about half the rate of long-time members. Some of the techniques described here can help you boost new-member retention, as may new-member outreach and involvement programs. However, in order to realistically anticipate future revenues and membership size, remember to discount your renewal rate for new recruits.

Re-engaging lapsed members

It's almost always easier and more cost-effective to reclaim a lapsed member (someone who has been a member in the past but has not responded to renewal notices) than it is to recruit a new member. Since the most common reason people do not renew is that they think they're still a member, it is logical to do everything possible to get them back in the door rather than have them feel they have been dropped, raising the possibility of ill will in your community.

Ill will is probably the worst legacy your membership program could be saddled with. So much of your organization's work is dependent upon trust and the goodwill of your community that once a poor opinion begins to circulate, undoing that damage takes untoward amounts of work. The best way to avoid this situation is to stay in close contact with your renewing members and especially your lapsed members.

Keeping in touch with letters

Page 63 shows an inspired letter from the Bicycle Alliance of Washington, written by Barbara Culp and Matt Canastrero for the purpose of staying in touch with lapsed members. This letter, written from the perspective of a dedicated volunteer, is engaging and effective. The Bicycle Alliance used this letter as both a standard renewal and as a "clean-up" appeal to bring in members who had not responded to five earlier efforts to renew them. Volunteers hand-addressed the envelopes, which went out with a first-class stamp. They also wrote the first name of the member in the greeting by hand and signed the letter personally. The response was terrific: 27 percent for the first use, much higher than their usual 11 percent. The Bicycle Alliance used this same approach several times, and the lowest return was consistently higher than that of past approaches.

Lapsed members are so likely to return (eventually) that I suggest that you never write "This is your last chance to renew." Instead, fold your lapsed list into your direct mail recruitment campaigns (more about those in Chapter Ten) and your special appeal mailings.

NARAL went one step further and included the "lift letter" shown in Exhibit 4.1 when they mailed their standard prospecting package to lapsed members. (A lift letter is a special message, sometimes from a celebrity, printed on a small piece of colored paper and included in a standard direct mail package.) In this approach, NARAL used the same prospecting letter, envelope, and response form as was used for their regular new-member recruitment. However, they included the small-format "Dear Former NARAL Member" lift letter to those who had not been active members for some time. When compared with sending the same packages to lapsed members without the lift letter, this approach increased both the response rate and the average gift from lapsed members. Better yet, this campaign saved time and effort by piggy-backing on an existing procedure.

Dialing for lapsed donors

Another effective way of following up with lapsed members is to phone them. Because this is such a time-intensive method of retaining members, phoning should only be introduced after you have given former members several opportunities to renew using less expensive methods.

After you have sent your standard number of renewal asks, consider including names of lapsed members in a pool to be called. These calls can be made quarterly or every six months. Ideally, board members, staff members, your membership committee, or other key volunteers involved with the organization will make the calls. This assures that the ask will be made by a peer and someone who is reasonably familiar with the work of the organization and the interests of your members. This

Bicycle Alliance of Washington
Renewal Letter to Lapsed Donors

Dear _____,

The truth is, most days I'd rather be out riding with friends.

But today is different. Today I'm volunteering at the Bicycle Alliance for a lot of reasons: they represent me in Olympia; they educate my state representatives; they advocate for bicycling funding for me in Washington, D.C.; they're working on bicycle safety education; and _they feed me chocolate._

I'm here today so that Linda can promote bicycle commuting and host a Bike Buddy training and Louise can write a letter to Senator Murray about the importance of the Klickitat Trail. I'm here today so that Mark can answer a score of e-mails with questions about bicycle routes in Washington and Barbara can meet with the director of Washington's Traffic Safety Commission. **I believe the work that the Bicycle Alliance does for you and me is important.** After all, the Bicycle Alliance is the only statewide bicycle advocacy group in Washington working fulltime to assure you and me more and better places to ride. And the Bicycle Alliance depends upon members like you and me to be successful.

Your membership in the Bicycle Alliance helps assure that Washington cyclists have access to scenic trails, bike lanes, and safe roads to ride. I'm sure that bicycling is important to you and your family, so please renew your membership today. All you have to do is complete the enclosed form and return it with your dues today in the envelope provided. Thank you for your continued support!

Sincerely,

Volunteer & Fellow Bicycle Alliance of Washington Member

P.S. Come on out on June 8th at 11:45 A.M. on the I–90 bridge path to demonstrate your support for this critical link across Lake Washington for cyclists and pedestrians. Proposals are afoot to narrow or eliminate this path; it's time to say "NO!" For more information, check out the illustration on http://www.bicyclealliance.org. (You can also renew your membership on-line at the same time.)

Vincent Wishrad
Membership Director

Dear Former NARAL member,

As the new membership director at NARAL, I have been reviewing our membership files. And, it has been a few years since we have heard from you.

<u>NARAL needs your support.</u>

For the first time in years, we have an anti-choice president, and anti-choice majorities control both houses of Congress. The 2002 elections could determine the fate of reproductive freedom for generations.

Your support in the past helped us successfully oppose the nomination of Robert Bork to the Supreme Court in 1987. This victory was also critical in the 1992 *Casey* Decision when the court reaffirmed the principles of *Roe* by a narrow 5:4 decision. You also helped us secure passage of the Freedom of Access to Clinic Entrances Act — signed into law under President Clinton. And, you were there for NARAL when clinics and abortion providers across the nation came under attack. We thank you for that support.

If NARAL ever needed a renewed commitment from you — it is now. Your reinstated membership will make a profound difference in our fight to protect women's reproductive freedom and choice — and help us prepare for the arduous battles ahead.

Please take a moment — today — and return the most generous contribution you can. I look forward to adding your name back to our list of valued members.

Sincerely,

Vincent Wishrad
Vincent Wishrad

Your support is critically needed to protect the freedom of choice in America. Please reactivate your membership today! Thank you!

EXHIBIT 4.1.
NARAL Lift Letter to Long-Lapsed Members

When NARAL added this lift letter to its standard prospecting package to lapsed donors, response rates and average gift from lapsed members increased compared with those who received the prospecting package without this letter.

can be a great volunteer job for someone who is eager to help out from home. Or you can turn it into a group activity by doing the phoning from your office or another site with several phone lines and enjoy the energy of success together. Here's how to manage such a group phoning activity:

- Schedule a calling night on a weekday evening.

- Around 6 P.M. bring your volunteer callers together in one place that has enough telephones and telephone lines so that each person or each two people have a telephone.

- Provide each caller with a script, private phone, and list of names and phone numbers of lapsed members to be called. If you have more volunteers than phones, the extra people can help look up phone numbers or put together follow-up mailings.

- Before calling begins, bring everyone together to discuss the purpose of the calls, how to answer typical questions, and what to do if an answering machine picks up (see the next paragraph) and to review the script and identify next steps.

- Begin calling. Let the group listen as you make the first few calls.

- After forty-five minutes of individual calling, regroup and quickly share accomplishments, feedback, and tips that are working.

- Get back on the phones.

- At 8:30 P.M. ask everyone to call back the folks they have tried to reach more than once and leave a message if there is an answering machine (for example, see the suggested message in the next paragraph).

- Prepare confirmation letters for follow-up mailing the next day.

- Total up your success and celebrate!

How to handle answering machines needs to be decided ahead of time. Many people screen calls, others are simply not home most evenings. Consider instructing callers to attempt three phone calls for each number during the evening. If a machine picks up on the first two calls, they should hang up without leaving a message. If on the third call they still are left with an answering machine, provide them with a message to leave such as the following:

Hi, I'm Willow Bynum, a fellow member of [organization name]. I'm sorry I missed you tonight. Several of us are volunteering to call members who have not yet renewed their membership. I wanted to make sure you know how important your continued participation is to the future success of [organization] and the work it is doing on behalf of you, me, and our community. Since I wasn't able to reach you tonight, I will go ahead and put a renewal reminder in the mail to you tomorrow. I hope that you will be able to respond positively and join us once again. Thank you for your past support of [organization]. I look forward to your continued support. If you have any questions about my call, please feel free to call [group's phone number].

All phone contacts in which the member agreed to renew or a message was left should be followed up with a reminder letter, a renewal form, and a response envelope mailed the next day. Ask your phone volunteers to address the outer envelopes by hand and add a personal note to the reminder letter as they complete each call.

A final question concerns credit cards. If your group can accept credit card payments (more on this later in this chapter), decide whether you want volunteers to be taking that information. If you are concerned about confidentiality issues or your volunteers are uncomfortable taking credit card information, you may wish to invite people to mail back their renewal dues when they receive your follow-up pledge letter. Another option is to invite your treasurer to participate in the evening to take credit card information. In that case, once the caller completes their discussion with the members, the member is transferred to the treasurer, who takes the credit card information.

Upgrading renewal gifts

Renewals can be a great opportunity not only to ask members to continue to support your organization and get more involved, but also to increase their level of support. One of the easiest ways to do this is to ask your members to increase their gift to the next level. If your database includes information such as expiration date and amount of the last joining gift (either initial membership gift or last renewal gift), incorporating this upgrade ask can be accomplished by programming an algorithm or if-then statements into your database or word processing program.

The sample renewal response forms in Exhibit 4.2 show how this can be done.

The Alaska Wilderness League's response forms are preprinted, three-up, on a standard 8½-by-11-inch sheet. In this example, the top form is a renewal, the bottom one is a special appeal, and the middle form shows what the preprinted form looks like before it is imprinted for a specific mailing. The beauty of this form is that you can use the same one for all of your member mailings. Just tailor the "Yes" statement for the specific campaign.

For renewals, information about the date and amount of the member's last joining gift is included, along with an invitation to join at the next level: "Your membership expires on 4/18/2002 [expiration date from database]. Thank you for your last membership gift of $18 [last joining gift from database]. Please consider renewing at $25 [selected by if-then statements in word processor]."

YES! **Please renew my membership today.** The Alaska Wilderness League is my voice for the Arctic National Wildlife Refuge and the Tongass National Forest in Alaska.

Your membership expires on 4/18/2002. Thank you for your last membership gift of $18. Please consider renewing at $25.00

☐$25 ☐$35 ☐$50 ☐$75 ☐$100
☐$15 Student/Senior ☐Other_____

Phone: _____

E-mail: _____

☐ Sign me up for automatic giving (see back).
☐ My check is enclosed, payable to Alaska Wilderness League.
☐ Charge my credit card: ☐VISA ☐MasterCard

Card #: _____ /_____
  Exp. Date

Signature: _____

Thank you for your support of Alaska Wilderness League.
Your donation is tax-deductible to the full extent of the law.

ALASKA WILDERNESS LEAGUE

122 C Street NW, Suite 240,
Washington, D.C. 20001
Tel: 202/544-5205 Fax: 202/544-5197
www.alaskawild.org

13850 - R4A0802RNL

Fran⌐ ᵀest ⌐nd
⌐53 1. ⌐ A ⌐E
⌐⌐vue, ⌐ 9⌐ ⌐-3⌐
‖.l‖⌐. ⌐l‖l‖⌐ .⌐⌐l‖. ⌐ll‖⌐. ⌐l‖⌐l‖‖.l‖l

Please make any address corrections above.

ALASKA WILDERNESS LEAGUE

122 C Street NW, Suite 240,
Washington, D.C. 20001
Tel: 202/544-5205 Fax: 202/544-5197
www.alaskawild.org

Phone: _____

E-mail: _____

☐ Sign me up for automatic giving (see back).
☐ My check is enclosed, payable to Alaska Wilderness League.
☐ Charge my credit card: ☐VISA ☐MasterCard

Card #: _____ /_____
  Exp. Date

Signature: _____

Thank you for your support of Alaska Wilderness League.
Your donation is tax-deductible to the full extent of the law.

Please make any address corrections above.

YES! **I would like to make a special contribution** to the Alaska Wilderness League. Please use my special contribution to ensure that the House-Senate Energy Conference Committee keeps Arctic Drilling out of the final version of the Energy Bill. Here is my contribution of:

☐$25 ☐$35 ☐$50 ☐$75 ☐$100
☐$15 Student/Senior ☐Other_____

Phone: _____

E-mail: _____

☐ Sign me up for automatic giving (see back).
☐ My check is enclosed, payable to Alaska Wilderness League.
☐ Charge my credit card: ☐VISA ☐MasterCard

Card #: _____ /_____
  Exp. Date

Signature: _____

Thank you for your support of Alaska Wilderness League.
Your donation is tax-deductible to the full extent of the law.

ALASKA WILDERNESS LEAGUE

122 C Street NW, Suite 240,
Washington, D.C. 20001
Tel: 202/544-5205 Fax: 202/544-5197
www.alaskawild.org

25041 - SPA0802MEL

M⌐ ⌐ M R⌐ ⌐ll
432 ⌐ ⌐te St
⌐in, l⌐ ⌐123-7⌐
l⌐. ⌐⌐⌐ll⌐. ‖l⌐l⌐l⌐. ⌐l⌐l⌐ll⌐⌐l⌐l⌐ll

4884

Please make any address corrections above.

EXHIBIT 4.2.
Alaska Wilderness League Response Forms

This set of three response forms shows how the same form can be used for several types of mailings. To the standard form, shown here in the middle position, is added language specific to the particular renewal (top) or appeal (bottom) it will accompany.

Although incorporating this kind of an ask will require some computer programming, it does increase the average renewal gift. For the four groups I have tracked that have used this approach, that increase has averaged $5 per person. If you are renewing one thousand members a year, you could expect an additional $5,000 simply by investing in a few hours of computer programming.

Including the upgrade information on the form rather than—or in addition to—in the letter saves you time and money. Usually you are already personalizing the form by including the member's name, address, and source code information. By asking for an upgrade on the form as well, you simply add one more bit of information to the personalization process. This may also relieve you of the need to personalize your renewal letters, especially in the first few asks when you are contacting a high percentage of folks who are likely to renew right away.

The second reason for asking for the upgrade on the form rather than just in the letter has to do with how people process bills and requests for money at home. Most people who decide to give generally keep the response form and return envelope in their pile of bills to pay. The outer envelope and the request letter get recycled or thrown out. Then, a week or two later, when they are paying bills, your well-crafted letter asking for an upgraded gift is nowhere to be found. Only the response form remains to let the member know what their last gift was and urge them to upgrade.

Accepting credit cards

An important goal of your membership campaign must be to minimize the barriers to the prospect saying "Yes." Being able to accept credit cards can make a difference by allowing a prospect to respond at the moment they are motivated by your invitation to join, even if they may not have the money in their checkbook at that moment. Also, many people prefer to pay by credit card if it will garner them frequent flier miles or other card benefits.

If your organization does not already accept credit cards, put researching this option on your priority list. Most banks discount their charges for servicing credit cards for nonprofit organizations. If you do not already have a relationship with a local financial institution, this is a good time to check out your options and set up an account with the one that is most responsive to your needs. Not only is the ability to receive credit card donations a convenience factor for your members, there is some indication that when paying with a credit card individuals may give a larger gift than if they were paying by check. In addition, allowing credit card payment is essential for establishing a monthly donor program, as discussed in Chapter Twelve.

Renewal premiums

Some groups use premiums—a special book, logo gear, or other merchandise exclusive to the organization—to encourage renewing. You should test this kind of program from time to time. One group I worked with had been offering an automatic renewal premium for every gift level for twenty years. When we tested the premium by offering it to only half the renewal list, the group that was *not* offered the premium actually had a (slightly) higher response rate and almost an identical average gift. The group will certainly want to test this response again over time, but they may be able to save money and staff effort by simply encouraging people to renew without offering them a premium for doing so.

This experience reinforces what you probably already learned from your members' survey: your members want you to spend their money on the work that they've hired or invested in you to do rather than on T-shirts and tote bags. That said, there are two situations in which premiums or exclusive services can make a difference. First, when you are trying to upgrade an individual's gift a unique premium might encourage them to take the leap from being a $50 member to a $100 member or even higher. Second, after you have already sent three renewal reminders, you may wish to test the power of premiums to sweeten the offer in future reminders.

Whenever you are offering a premium, provide the member with the opportunity not to receive it by including a check box on your response form where they can decline: "☐ Please keep my premium and devote all of my membership dues to [your organization's name]'s good work."

Tracking your responses: source codes

The classic method for tracking the effectiveness of your various campaigns is to use source codes. As shown on the Alaska Wilderness League response form in Exhibit 4.2, a source code should be included on each of your mailings and publications. (In these examples, the source code begins with R for renewals and SP for special appeals. The preceding number is the member's ID number, included as an aid to data entry.) Resource C suggests a protocol for designing source codes.

In addition, you should assign a source code to other activities that generate contributions or inquiries about your organization. These include e-mail campaigns, special events, and perhaps even editorial pieces in your local newspaper—any effort that may inspire a significant number of individuals to join, send you a gift, call you up, or otherwise register their interest in your organization. Source codes will allow you to use many of the techniques identified in this and future chapters. Here are some examples of how source codes can be used:

- Source codes allow you to send one bulk mailing, using the same letter and response form, to those receiving first, second, third, fourth, and fifth renewal notices and still keep track of which notice the respondent sent back with their donation.

- Source codes will help you identify whether your longer, special-appeal-type renewal letters are more, less, or equally attractive to those who receive them as shorter, one-page approaches.

- Source codes will help you identify which topics draw the greatest response from members. For example, knowing whether the renewal letter about your food bank was more or less popular than the one about job training may gain you some insight into which topics members are most likely to respond to, as well as some tips on how to communicate most compellingly in the future.

Most databases include a function for logging your source code list and description. In addition, it is useful to keep a notebook or file with samples of each of your communications by source code. See Resource D for a Membership Activities Report form that can help you retain important data about each of your campaigns. This kind of information will help you be even more effective in the future by providing examples of best practices and documentation for you and your successor.

Calculating your renewal rate

Your renewal rate provides you with a useful measure of the effectiveness of your renewal efforts, the loyalty of your members, the resonance of your programs and messages, and the number of new members you need to recruit each year simply to retain your current membership level. To calculate your renewal rate, use the Renewal Rate Calculation Worksheet. A sample is shown in Worksheet 4.3. Keeping track of your renewal rate is simply a matter of reliable recordkeeping and regular updating.

Here are the steps for using the worksheet:

1. *Log the number of first renewal notices you mail each time you send renewals.* For example, if you're using the every-six-week renewal schedule suggested earlier, the Date Mailed column should reflect the actual dates you mailed four renewal only and four renewal/special appeal campaigns throughout the year. In the example on the worksheet, first renewal notices were mailed on 2/01/04 to one hundred members with expiration dates between March 1, 2004 and April 15, 2004. For each subsequent renewal mailing (those shown for 3/15/04 and 5/1/04, for example), you add the corresponding first-notice date range and total of packages mailed. (See Worksheet 4.2 for the schedule and date range for each

Renewal Rate Calculation Worksheet

By following the instructions for this worksheet, you will be able to calculate your renewal rates for each renewal notice mailed, as well as an overall average.

Date Mailed	Number of 1st Renewal Notices Mailed	Expiration Dates Mailed	Renewal Rate After 3 Months			Renewal Rate After 6 Months			Renewal Rate After 9 Months		
			Date	Number with Same Expiration Date	Renewal Rate	Date	Number with Same Expiration Date	Renewal Rate	Date	Number with Same Expiration Date	Renewal Rate
2/1/2004	100	3/1/04–4/15/04	5/1/2004	72	28.00%	8/1/2004	49	51.00%	11/6/2004	39	61.00%
3/15/2004	142	4/16/04–5/31/04	6/13/2004	96	32.39%	9/18/2004	63	55.63%	12/14/04	45	68.31%
5/1/2004	78	6/1/04–7/15/04	8/1/2004	54	30.77%	11/6/2004	31	60.26%	2/1/2005	15	80.77%
Total	320			222	30.63%		143	55.31%		99	69.06%

renewal mailing.) Note that second, third, and other notices were probably also mailed on each of these dates; however, only the first notice count is used for calculating the renewal rate.

2. *Check your database on a quarterly basis* for how many members retain their initial expiration date. It's probably most convenient to do this check when you are pulling data for your next renewal mailing. By subtracting the number of members who still have the same expiration date from the initial number the first renewal mailing went to, then dividing by the initial number mailed, you get the number of members who have renewed their membership in that quarter. The six-month and nine-month baselines that you will come up with, and that are included in the renewal rate worksheet, allow you to track trends and patterns in your renewal rate and identify any trouble spots.

3. *Estimate your annual renewal rate* by calculating the average renewal rate for mailings nine months out. You can go back and calculate your past renewal rate the same way, if you know the number of first notices mailed each round and the number of (now-lapsed) members still within that range of expiration dates.

Once you have estimated your renewal rate, use the Renewal Planning Calendar shown in Worksheet 4.4 to project renewal income and cash flow.

Here is the way to use the worksheet:

1. *In column A, enter the number of members whose membership is set to expire in each month.* For most membership databases, this means asking the program to tally the number of members with expiration dates between the first and the last dates of each month.

2. *In columns B and C, calculate the average gift:* first, total the amount of all joining gifts of both new and renewed members with expiration dates during that month, then divide by the number of members who sent gifts. In most databases, this means asking for the total amount recorded as the most recent new-member or renewal contribution when you collect the number of folks to be renewed each month. By dividing that total by the number of members with the same expiration month (column A), you can find the (past) average renewing gift for members whose membership is set to expire during each month.

The Web-based version of this Excel worksheet integrates with a bar chart. The bar chart will show you immediately how your unrestricted income dips and climbs throughout the year. This is valuable information for planning your budget and expenditures as well as for anticipating your need for additional administrative assistance.

The bar chart can also highlight planning opportunities. For example, if you see that your membership renewals are concentrated in one, two, or three months, ask yourself why. If your recruitment efforts, as discussed later in Part Three, are relatively consistent during every month of the year, this chart may be telling you that

Renewal Planning Calendar: Estimating Revenues and Member Continuity

This worksheet provides a snapshot of the ebbs and flows of your renewals throughout the year—and the resulting surges and lulls of your cashflow. For this chart, focus on member joining gifts rather than the total of all gifts. For the most accurate projections, begin with the expiration month you are just now starting to renew and continue through a year from the current date. Months before that will have fewer renewing members, since you have already renewed some, and months after will have more, because you are still adding members.

Expiration Month	(A) Number of Memberships Expiring	Current Giving as of ___/___/20___, based on last membership gift		Projected Retention based on renewal rate (R) from Worksheet 4.3: ___%	
		(B) Total Dollars	(C) Average Gift (B ÷ A)	(D) Estimated Number of Members Renewing (A x R)	(E) Estimated Dollars (C x D)
January 2004					
February 2004					
March 2004					
April 2004					
May 2004					
June 2004					
July 2004					
August 2004					
September 2004					
October 2004					
November 2004					
December 2004					
January 2005					
February 2005					
March 2005					
April 2005					
May 2005					
June 2005					
July 2005					
August 2005					
September 2005					
Total					

your cause has some seasonality. In that case, consider focusing future new-member prospecting efforts during those most successful months.

However, peaks in the renewal planning bar chart may indicate that most of your members come from existing campaigns traditionally held in those months. For example, a surge in November may be caused by the number of new members you recruit through participation in your annual dinner and auction. If you are looking to even out your workload and your cash flow, consider testing membership recruitment campaigns in the months when renewals are lower.

Plan to update the Renewal Calendar worksheet regularly, at least before each budget cycle, to provide a reality check on the revenue and cash flow your renewals are producing.

Thank you and welcome!

Gratitude; appreciation; many thanks. Mom drilled it into us and it still is true: thank-you notes count. However you express it, a prompt acknowledgement is an important response to any contribution: renewal, special appeal, new member, or other gift.

Thank yous first and foremost should be prompt. A best practice, as Kim Klein says, is to "Thank before you bank." Make sure you send your gift acknowledgement before you even cash the check. By adopting this policy, your organization honors its members' donations—and provides an incentive to make sure that thank-you notes are produced and mailed promptly (or deposits can't be made).

Many membership database systems include the ability to produce thank-you notes once you document the contribution. Such functionality also allows you to include the amount and deposit date of the contribution right in the letter, so the letter can also serve as a receipt. If you have a 501(c)(3) tax status, your member may be able to deduct their donation if they itemize on their tax return. Technically, the IRS only requires donors of gifts of $250 or more to produce a tangible receipt for tax purposes. However, it is a helpful courtesy to your members at all levels to confirm in writing the size and date of their donation.

Be sure to mention that "no goods or services were exchanged for this contribution." If, instead, the member received a premium or gift with a cost to your organization of more than about $8.00 (the IRS's threshold for determining significance), recognize that the amount of the donation, less the market value of the premium, is "tax-deductible to the full extent of the law."

Your thank you shows your values

There are almost as many ways of thanking your contributors as there are organizations. Some lean grassroots groups use a pre-printed postcard with blanks to fill in name, gift amount, and date. Some board chairs send personal notes of thanks, especially in recognition of gifts of more than a certain amount.

When the Rails-to-Trails Conservancy began, executive director David Burwell adopted the policy of phoning every new member who joined at the $100 level or higher. As a new, growing organization, Rails-to-Trails was extraordinarily appreciative of each new member, especially those with the vision to make a significant investment in the group. With David's phone call, those members learned firsthand and quickly that their support was making a difference. (They got a written thank-you note and receipt, too, of course.) I have no doubt that many of those early, personally thanked members are still active in the Conservancy now, fifteen years after that initial enthusiastic thank you.

Whatever approach you choose to thank your members, be sure to systematize your routine and check it regularly for efficiency and timeliness. Thank yous are too important to get sidetracked or delayed. Besides the ill will such oversights can cause, the backlog can soon grow to overwhelming proportions. Stay up to date.

Public recognition

Many organizations also thank their members by listing the members' names in their newsletter, annual report, or other publications. This listing has the added value of documenting the number and influence of your supporters. For this strategy to be most effective, keep an eye to proportion. If your list of new members between campaigns is short, postpone your recognition until you have an impressive number. Another option is to frame your introduction so that it creates an empowering context: "The 620 other members of Gay Pride Dayton welcome February's new members."

Do you need to ask permission to recognize your members publicly? In most cases, probably not. But there are exceptions. Most people who prefer anonymity will let you know their preference when they send a gift. Some organizations serve individuals, such as government or corporate whistleblowers, who could face serious repercussions should their identity become known. In such a case, handle public acknowledgment sensitively. Also, it is a courtesy to check with your major donors before you list their support. Most will welcome the appreciation, but your phone call or e-mail will show that you are thinking of them and confirm the way they prefer to be listed.

New and renewal welcome packets

A thank you in response to a new or renewing member is also a wonderful opportunity to enlist additional assistance from that member. The adage that your last customer is most likely to be your next customer can apply to membership, given a little encouragement on your part. Something you wrote or did in the past several weeks resonated strongly enough with your member to encourage him to join or rejoin. Your new and renewing member welcome packets are the perfect opportunity to invite this recently enthusiastic member to invest their time as well as their money. Here are some features to consider including in your welcome packets:

- *Give the inside scoop.* Becoming part of a community of people with shared values is a major motivator for many joiners. Your job is to help the newcomer (or renewer) feel like an insider. Use your welcome packet to explain what benefits the member will be receiving (newsletters and discounts, for example). Invite them to save the dates for your annual meeting, monthly potlucks, auction and dinner dance, or other event. Share whatever else a member needs to know to be one of your gang.

- *Explain who's who.* Put some faces with the name of your organization. Invite the member to visit the office, by appointment or at a regularly scheduled members' open house. List the officers and staff and their responsibilities. Whom would one contact for what? Idaho Conservation League includes a listing of staff members, their responsibilities, and contact information on the back of each thank-you letter.

- *Ask for action.* If your group is involved with advocacy, consider including tips on how to get involved. Invite members to send you their e-mail address to receive action alerts. Announce plans for Lobby Day or agency watchdog training. Alaska Wilderness League includes a helpful primer on contacting Congress called "Exercising Your Right to Write" on the back of each of their thank-you notes.

- *Invite people to volunteer.* Does your food co-op need more help around the store? Can your literacy guild use another tutor? Does your PTA need assistance with the new Safe Routes to School program? Your new and renewing member packets are a great place to publicize volunteer opportunities, with this caution: be sure that you have a system in place for following up with every volunteer offer. It is frustrating for a member to offer their services as a volunteer and never be contacted; such treatment can cause them to lose faith in the organization. If you end up unexpectedly being overwhelmed with such offers, at least send an e-mail or postcard explaining the situation and asking for patience.

- *Ask for referrals.* Consider including a postcard in your welcome packets inviting members to send you the names and addresses of other people they think might be interested in your organization. Ask for permission to use the member's name when you make contact. Then, send out a letter to these prospects that begins, "I am writing you today because [member's name] is a member of our organization and thought you, too, would be interested in our work." The strength of this trusted connection and the personalized letter should gain a significant response.

• *Provide something of value.* A calendar of art center events, a guide to hikes on your land trust's properties, or a bring-a-friend-for-free coupon for the World Affairs Club's next lecture—each of these additions to your thank-you packet reinforces the value of your organization's work and encourages new and renewing members to participate again soon. The Access Fund sends members their "Membership Handbook," an informative, twenty-four-page reference booklet with everything one needs to know to be a responsible climber and get the most out of one's Access Fund membership. Decals, bumper stickers, and refrigerator magnets are inexpensive, mailable premiums that allow your members to show their affiliation while they help spread the word of your organization's existence to neighbors and friends.

Plan now to review your organization's thank-you process and make sure it is prompt, accurate, and thorough. Then, tackle those welcome packets and see how successful you can be at encouraging members to get more involved.

CHAPTER 5

Inviting Member Action Through Special Appeals

Special appeals are periodic communications that you send to your members to provide added value and information about your organization and the issues they care about, as well as to give members an additional opportunity to contribute to your work. There are several advantages to special appeals:

• Special appeals provide in-depth, timely updates for your members about one of your group's special projects or programs; each special appeal provides additional information you have reason to believe the member will find valuable.

• Special appeals can offer members a legitimate involvement action to help assure the success of the campaign you are informing them about. Such actions include signing a petition or letter of support, completing a survey or questionnaire, volunteering for an action alert team, or signing up to send a letter to the editor.

• Special appeals document the need for funds to accomplish your objectives; the more specific they are, the more convincing.

• Special appeals provide an easy way for members to provide financial support for this latest undertaking.

When an individual joins your organization, they have, in essence, invested in the promises you have made for change, community connection, a better life, fun, or services. By joining, your members have acknowledged that they can accomplish their personal goals more effectively as part of your organization than they can alone. Your job is to invest their contribution wisely, responsibly, and effectively, and remind them of the good work their investment has made possible.

Whether you have conducted your membership survey yet or not, there's one thing that you already know about each of your members: each has given you money. Special appeals are an important opportunity for your members to exercise that preference to give you money once again.

An often-quoted adage of the for-profit world is that your most recent customer is most likely to be your next customer. (That's why when you order something from a catalog there's always another catalog at the bottom of the delivery box.) If you are in fact doing the great work that you have promised your members and you have a legitimate need for additional funds to allow you to do even better on their behalf, it is appropriate to invite them to make an additional investment in the issues they care about. Your job is to make your members feel great about their past investment in your organization and to encourage them to give again and again. Special appeals are a proven, effective method for educating your members and soliciting contributions.

Quarterly is not too often

The answer to the frequent question, "How often can we ask for additional gifts?" is based in the sincerity of your request, the immediacy of your need, and the power of your communication. General fundraising wisdom tells us that organizations can easily and effectively ask their members for additional investments once a quarter, and sometimes more frequently, *if* your requests are informative, engaging, and about something your members care about. (It's only junk mail if the reader thinks it's junk.)

Someone on your team may balk at the concept of mailing special appeals quarterly. Someone will invariably come up with the horror story of joining a national organization and being deluged with requests for additional contributions every month or six weeks. However, if your special appeals follow the four value-added requirements detailed in the preceding section, you will be assured that your communications will inform your members more about the work that you are doing, explain to them how they can have an impact, and build loyalty—as well as raise additional funds. If your naysayers remain unconvinced, try adding appeals gradually and document the response, both for and against.

To put this in perspective, you can expect from 6 percent to 20 percent of your members to contribute to each of your special appeals. However, many, many more of your members are opening your letter and at least skimming the information in it about the important work your organization is undertaking. We know this because when a special appeal also includes a request for action, responses without a contribution will almost always equal or exceed the number of responses with a donation—sometimes by as much as two or three times.

Keep these numbers in mind when you receive complaints—and you *will* receive a few complaints from members about too much mail. By comparing the number of complaints to the number of donations and actions that result from special appeals, you can appropriately gauge your members' comfort with your special appeal program. Take the time to respond to each of those complaints, explaining the importance of your special appeals as education tools and offering the member the option to get only one appeal or none a year.

In the United States, your group gets an additional benefit from including a legitimate request for involvement with your special appeal. The Internal Revenue Service has determined that, under certain circumstances, communications with a request for action can be considered program activities rather than fundraising activities and should be reflected as such when you report on program expenses at the end of the year. This can make a big difference as you try to minimize the percentage of expenditures designated for fundraising and administration. (For more on this topic, see Chapter Fourteen.)

How long should your letter be?

How long a fundraising letter should be is probably one of the most frequently asked questions in fundraising. The answers might surprise you: in most cases, longer letters increase response—and every group and program is a little bit different. For that reason, you will see samples throughout this *Toolkit* of two-page letters, four-page letters, and letters of other lengths. Resource E further details the steps in writing a fundraising letter, and Resource A recommends some specific copywriting references.

We don't have a lot of information about exactly why longer letters work, but here are some patterns I've observed:

• Your issues are complicated and may be difficult to understand. It takes space to provide enough background for your members to feel adequately informed about a topic they care about.

• Those of us who are over forty probably represent a substantial portion of your membership—and are also members of the bifocal generation. An additional sheet of paper allows you to tell your members what they want to know, in a type size that they can read!

• Although most of your members are not going to read every word of your appeal, by using subheads, bullets, bold face, short paragraphs, and other techniques, you can help them glean the highlights of your message quickly. They can then read more if they wish. It takes space to make your letter readable.

Shorter (two-page) letters work best in the following cases:

a. The issue you are writing about is so central to the purpose of your group that everyone is already familiar with it

b. You have such a small, tight, dedicated membership that you expect your appeal to get a high response—the letter is simply a reminder

c. You are writing about such an immediate, time-dependent issue that you don't have time to prepare a long letter—or have someone read one

To find out what works best for your organization, review the samples in this chapter and test various approaches internally. As long as your letter is sincere, informative, and worth the time the member spends to read it, you should have success. Exhibit 5.1 shows the appeal the Alaska Wilderness League used to update their members on a fast-moving topic, explain a complicated issue, and enlist help with their letter-to-the-editor campaign. This special appeal garnered an excellent 9 percent response and recruited many valuable letters to local newspapers.

Choosing your special appeal topic

Worksheet 5.1 presents the aspects to be considered as you choose your next special appeal topic.

For each topic that may provide a subject for a special appeal, consider the items in the left-hand column to analyze its potential for success.

• *Current program priorities.* Ethically, your special appeal needs to ask for support for work that you are currently doing or, in some cases, would do if you had the resources. If, for example, you have a project that is popular with your members but for which you already have funding from foundation grants and perhaps in-kind services, that would not be a legitimate topic for a special appeal. By only asking for what you really need, you keep building trust and accountability. Similarly, if you are seeking funds for a project not yet fully funded and you suspect you may be able to raise more money than you actually need for this project, include in the letter a statement such as, "Your donation now will help assure the success of this important project and others like it in the months ahead."

• *Timeline.* Because special appeals go only to your own members, you can and should expect a relatively high rate of members opening your envelope and a relatively prompt response. To increase that response, as with all communications, having a goal that is time-limited helps to provide your members with a reason to respond today. When planning appeals with such a deadline, requesting action within a minimum of six and a maximum of sixteen weeks works best. A deadline

Special Appeal Strategy Planning Worksheet

Use this planning tool to analyze possible appeal topics for their potential for success. Most topics will not have (or need) every asset, but each addition will strengthen your appeal's attractiveness.

Mail Date: _____	Possible Topic: _____	Possible Topic: _____	Possible Topic: _____	Possible Topic: _____
Current program priorities				
Timeline/need for urgent action				
Do we own this issue?				
Coverage in our communications				
General media awareness				
History of membership interest in issue				
Emotional message/ future generations connection				
Personification potential				
Funding needed				
Incentives?				
Distribution				

ALASKA WILDERNESS LEAGUE

February 20, 2002

Dear Alaska Wilderness League Member,

If you have picked up a newspaper recently, you know the debate about the future of the Arctic National Wildlife Refuge remains front and center.

At the Alaska Wilderness League, we take seriously our commitment to be your eyes, ears, and voice here in Washington, D.C. Now, it is just a matter of days before the United States Senate begins debating energy legislation and the fate of the much-contested Arctic Refuge. By the time you read this letter, they may even have started.

Today, I am writing to you — as a member of the Alaska Wilderness League — to update you on this crucial upcoming vote and to again ask for your help.

The stage is set for a face-off between people like you and me who support protecting the wildlife and wilderness lands of this magnificent country — and oil drilling proponents who would sacrifice this last, still-pristine public legacy for six months worth of crude ten years from now.

This is a classic example of Big Business vs. the will of the American people. Your actions now can help make sure your voice – and the voice of all who cherish the natural treasures of the Arctic Refuge – is heard above the moneyed shouts of Big Oil.

Last time I wrote to you, I mentioned that drilling proponents were trying to attach drilling language to any legislation moving in the Senate. In fact, three times they attached drilling language to "must-pass" relief bills. And three times the Alaska Wilderness League and our allies rallied to defeat them.

Believe me, we couldn't have gotten to this stage of effectiveness and national attention without support from you and your fellow

122 C St NW Ste 240, Washington DC 20001 • Phone: 202-544-5205 • Fax • 202-544-5197

Use a real date to
show timeliness.

Put "you" in the
first sentence or
paragraph.

Write in the first
person.

Acknowledge past
relationships.

Break pages
mid-sentence.

EXHIBIT 5.1.
Alaska Wilderness League Special Appeal

This special appeal by Alaska Wilderness League provided members with valuable, timely information about their core issue and an opportunity to take action in addition to giving.

members. Yet, these earlier fights were just a precursor to the much larger battle looming ahead in the coming days.

Now that the New Year has arrived, Senator Majority Leader Tom Daschle has promised to bring an Energy Bill to a vote. Simultaneously, several Senate Committees will have hearings on aspects of the bill. Ultimately, pieces of the bill will be voted on and amended.

The Arctic Refuge debate will happen when a pro-drilling Senator files an amendment to Senator Daschle's Bill. Then, our Senate champions, who have vowed to stop any such amendment, will begin to filibuster.

Like a chess game, each action has a reaction. A cloture petition will be filed to end the filibuster. **The Arctic Refuge vote will be a vote for or against the filibuster.** The other side needs 60 votes to overturn a filibuster. Alaska Wilderness League is determined to make sure Big Oil doesn't get its 60 votes. I am confident that, with your continued support, we will be successful.

Whatever happens with the Arctic Refuge vote in the Senate, the story isn't over. We will continue to need the collective strength of members like you, as well as the rest of the environmental community, to help protect the Arctic National Wildlife Refuge.

The next step will be a Congressional conference committee where the differences between the Senate and House energy bills will be ironed out. This process may be so contentious it takes until Fall to reach a compromise. Your help now will make sure we go into the conference committee with a clean, protective Senate bill, giving us the strong position we need for successful negotiations.

Sometimes the fate of the Arctic Refuge seems like a David vs. Goliath scenario. Even though the Arctic Refuge is the Alaska Wilderness League's number one priority, we still are being vastly outspent. We just don't have the other side's seemingly endless resources.

Just the other day, the *Wall Street Journal* reported (January 20, 2002) that the:

"[Alaska] State House panel Tuesday approved spending $1.1 million more this year to push opening the Arctic National Wildlife Refuge to oil-drilling...The House Finance Committee bill would give $1 million to the nonprofit lobbying group Arctic Power and $100,000 to the city of Kaktovik. The spending would bring to $3 million the state money provided to Arctic Power in the fiscal year that ends June 30, said Arctic Power Executive Director Kim Duke."

Yet, even though Big Oil and its allies outspend us more than ten-to-one, the Alaska Wilderness League is still effective – thanks to the thousands of voices like yours that we bring to this debate. In fact, the **Alaska Wilderness League is obviously so effective that Big Oil is trying to intimidate us.**

Beginning last October and continuing this year, our opponents have attacked the credibility of the Alaska Wilderness League with nuisance suits and administrative filings.

Help your members understand your complexities.

Tell your members why they make a difference.

Use familiar comparisons.

Insert quotes rather than reprint articles.

Maximize your type size for easy reading.

EXHIBIT 5.1. (continued)

Their goal is to divert staff resources with their endless requests for documentation – hoping to shake our commitment to protecting the Arctic Refuge.

Well, we won't be so easily distracted. With your help, we are committed to promoting and protecting the Arctic National Wildlife Refuge for today and generations to come.

Right now, as the Alaska Wilderness League faces some of our greatest threats, I invite you to take a moment to congratulate yourself on the success you have helped make possible.

Emphasize past success.

Who would have imagined that a scrappy, independent, non-profit organization could have withstood — and even stopped — this past year's assaults on the Arctic National Wildlife Refuge?

Yet, despite the Bush Administration's continued call for drilling in the Refuge;

Despite the literally tens of millions of dollars that Big Oil and its allies have spent on lobbying, nuisance suits, and misinformation;

Despite behind-the-scenes dealings by energy cartels –

Despite all this, the Alaska Wilderness League and our allies have succeeded in protecting the treasures of the Arctic Refuge — for the time being.

Bold, indents, and short sentences ease readability and add emphasis.

We have had this success because of your willingness to speak out and take action on behalf of your beliefs. This is truly a situation where voices count. And now I'm going to ask for your support once again. Here is what you can do now to aid our efforts:

Tell your readers what you want them to do.

#1: **Donate to the Alaska Wilderness League.** Your special contribution now funds travel expenses for Arctic activists, meetings with key Senators, advertisements in swing-state newspapers, and other efforts to prove the public's support for protecting the Arctic Refuge. Return the enclosed response card, with your check, money order, or credit card donation, in the pre-addressed envelope enclosed. Faster yet, fax the enclosed form with your credit card information to (202) 544-5197. Every donation will go directly to help protect the Arctic Refuge.

Make it easy to give.

#2: **Write a Letter to the Editor** of your local newspaper to encourage others to take action on behalf of the Arctic National Wildlife Refuge. Congressional staffers rely on local letters to the editor to give them a snapshot of their constituents' concerns. Your letter now will help provide the political support your Senators need to hold the line on the Arctic. At the end of this letter, I've included a sample to get you started (feel free to write your own, too).

Number action items to emphasize their importance.

Thank you again for your support of the Alaska Wilderness League, the Arctic National Wildlife Refuge, and other wild places in Alaska. Together, we will make sure the

Give your members a chance to participate.

EXHIBIT 5.1. (continued)

Senate knows that Americans want this magnificent natural treasure – and the polar bears, caribou, musk oxen, and millions of wild birds that call it home – protected for generations to come.

Sincerely,

Cynthia D. Shogan

Cindy Shogan
Executive Director

P.S.   Your continued support now is critical. This is the time to show oil-drilling proponents that the American people want to protect our natural heritage. And, because we were so successful during 2001, now is the time when Big Oil is pulling out all the stops to make sure they overwhelm us with overspending and misinformation. Please send in your donation and write your letter to the editor today. I look forward to hearing from you soon!

> The Arctic National Wildlife Refuge is an irreplaceable natural treasure, home to birds, grizzlies, rare musk oxen, polar bears, and other wildlife. The Arctic Refuge is too valuable to sacrifice for six months of oil (perhaps) ten years from now. The coastal plain of the Refuge is also the birthing and nursery grounds for the 130,000-member Porcupine Caribou herd, one of the hemisphere's largest caribou herds. The Gwich'in Indians have called this land sacred for more than 20,000 years. This tribe depends upon caribou for food and as the foundation of their culture and traditions.
>
> What our country really needs is true energy security, not an approach that continues our pattern of increasing oil imports and consumption. Energy security for America <u>can</u> be achieved. We can and must use existing conservation technologies and renewable energy sources to end our dependence on foreign oil. According to the EPA, increasing fuel efficiency for cars, mini vans, and SUVs by just three miles per gallon would save more oil within ten years than is ever expected to be produced from the Arctic Refuge.
>
> Multinational oil companies lobbied aggressively to pass an energy bill out of the House of Representatives that allows oil drilling and development in the entire coastal plain of the Arctic Refuge. These special interests continue to push for Arctic Refuge drilling as the Senate now considers its version of the energy bill.
>
> You can help protect America's last, best pristine landscape. Call your Senators _____ and _____ today and urge them to keep oil-drilling language out of any Energy legislation and keep alternative solutions in.
>
> Sincerely,
> (Your Name)
> (Your Address

P.P.S.   *You can learn more tips on writing and placing letters to the editor on our website at www.alaskawild.org/newspapers.html. When your letter is printed, please mail or fax me a copy, along with the editorial page masthead showing the date. We will then provide a follow-up copy to your Senators when we meet with them. (And please send in your contribution today.) Thanks!*

Use one signer.

Summarize your letter and call to action in the P.S.

Identify your strongest message and keep repeating it.

EXHIBIT 5.1. (continued)

that is shorter than six weeks runs the risk that individuals will not be able to respond before the deadline has passed (because of slow mail delivery, their own financial situation, their tendency to put off opening such mail, or other reasons). Beyond three to four months you lose the sense of immediacy that encourages people to act today.

Your deadline can be established internally or externally. For example, a deadline could be a city council budget hearing, the reconvening of the state legislature, or the date of an upcoming agency public hearing. It could be seasonal: return of children to school, holiday hunger pains, the onset of winter, or the return of migrating birds. You can create your own deadline by setting a fundraising goal: "Our goal is to raise half of these funds from our members by May 21st, before we launch this campaign publicly," or the need to fulfill a matching grant: "Our board has pledged to match all donations received by August 31."

• *Do we own this issue?* This factor considers both your members' perception and knowledge of your organization as well as your program activities. For example, if you are a state- or province-wide advocacy group that members value in part because of your activism in the legislature and your special appeal is asking for support for your legislative work, you clearly own this issue and your members are aware of it and care about it. On the other hand, you can certainly send a special appeal about a new campaign you are initiating. In that case, help your members understand the place of this new issue in your work by explaining how the fundamental issues your members care about benefit from this new direction.

• *Coverage in your communications.* Ideally, one to two weeks before they receive your special appeal, your members will receive your newsletter featuring an article on the topic of your appeal. (More about newsletters in Chapter Six.) The special appeal then provides them with additional, up-to-date information about the issue, along with some specific action steps they can take to assist with your success, including the opportunity to make a donation. Your newsletter article raises the visibility of the issue; your special appeal provides an opportunity for your member to act on that awareness.

One cautionary note here: Some organizations have perpetual difficulty meeting deadlines for newsletter publication. Do *not* delay sending your special appeal because the newsletter is running late. Your organization's cash flow and ability to be successful depend on revenues you solicit through your renewals and special appeals. The ability to reinforce your special appeal's power with an introduction through the newsletter is valuable but far from required. Consider instead, or even in addition, sending a brief informational e-mail to all members for whom you have e-mail addresses on the day you mail your special appeal, telling them to expect a letter from you soon, with detailed information about your important project.

- *General media awareness.* Coverage in local, regional, or national press of your planned or proposed activities—or something reinforcing the need for them—can certainly enhance your members' awareness of and concern about your special appeal topic. The more your members hear about your special appeal topic in advance, the more likely they are to take action when you ask them. Whenever possible, coordinate your special appeal's theme, message, and timing to complement your group's other public information and communication efforts.

- *History of membership interest in the issue.* Do you have a special topic that is a favorite of your membership? Is there a program or project that always seems to be the topic of conversation at meetings or volunteer nights? If so, chances are this will be a great topic for a special appeal; this is your chance to tell your members in depth about new developments and ask for their financial support. This is another good reason to track the relative response to past special appeals and other campaigns through source codes (see Resource C). A strong understanding of the performance of past appeals provides analysis you can build on for future success.

- *Emotional message and connection with future generations.* Special appeals present a wonderful opportunity to speak in an intimate, collegial, friendly voice with your members. The tone and attitudes that you incorporate into your special appeals can enhance your organization's sense of community. One of the best ways to do this is to tell a story. Speaking in the first person, the letter signer—usually the executive director or president—can speak from the heart about why she personally cares about this issue and why it makes a difference to her family and the reader's. Explaining the impact of this project on future generations can add to the letter's effectiveness.

- *Personification potential.* The writer can also discuss how someone related to the organization has had—or could have, with the member's help—a profound impact on the issue at hand. The person featured in your letter could be the staff scientist who has dedicated a dozen years to becoming the expert on wildlife protection in your state. Or you can tell the story of how your mentoring program has changed (or will change) the life of a child or family in your community. Another possibility is to highlight the qualifications, training, and accomplishments of your new executive director or other staff person, with the purpose of the special appeal to secure the funds needed to keep this person on staff for the full year. The objective of personification is to take what might be a rather esoteric and potentially obscure program (the techniques for reaching your goals) and make it real by explaining how it makes a difference in the lives of people the member can relate to (the benefits).

Jessica Hixson, outreach coordinator for The Snake River Alliance, used the power of personification in a special appeal to support volunteers who were traveling from Idaho to Washington, D.C., to lobby for cleaning up nuclear wastes and ending U.S. nuclear weapons production.

The following paragraphs, excerpted from Snake River Alliance's special appeal, help readers understand the importance of this project and the dedication of participating volunteers:

> Our annual DC Days are a great opportunity to join activists from around the country for four days in Washington, D.C., to focus on cleaning up nuclear wastes and ending U.S. nuclear weapons production.
>
> Participants take part in skill-building and issue workshops; hold a media event; meet with senators, representatives and other government officials; honor people who have made special contributions to the cause; and network with fellow nuclear and peace activists from around the world.
>
> **We'd like you to join other Alliance members and staff in DC Days 2002.** What is required of each participant is a commitment to help raise the $700 cost to attend DC Days. In addition, participants need stamina for long days on Capitol Hill, flexibility in dealing with changing circumstances, and a good sense of humor. The Alliance assists participants' efforts by asking our current members to contribute to DC Days.
>
> **If you are unable to join us this year, please help enable someone else to go.** A donation of $25, $50, $100 or more would be a great help to get us on our way. In the past, members also have donated frequent-flyer miles or tickets or helped find someone to house or host us in D.C. An envelope is provided for your donation. **Please be generous!**

The letters were preceded by telephone calls telling members about the campaign. Five volunteers and four staff members who were going to Washington reached about a quarter of the membership by phone to ask for support for their trip. They followed a script Jessica had created and watched her make the first calls. They did not accept money over the phone, but alerted members to the letter and asked for their help. Jessica then mailed 852 letters (at a cost of $682). She received 143 responses (an impressive 16.8 percent return) and gifts totaling $5,779 (for an average gift of $40.41); net income was $5,096.

• *Funding needed.* Be as specific as possible in communicating to your members the costs involved in accomplishing a special appeal project. Sharing this information reinforces your members' trust by letting them know that you value their contribution, will be accountable for its investment, and will use it efficiently. Being forthright about the amount of money you need enables the member to place his ability to give in the scale of your needs. This cost factor should include all of the costs of accomplishing your project: direct costs such as travel, phone, printing, and supplies, as well as direct staff time, and overhead costs including a portion of the rent, computers, heat, light, and the time it takes other personnel to oversee and participate in the success of the program. Ideally, the number you end up with will be a bit more than you usually attract to your special appeals, but not so large that the individual cannot see his ability to affect your goal.

Idaho Conservation League's experience with a year-end appeal is a great example of the power of telling your members what a program will cost. Staff estimated it would cost $25,000 to support the League's presence during the upcoming state legislature's session. This seemed like an unattainable goal, as their most successful past appeal had raised just under $12,000. Yet the letter shown in Exhibit 5.2 was a great success. It was used both as a year-end appeal and, slightly tweaked, as a renewal request (in a scheme similar to that recommended in Chapter Four). The letter, with its request for both a survey response and a contribution, went to a total of 2,538 members. Nearly one-quarter of the recipients sent back the survey, and a very healthy 12.9 percent sent donations as well. The total income was an astounding $35,943, including two $5,000 gifts. On the third day following the appeal mailing, executive director Rick Johnson received a call from a steady supporter. He wanted to understand more about the organization's plans for working with the state legislature. After a short conversation, the member shared that the past year had been quite a successful one for him. In appreciation of the work the League was doing, the member committed a gift of $5,000 and offered to recruit another member to match that gift. The member specifically credited knowing how much the project would cost and how big an impact his gift could make as motivation for increasing his contribution tenfold. As a result, the League not only exceeded its fundraising goal, it also gained two new significant major donors.

You can also communicate the impact of a single gift using the "UNICEF approach." This technique, used successfully by UNICEF and other groups, reinforces the impact of each donation by assigning a gift value to specific program activities. For example, "Your gift of $36 will feed a homeless family of four for seven days." When using this approach, be sure to provide a wide range of gifts, from $20 up to $1,000 and more. Then, make sure that the gift amounts suggested on your response form match the gift amounts described in your letter.

• *Incentives.* Some organizations have successfully used matching gifts as an incentive for a special appeal. Such an arrangement can frequently be arranged with a current donor on a no-lose basis for your organization. For example, when the Carlson Foundation announced a $10,000 gift to the Bicycle Alliance of Washington, Alliance executive director Barbara Culp worked with the foundation to position the gift as a matching grant for the group's bicycle commuting and education programs. The Alliance then developed a special appeal around these programs that announced that gifts would be matched up to $10,000 by the Carlson Foundation. The result was a welcome leverage for the foundation's gift and added incentive for members to contribute to this program.

Some groups have also used premiums effectively to encourage larger-than-usual special appeal gifts. Consider offering a premium gift to anyone giving about one-third more than your average special-appeal gift. This will encourage donors

November 12, 1997

Dear Friend of Wild Idaho:

Snow has settled on the wild heart of Idaho. Cottonwoods along our rivers stand bare and fingers of ice are reaching into pockets of still water. The brilliant tamaracks of the north have flared with autumn color. Ducks and geese are on the move, and the long evenings are bringing friends and family together. Another year is passing by.

For the Idaho Conservation League, our 24th year of working together to protect the water, wildlife, and wild lands of Idaho is drawing to a close.

And for another year, the wild heart of Idaho beats strong in this increasingly unwild world surrounding us. *Wilderness!* For Idaho it defines us. *Clean, clear water!* It is the blood of our economy and way of life. *Wildlife!* How many of your out-of-state friends and family live where wolves howl, herds of elk and pronghorn roam mountains and grasslands, and wild trout, salmon and steelhead can be found? *We are very lucky.*

At this time of year we traditionally give thanks and show appreciation. Now is a perfect time to remember how wonderful Idaho is, what it has given to you, and how much poorer we'd be in a less rich Idaho, a less wild Idaho.

In January 1998, we will represent you and your family before the Legislature for the 25th time. *With your help, the Idaho Conservation League will once again be there to voice your concerns.* Some legislators have already begun an effort to weaken the public's ability to protect neighborhoods through local land-use planning. This is no time to just wait and see what happens. We are already building a broad-based coalition to stop this damaging bill. More and more, issues once debated on a federal stage are being handed to the states. We will also be working during the Legislature to pass bills to protect Idaho's clean water and address Idaho's thousands of abandoned mining sites.
For you, your family and the Idaho we love, the Idaho Conservation League plans to be there, and be well prepared.

As the Idaho Conservation League begins its 25th year, I'm writing to ask you to do two things to make sure the Idaho Conservation League is as effective as possible in 1998.
#1. Please fill out the enclosed survey and return it by November 30. This will give us information about what you think our legislative priorities should be before the session begins in January.
#2. Please renew your membership with the Idaho Conservation League so we can count on your membership support during the 1998 legislative session.

We're making a special effort to raise $25,000 to face the threats before us this legislative session. Why is this so important? The Idaho Conservation League is before the Legislature each and every year because you provide us the support to represent conservation.

P.O. Box 844, Boise, Idaho 83701 • 413 W. Idaho, Suite 203 • (208) 345-6933 • Fax (208) 344-0344
E-Mail: icl@icl.desktop.org
Coeur d'Alene Field Office: 103 S. 4th St., Rm. 259, Coeur d'Alene, ID 83814 • (208) 664-9184 • Fax (208) 765-5117
Ketchum Field Office: P.O. Box 2671, Ketchum, ID 83340 • (208) 726-7485 • Fax (208) 726-8437
Moscow Field Office: P.O. Box 9783, Moscow, ID 83843 • (208) 882-1010 • Fax (208) 882-1010

EXHIBIT 5.2.
Idaho Conservation League Special Appeal

This special appeal/renewal combination specified the amount of money needed for the project ($25,000) and doubled the income of any previous appeal this group had sent.

And let me tell you, representing conservation in the Statehouse is not easy! But, we have a long list of accomplishments to show why it's important. Last year we helped pass state mining law improvements and a bill to protect streamside habitat, just to name two.

And early 1998 will bring more than just the Legislature. Have you been to Copper Basin? It's an extraordinarily beautiful circular valley ringed by the Pioneer, White Knob and White Cloud Mountains in between Ketchum and Mackay. Phelps-Dodge, one of the world's largest mining companies, wants to begin exploratory drilling for copper here.

Imagine an open pit copper mine scarring this gorgeous landscape. This kind of mine is massive. Huge. Destructive. Even the possibility of one in the Copper Basin is crazy. When the Idaho Conservation League learned of the threat to Copper Basin this summer, we jumped in immediately and brought it to the attention of thousands. We are currently gathering information to counter the next move by Phelps-Dodge, expected in the spring of 1998.

Does your heart hold a special place in the public lands of Idaho? Chances are, that place is not fully protected. The *Owyhee Canyonlands* is still threatened by a bombing range, mining claims are still scattered throughout the *White Clouds*, and the Lewis and Clark country on the *Clearwater and Lochsa* is threatened with large-scale, industrial logging, including one creek which is home to 15% of all remaining wild salmon in the Snake River system. As a result of your continued support, you can count on the Idaho Conservation League to represent you by tracking the paper trails, attending important meetings, and, if necessary, going to court to protect these and other treasured places.

Your special contribution is particularly important now, as we prepare for this upcoming session of the Legislature. Please help us keep Idaho wild by returning the enclosed survey, with your donation by November 30.

We all have much to be thankful for—including Idaho. Our state will only stay this wonderful if people like us work together to keep it so. **You and your family are partners in our work for clean water, wilderness, and wildlife. Together, we make a difference.** Thanks for your past support.

for the wild,

Rick Johnson
Executive Director

P.S. Remember this magic place we call home. The wild heart of Idaho will beat strong so long as we work together to protect it. On behalf of all of us at the Idaho Conservation League, we wish you and your family an enjoyable holiday season, and we sincerely thank you for all your help. Your gift is tax deductible, and will help ensure our effectiveness at the Legislature in January. I look forward to hearing from you soon.

EXHIBIT 5.2. (continued)

to stretch their giving in order to receive the premium. The premium should be tied directly to the issue at hand. For example, the Colorado Environmental Coalition has had considerable success with offering a book featuring hikes and photographs of the Colorado canyon lands when their special appeal and new-member recruitment campaigns feature canyon lands initiatives.

Your special appeal topic need not have all of the factors on the worksheet in order to be successful. However, the more of these factors that pertain to a topic, the more likely you'll have an appreciative response from your members.

The power of year-end giving

Most nonprofits enjoy a significant boost in giving levels during the last two months of the year. Historically, November and December are the most common times for members to send you a gift. It may come as a surprise to learn that the end of the tax year is not much of a factor here: *The Chronicle of Philanthropy* reports that the tax deductibility of a gift ranks about fourteenth on the list of motivators for people to give at non–major donor levels. This is partly because only about one-third of the U.S. population actually itemizes on their tax returns, enabling them to benefit from the tax-deductibility of charitable giving.

A big reason that special appeals in the last quarter of the year are so successful is that the mainstream culture and media reinforce your message of making a contribution. November and December are for the celebration of thanksgiving (Canadians get an October boost on this one) and the season of giving. Your special appeal, arriving at a time when your members are repeatedly hearing about the importance of giving and are in holiday gift-giving mode, provides a convenient opportunity for your supporters to respond to these cultural, societal—and, yes, commercial—directives. That's why the Special Appeal Calendar (see Exhibit 4.2 in Chapter Four) recommends mailing a special appeal in early- to mid-November.

On years when there are November elections, time your appeal to arrive shortly after Election Day in order to avoid competing with the deluge of electioneering mail and no later than the week before Thanksgiving. Many families make their giving decisions at Thanksgiving, so you want them to receive your message before the holiday. If, however, you find that you simply cannot make that pre-Thanksgiving window, mail your year-end special appeal as soon after Thanksgiving as possible. Responsiveness begins to drop precipitously after about December 15, when people are overwhelmed with family activities, special celebrations, and the myriad obligations of the year-end holidays.

Distribution and personalization

In general, your appeal should go to all your members. Those who are being renewed at that time receive the same information, but with a renewal ask. If your topic is particularly hot, you could also send this appeal to prospects who have contacted you or otherwise registered an interest in your organization, but have not yet joined. A powerful appeal might be just the ticket to convince them to make an investment and join.

If you have used this same topic in an earlier appeal, consider personalizing your letters to members who gave to that appeal. Kirsten Lee, former membership director at Audubon Society of Portland (Oregon), sends a personalized version of the appeal letter to people who have given $50 or more to an appeal on the same topic in the past. These members respond far better than other segments of the mailing: 13 to 16 percent instead of an average 2 percent.

Finally, if you find that your special appeal brings an extraordinary response, consider using it as the basis for a new-member prospecting piece (see Chapter Ten). The topic's popularity with your members is a good indication that it will also work with the allied public. (Similarly, if a special appeal meets with lackluster results from your members, it is a sure indication that it will do even more poorly with the public.)

Special appeals and major donors

People in my workshops often ask whether special appeals should go to major donors. The answer is yes. Your major donors are among your most enthusiastic and dedicated—as well as generous—members. You definitely want them to know about your most exciting and current projects, and that's what your special appeals highlight. Personalize these requests to reinforce the heightened relationship you have with these folks by using a closed-face envelope (no window), first class stamp, inside address and personal greeting, and a real signature, preferably accompanied by a short note from the signer.

If you are in the midst of a major donor campaign (see Chapter Twelve), consider sending your special appeal with a Post-It note saying something like, "Here's our latest project. I look forward to talking with you next week regarding this most recent development. I'll give you a call." Alternatively, you could rewrite the letter without the ask and use it simply as an update. This approach is especially appropriate for members who have recently given you a large gift. Your appeals are a valuable update on your work, reinforcing the pride donors feel in having made such a smart investment in your organization. Make sure your best donors also get this reinforcement.

Save time with a mail shop

Like the vast majority of membership staff and volunteers, you probably have far more work to do than time to do it in. Here's one way to lighten your load: find yourself a reliable mail shop and use it.

A mail shop is a commercial service provider that takes your printed pieces (letter, response form, outside envelope, and return envelope), along with your mailing list (electronic or labels), and prepares your mailing for the post office. Mail shop vendors will, in most cases, fold your materials, insert them, seal the envelopes, apply addresses to the envelope or response form, sort for bulk mail, and deliver your mailing to the post office. To save yourself even more time, many mail shops will even manage the printing for you. In that case, you e-mail them the text of your letter and response form along with your mailing data; you never have to touch a printed piece, lick an envelope, or stick on a stamp again.

By checking with your colleagues from similar-sized organizations in your community, you can probably identify one or two mail shops that fit your needs. It is particularly efficient to use a mail shop for mailings of one thousand pieces or more. The cost and convenience far outweigh the time and energy you put into recruiting volunteers (or your school-aged children) to stuff envelopes and prepare your mailing for the post office. For larger mailings, a mail shop may actually end up saving you as much as it costs, by taking advantage of bar-coded postal discounts.

Meanwhile, you can be spending your time on the important work of drafting that next special appeal, fine-tuning your renewal program, and otherwise improving your membership program (and your revenues).

Raising money for operations

Contributions from your members are your best and quickest source of unrestricted revenue and, for advocacy organizations, can be used for lobbying efforts that foundations are prohibited from funding (see Chapter Fourteen for more on lobbying restrictions). The catch in raising operating revenue is that appeals that focus on program are more likely to be compelling to your membership than those seeking funds to cover your on-going operations. Here are two ways to ensure that you can maintain the balance between direct benefit and general support:

• *The overview appeal.* This classic is most commonly used at year-end, but could be used any time. In an overview appeal, the president or executive director summarizes a range of past accomplishments and thanks the member for making those successes possible. The appeal goes on to describe the similar range of challenges and opportunities the organization will be presented with in the months ahead. The member is invited to make a gift to help the organization sustain its effectiveness in the future. Because this appeal features just about everything the organization is involved with, it is legitimate to allocate the monies raised on an as-needed basis.

• *Quantify staff and overhead costs by the products they produce.* This approach is especially effective on an anniversary date or as a year-end appeal. For example, a mental health clinic could craft a special appeal for its executive director's salary and office expenses by quantifying the benefits the community has accrued by having the office available full time. Specifically, the board president (the letter signer) can explain that, prior to hiring the clinic director, the organization had difficulty just keeping up with phone calls; outreach programs were virtually impossible. Now, in only the first eight months of the clinic director's presence, she has enabled the organization to begin four weekly support groups, provide one-on-one care to more than one hundred clients, and initiate partnerships with health professionals in the county's major hospitals—as well as answer phone calls. All of this was possible because there is someone as qualified as your clinic director on hand full-time to respond confidentially and quickly to community residents on their own time and schedule. Members' gifts now will help this much-needed success continue.

The signer

In most cases, only one individual should sign your letters. This allows the letter to be written in the first person, enhancing the one-to-one connection between the member and the leadership of the organization. It also allows the writer to share a personal experience or story that intensifies the connection.

Plan your next special appeal now!

As foundation and corporate funding diminishes, healthy organizations will increasingly depend on their members as sources of speedy support. Worksheet 5.2 is designed to help you plan ahead for quarterly special appeals throughout the year. Start by filling in the topic of your appeals, as you know them. (Try to coordinate with your newsletter's editorial coverage, mailing an article on the same topic one or two weeks before you mail your special appeal.) Then identify your target mail dates, coordinating with your newsletter distribution plan whenever practical (see also Worksheets 4.1 and 4.2 for mail dates). Be sure to plan a fourth-quarter appeal in that all-important window in November just after Election Day and before Thanksgiving (in the United States)—by November 15, if possible.

Work backward from your mail date to schedule the specific tasks identified in the left column. This planner estimates that it will take seven weeks from the

Annual Special Appeal Planner

Use this planner to schedule the time you will need to send quarterly special appeals to your members.

Tasks/Timing	Week	First Quarter: _____	Second Quarter: _____	Third Quarter: _____	Fourth Quarter: _____
Subject/topic: _____ _____					
Mail date: _____ (postage check deposited)	0				
Labels/disk and printing to mail shop	–1				
Artwork to printer	–2				
Newsletter mailed	–2				
Final copy approved	–2.5				
Final copy circulated	–3				
First draft comments received	–4				
First draft circulated	–4.5				
Printing/production bids	–5				
Segmenting/quantities set; incentives confirmed	–5				
Mail to: _____ _____ _____ _____					
Research	–6				
Topic determined	–7				

time you determine your appeal's topic to the time it actually goes in the mail. The first three weeks of this schedule are most important for your first special appeal. Once you and your team have a production process in place and are comfortable with review and approval procedures, you may be able to shorten this time frame considerably.

Special appeals provide an important, reliable, and lucrative opportunity to raise funds from your members while sustaining intimate communication with them, presenting your issues and concerns in your own words. Your special appeals can also offer an opportunity for your members to become involved in your campaign by signing a petition or statement of support, volunteering, registering for action alerts, or pledging to send a letter to the editor.

CHAPTER 6

Creating Effective Member Publications

This chapter is not intended to supplant the dozens of excellent publications available on how to design newsletters and other effective communications; rather, it consolidates some of this information and focuses on some of the specifics that have been most helpful to participants in my classes. The chapter will help you steer clear of common pitfalls, while providing a context within which to strategize effectively about your group's communications.

There are three additional reasons for this chapter. First, in many groups, responsibility for communications (especially newsletters, annual reports, brochures, and sometimes even a Web site) falls to the membership person or team. Second, once you consider the volume of communications you distribute—member and new-member letters, other recruitment devices, newsletters, direct mail campaigns, public service announcements, responses to information requests, and more—you will probably find that you are the one telling folks about your organization most often. Third, and perhaps most important, as discussed in Chapter Two, your membership and program work will be much more effective if the messages that come from your organization are clear and consistent. This chapter will help you accomplish that.

The production considerations discussed in the first two sections of this chapter apply whether you are developing a new brochure, publishing your first annual report, establishing or upgrading your Web site, or putting together a feature outreach piece about your latest campaign. Use Worksheet 6.1 to record the decisions you make in this chapter.

Publications Development Strategy Worksheet

Use this worksheet to record your publication strategy and the production considerations for every publication you plan to develop.

Why? (purpose):

_____

Who? (audiences):

_____

What? (message):

_____

How? (distribution):

    Where?

    How many?

    Requirements?

_____

What next? (follow-up):

_____

When? (timeline):

How much? (budget):

Production parameters:

Production review team:

    Project manager:

    Research and testing:

    Copywriting:

    Fact checking:

    Editing:

    Design:

    Final approval:

    Other:

Notes:

Develop your production strategy

Begin the discussion of any publication—whether new or a new edition of a recurrent publication, whether print, electronic, or some other media—by concentrating on a series of questions: Why? Who? What? How? What next? When? How much?

- *Why?* What is the purpose of this publication? Are you hoping to provide information, educate, raise the visibility of your organization, inspire readers to take a direct action—or more than one of these? The more focused you can be about the purpose of the publication, the easier it will be to create the outline for the text and plan its appearance. If you have more than one purpose for a single publication, prioritize those purposes to help direct you to success.

- *Who?* Define the audience or audiences for your publication as specifically as possible. Some questions to ask: Are they members or non-members? Are they residents of your community, workers, visitors, or people who dream of coming there someday? Do they have similar demographic, socioeconomic, or lifestyle characteristics? (Reviewing the results of your membership survey from Chapter Two can help here.) How familiar are they with the issue you are focusing on? How many potential individuals are there in your target audience(s)? How many of them do you want to reach with this publication?

- *What?* Before you start writing, try to distill the prime message of your publication into a single phrase or sentence. Marketers sometimes use the term "single net impression" to summarize the information or action they want the reader to retain from the publication. To fine-tune your message, refer to the results of your membership survey and any polling or opinion data your group has available. Depending upon the specificity of each audience, you may wish to pre-test your message with some members of that group through a focus group (formal or informal), test mailing, or telephone calls.

- *How?* The biggest challenge with most publications is distribution. Again, answer the following questions: How will you get your publication in the hands of or before the eyes or ears of your targeted audience? What will be the cost of that distribution? How will you follow up to replenish displays or other off-site distribution locations? Can you take advantage of existing distribution systems or will you need to enlist the help of volunteers or paid associates to get your publications to those you're trying to reach? How many pieces will you need to distribute and what kind of response to the piece is reasonable to expect?

- *What next?* Consider what, if any, follow-up you may need in response to this communication and how you will provide it. Will you need to send an information packet or thank you? How much of your next-step response material can you prepare in advance? Try to estimate a range of responses, from a disappointing outcome to your best-case scenario. Talk with colleagues who have undertaken similar communications to see what range of response is reasonable.

• *When?* Timing can have a significant effect on your success and your ability to take any needed next steps. For example, will the presence of a holiday help or hinder your ability to get your message to your targeted audiences? (If your newsletter is not in the mail by the first week of December, postpone mailing it until early January.) Are there seasonal advantages or disadvantages? Can you roll out your distribution in stages to allow a more gradual response load, rather than risk being buried by a tidal wave of response all at once? Also, check with your colleagues to make sure that your timing does not conflict with another major demand on the organization.

• *How much?* How much money you have to spend on this communication will determine, to a great extent, the media you'll use, the format, the number of pieces or breadth of distribution, and other factors, such as color on a print piece, or the extent of the "bells and whistles" you can install on your Web site. Do you have an option for in-kind services or contributions? By donating services, a generous designer or Web site programmer can save you a great deal of money. However, it can be difficult to disagree with a volunteer in this situation. To minimize problems and make sure that you end up with a product that will really work, ask to see the kind of pro bono work your volunteer has produced in the past; talk with past clients to get a feel for how comfortable the working relationship was.

If possible, develop and agree to a budget before investing a great deal of time in the project. This should include identifying the vendors who will produce the communication for you and securing pricing bids on a range of formats and quantities. For publications, meet with your printer and designer early on to discuss options. Though a good printer will competently print whatever you and your designer come up with, by involving the printer early in your design process he or she can help you maximize the use of paper, introduce you to time- and money-saving technologies, and generally make sure that you get the most for your investment. (Setting a budget and working with printers are both discussed in more detail in Chapter Ten.)

Put together your production team

Once you've confirmed the communications strategy for your new publication, put together a production team and assign responsibilities on the worksheet. You want all of your leadership to have ownership in the ultimate product. Establishing each team member's involvement at the beginning of the process and identifying when that responsibility will be required will help ensure an effective product on a schedule you can stick with. For example, you will need and want to consult with program staff to make sure that all of your facts are accurate. That does not mean, however, that they are also responsible or even involved with final editing and format. Similarly, although you may hire a designer to manage graphics and layout, it's certainly appropriate—even required—for you to be involved in setting the parameters for that design and reviewing and approving the final layout before it goes to press.

- *Set production parameters in advance.* Early in your process, identify the basic requirements of your project. These could include making sure you print only on 100 percent recycled or non-chlorine-bleached paper, use only union vendors, use only American-made products, restrict the size and weight of a publication to fit certain mailing requirements, or assure that your Web site improvements will be easily accessed without a high-speed modem connection.
- *Establish a timeline.* Prepare a calendar itemizing each project task, defining the responsible party or parties, and setting a completion date. At this stage, provide several additional days for each of the final two or three tasks. Every project tends to take longer than you expect (especially if it is a new undertaking), and you will need this "make-up" time to ensure delivery on schedule.
- *Do some research.* Collect examples of publications that illustrate how others have developed pieces similar to yours. Ask your co-workers and board members to collect and share with you samples that they have seen or received and found effective. Contact organizations you admire or designers and vendors you've worked with in the past and ask for samples. Then, follow up on the best of these to learn from the producer how effective they've been. Ask what they could have done differently to improve the final product. Most of these contacts will be generous in sharing their experience.
- *Test your publication before printing it.* Today's near-photo-quality desktop printing and high-technology copying make it relatively easy to prepare several versions of a new brochure or other publication, distribute them to testers, and gain feedback before going to press. Similarly, you can enlist visitors to your Web site to compare, contrast, or rate different ways of presenting your information. Also consider testing your distribution methods. If you are unsure of the volume of response to expect and your ability to manage that response, see if there's a way you can test your program with a portion of your outlets rather than beginning with a total launch.

By following these steps, you should be assured of a successful publication arriving on time and on budget.

Using your newsletter to build member loyalty

For most organizations, the newsletter is their most consistent communication with members. Review your newsletter and identify ways to assure its effectiveness for retaining membership and, to a lesser degree, attracting new members. Here are some tips for making your newsletter more membership-friendly.

- ***Blow your own horn.*** Everyone who sees and reads your newsletter knows it is a publication of your organization. Therefore, they expect and need to see information about your organization. This may sound simplistic, but many newsletters try to adopt an independent, unbiased, journalistic style. Yes, your information has to be truthful and accurate, but keep in mind that it is almost the only place where members learn what your organization is doing through your own words and images. Your members are receiving more than three thousand marketing messages each day (David Shenk, *Data Smog.* New York: HarperCollins, 1997). If you are producing a quarterly newsletter, this is your one chance out of more than 270,000 other marketing messages (minimum!) to reaffirm to your members the importance and value of your group. Your newsletter does not need to be boastful or falsely aggrandizing. However, it does need to be positive and enthusiastic and to underscore the real benefits that your organization is providing to each member.

- ***Use language your members relate to.*** Here's where the results of your membership survey and elevator statement come in handy. Share these with everyone responsible for writing and editing your newsletter. Consider putting together a list of key phrases and nuances that should be reflected in your newsletter articles, keeping in mind that every issue of your newsletter is going to be the first issue seen by at least one reader. Are you providing enough background so that they can understand your issues and actions? Are there themes or priorities you want to feature in photos and other graphics? Are they inundated with acronyms and confusing government agencies and other references? Make sure that your newsletter will be understandable and appealing to someone who is just becoming one of your insiders.

- ***Highlight "people like me."*** Every page of your newsletter—sometimes subtly, sometimes dramatically—affirms the culture of your organization. Your goal is to make sure that the signals your newsletter sends resonate with the audiences you're trying to involve. For example, do the people shown in your photos reflect the breadth of audiences that are represented in your membership (or you wish to have represented in your membership) by gender, race, ethnicity, age, and economic group? You can reinforce your diversity of geographic focus by highlighting a variety of place names. Consider including people features, such as photos and write-ups of new board members and staffers, the stories of key volunteers or interns, photos and comments by attendees at your latest special event. If you are having trouble recruiting new volunteers for a specific project, include an interview with an active volunteer highlighting how that person got involved. If your goal is to attract families, consider including kids' activities or feature a family "outing of the month."

- ***Focus on news they can use.*** Before writing even begins, assign each newsletter article a clear purpose and benefit to the member-reader. How is this information going to make a member's life better? Why should the reader care about this feature? What will the impact be on your readers' family, business, and quality of life? If possible, end each article with a recommendation for action the reader can take, such as hike a newly acquired piece of land trust property, attend a new-volunteer night at the food bank, write a letter to the editor, attend a public hearing, or bring a friend to a slide show to help spread the word.

The second mostly frequently read space on a newsletter is the back page (or back cover), so use that for critical information. Planned Parenthood of Southwest and Central Florida uses that space to clarify some frequently misunderstood facts and tell members where to get more information. Exhibit 6.1 shows one way they used that space.

- *Tell me what I need to know, not everything you know.* Perhaps the most difficult task in creating a newsletter is condensing the extraordinarily complicated and time-consuming work that your organization undertakes into readable, succinct, and informative articles that can fit on one page or less. Combine this with the challenge that newsletters need white space and graphics, good-sized photographs, captions, and other design elements to make them readable, and the space for text shrinks. One way to accomplish clarity is to use your newsletter to summarize the highlights of an issue. Then, at the end of the (brief) article, direct readers to your Web site or invite them to call or write for a copy of a fact sheet that elaborates on the issue. Another possibility is to feature a single in-depth article in each newsletter. This will assure each of your key programs one chance to gain the limelight and greatest attention from your members. Keep in mind that you can also expand in-depth coverage through a special appeal.

Cocktail Party Conversation

You're at a party and the Martinis are flowing. Someone mentions something about emergency contraception, and your date says, "Oh, ya, that's that RU-something or other, you know the abortion pill." You gently put your glass down and calmly say:

"Wait, you've got two things confused. First of all, emergency contraception is something you take to prevent getting pregnant if you've had unprotected sex. RU-486, called Mifepristone in this country, is something you take once you are pregnant. Emergency contraception, sometimes just called EC or the 'morning-after pill', is a series of hormone pills that must be taken within 72 hours after unprotected sexual intercourse. They prevent a fertilized egg from implanting in the lining of the uterus. EC does not interrupt or disrupt an already-established pregnancy. RU-486 (from France), also called 'medical abortion' is a series of two pills taken within the first seven weeks of a pregnancy, which induce an abortion. Got it?" ■

IF YOU HAVE QUESTIONS FOR
PLANNED PARENTHOOD   call 365-3913
ABOUT . . .   and ask for

DEVELOPMENT .... Jan Chester
EDUCATION .... Marilyn Anderson
PATIENT SERVICES .... Sue Westcott
PUBLIC AFFAIRS .... Wendy Grassi

If you receive more than one copy of this newsletter, please share it with a friend.

EXHIBIT 6.1.
Planned Parenthood of Southwest and Central Florida Newsletter

Planned Parenthood of Southwest and Central Florida used the back mailing cover of one newsletter to clarify some frequently misunderstood facts and tell members where to get more information.

Determine schedule and regular features

Plan now to sit down with your executive director and your newsletter editor or coordinator to develop an annual schedule for each issue's features and themes. By planning the year in advance, you can coordinate introducing a topic in your newsletter that is the subject a week or two later of a special appeal, thus heightening your members' understanding and enhancing the likelihood of response to the appeal.

Get your newsletter out on time

Virtually every organization is challenged at one time or another with simply being able to get their newsletter out on schedule. Here are two examples of approaches to solving that problem. Greater Yellowstone Coalition held a staffwide meeting to discuss corporate values. A highlight of that discussion was the importance of punctuality. By emphasizing the impact one person's delay could have on all the other members of the team, they reached an agreement that meetings would start on time and deadlines would be met. They also established a system for amending deadlines, when necessary, far enough in advance to avoid affecting other staffers.

At the beginning of each year, Alaska Wilderness League schedules quarterly newsletter days, when each staff member involved in writing or producing the newsletter has to be in the office. On that day, they put the telephones on the answering machine and meet first thing in the morning to discuss the outline for the upcoming issue. They then assign responsibility for drafting each article to one of the people in attendance, return to their offices, and write their articles. They meet later in the day to review text, do some editing, and fill in as needed. In this system, the entire newsletter is put together in a day and sent to the designer for layout. As a result, their newsletter is in their members' hands within two weeks of the time they actually write the articles, ensuring that members receive timely information and reaffirming the value of their membership as a source of current news and strategy.

Include regular membership features

Establish a list of membership-enhancing items that should appear in every issue. They should include as many of the following pieces as possible.

• *A remit envelope inserted into the newsletter.* These envelopes often pay for themselves the first time they are included. (Details on designing remit envelopes are given later in this chapter.) Remit envelopes come in handy for members to share with someone who saw your newsletter sitting on their counter and was interested in membership. They also provide a reminder for your members that you are supported by their generosity. When Oregon Natural Desert Association first inserted remit envelopes into their newsletter, they received thirty-seven responses from a distribution of about 1,500. This is more than a 2 percent response rate—a very good response (see Chapter Ten for more on response rates). The revenue raised covered the cost of the envelopes in three issues of the newsletter, and the organization recruited several new members. Before they added their remit envelopes, this group usually received only one or two contributions in response to its newsletter.

- *A membership form.* Ideally, this form should be printed on the back of the address block, so you can see who it came from and so that respondents are not required to cut out valuable information to send the form back to you. Although you will not get many responses to this form, it reinforces your organization's commitment to membership. (If you have to choose between this form or a remit envelope, use the remit.)

- *An invitation to join your monthly donor program.* Monthly donor programs are discussed in Chapter Twelve.

- *A reminder of the opportunity for memorials and sample bequest wording.* These giving opportunities are also discussed in Chapter Twelve.

- *A list of board and staff members.* Be sure to include the functions or programs that each is responsible for (see Exhibit 6.1).

- *Complete contact information for your organization.* This should include name, street address, mailing address (if different), telephone numbers, fax number, Web site address, and e-mail address for general information.

Some tips for getting the reader's attention

Here are two ideas for encouraging the reader to look inside your newsletter and directing him or her to key points once there:

- *Use the address block panel to bring the reader inside.* Most newsletters arrive in the member's mail with the address label up, because that's what the letter carrier needed to see. This panel becomes the reader's first impression of your newsletter. Consider it your "billboard" for convincing your member to open the newsletter and read inside. What's the most important and compelling message inside that you can "advertise" in this prime space? (Hint: the answer is not your board and staff list.)

- *Reinforce your message with captions.* Powerful photographs will grab your readers' attention. Reinforce the impact of the visual by summarizing your story with a caption. Follow *National Geographic* magazine's very successful formula: subscribers can learn the main points of the articles simply by reading the captions and looking at the pictures.

Remit envelopes

One of the most powerful and versatile membership publications you can use is a remit (or remittance) envelope. This format combines the convenience of a return envelope with a super-sized back flap, which can include a marketing message about your organization along with space for the respondent to complete her contact information and indicate a donation. Remit envelopes come in two basic sizes, indicated by numbers: No. 6-1/2, which measures 6.25" x 3.5", and No. 9, which is 3–7/8" x 8–7/8". To create other sizes may be more expensive, but an envelope manufacturer can work with you to produce remits in just about any size you desire.

Remit envelopes can function splendidly as an inexpensive, effective brochure, with a clear ask for contributions. Depending on the number of remit envelopes you print, prices may run between $50 and $100 per thousand—a lot less than what groups normally spend on their brochures. You can use remit envelopes in myriad ways to attract new members and additional gifts. Here are just a few:

• As discussed earlier in this chapter, insert a remit envelope into your newsletter and other publications, to encourage additional contributions and one-to-one membership recruitment. My college alumni association, for example, includes two remit envelopes in each edition of the calendar mailed every year to graduates, parents, and friends of the college.

• Make sure board and staff members keep remits handy at all times to pass along to potential members they meet. Five or six envelopes are easy to slip into a purse, briefcase, or backpack.

• Place a remit envelope on chairs at your slide shows and other presentations and on tables at special events. When coupled with a request for support from the podium and an enthusiastic statement from each table captain, remit envelopes will generate additional gifts even at an event with an admission charge.

• Consider including a remit envelope in your new-member and renewing member welcome packets. Invite the member to pass it along to a friend or colleague they feel would be interested in your organization's work. A leading children's hospital raised more than $80,000 in a year just from remit envelopes they included in their thank-you notes, even though there was no direct ask for an additional gift in the thank-you note itself.

The remit envelope in Exhibit 6.2, designed by Wisconsin's Environmental Decade (now known as Clean Wisconsin), functions as a brief and attractive brochure that encourages immediate gifts.

**WISCONSIN'S
ENVIRONMENTAL DECADE**

Your environmental watchdog since 1970.

To protect the environment and preserve the quality of life in Wisconsin through · the enactment of progressive public policies · the enforcement of laws, and · the active participation of people.

YES! I want to defend Wisconsin's water, air and wild places with my membership in Wisconsin's Environmental Decade.

☐ It is my/our pleasure to enclose a **tax deductible** gift of $ _____ for Wisconsin's Environmental Decade.

Name _____

Address _____

City _____ State ____ Zip _____

Email _____

☐ My check is enclosed   ☐ Please charge my account

_____ VISA   _____ Mastercard

Credit Card # _____

_____ Exp._____

Signature (required for credit cards)

_____

Thank you for your support!

Contributions to Wisconsin's Environmental Decade are tax deductible to the full extent of the law.

(inside)

**YOUR SUPPORT
WILL ENABLE US TO—**

RESPOND to sudden threats to Wisconsin's environment.

FIGHT the constant attempts to eliminate, weaken, or sidestep important environmental safeguards.

WORK on Wisconsin's behalf — for the sake of our children and grandchildren.

residents on the health risks associated with air and water pollution.

ENFORCE existing, common-sense environmental laws.

**WISCONSIN'S
ENVIRONMENTAL DECADE**

Your environmental watchdog since 1970.
122 State Street • Suite 200 • Madison, WI 53703-2500
608.251.7020 • Fax 608.251.1655
www.environmentaldecade.org

(outside)

WISCONSIN'S ENVIRONMENTAL DECADE
122 STATE ST   STE 200
MADISON WI 53703

PLEASE PLACE
FIRST CLASS
POSTAGE HERE

WISCONSIN

CLEAN AIR

CLEAN WATER

HEALTHY COMMUNITIES

Help us defend it for generations to come

EXHIBIT 6.2.
Wisconsin's Environmental Decade Remit Envelope

A crisp design makes this one-color remit envelope into an inexpensive brochure for Wisconsin's Environmental Decade.

Northwest Coalition for Alternatives to Pesticides PO Box 1393, Eugene, OR 97440-1393

(541) 344-5044, FAX (541) 344-6923

E-mail: info@pesticide.org   http://www.pesticide.org

3748

| | Becky Long | | | September 25, 2002 |

Quantity	Description		Price	Ext. Price
1	THIS IS A TEST INVOICE			$0.00

Sub Total	$0.00
Research	
Postage	
Proc. Fee	
-Paid	
Total	**$0.00**

To answer some information requests, we send materials not written by NCAP.
NCAP does not endorse all of the contents of these materials, nor do we endorse products.

Save this portion for your records

- -

Please submit this portion with your payment

Northwest Coalition for Alternatives to Pesticides PO Box 1393, Eugene, OR 97440-1393

(541) 344-5044, FAX (541) 344-6923

E-mail: info@pesticide.org   http://www.pesticide.org

THANK YOU for your information request. We hope the information is
useful. If any of these materials are not what you need, simply return them
to us in good condition, and we will adjust your billing accordingly, or work
with your request to your satisfaction.

Record #	Invoice #
5255	3748

Balance Due $0.00

WE NEED YOU! Become an NCAP member and support our work
to provide healthy solutions to pest problems. All members receive
NCAP's quarterly *Journal of Pesticide Reform.*
($25 Basic Membership, $15 Limited Income)

Amount
Enclosed

Please charge my Visa or Mastercard

Acct. # _____

Expires: _____

Signature: _____

ᵓcᴋ Loᵢ

31ᵧ '2 E t Avₑ

ᴸ ᵢne 9ᵢ 5-374

EXHIBIT 6.3.
Northwest Coalition for Alternatives to Pesticides Invoice

Almost every communication can be an effective membership communication. Northwest Coalition for Alternatives to Pesticides
uses their invoices to recruit new members.

Every communication is a membership communication

Building on the membership partnership you articulated in Chapter One, it is in your organization's best interest to reemphasize the role, importance, and value of members and membership in all your publications. As you work with your team, identify ways that you can incorporate your membership message into all your publications. As inspiration, Exhibit 6.3 shows how Northwest Coalition for Alternatives to Pesticides uses their invoices for brochures and publications they sell to recruit members. In the first eleven months of 2002, they received 106 memberships from 683 invoices mailed. Wow!

PART THREE

Expanding Your Membership Base

Most organizations need new recruits to expand their influence, increase access to resources, support program initiatives, and make up for the natural attrition of current members. Chapter Seven presents an overview of the types of membership recruitment techniques available, then uses case studies and examples to help you decide which approaches will work best for your group, when to use them, and with what audiences.

Chapter Eight suggests several proven ways to convince your in-house prospects—people who have registered an interest but not yet joined—to become members. Chapter Nine addresses asking one-on-one for membership gifts and will be especially helpful for organizations that are small, new, or focused on local issues. Chapter Ten reviews direct mail, the workhorse of nonprofit recruitment. This technique will be particularly applicable to state and national organizations and larger local and regional groups, although the techniques are standards for every organization. Chapter Eleven provides some additional tips for recruiting through cyberspace and special events.

CHAPTER 7

Recruiting New Members

New-member recruitment is the art of convincing someone whom you think *should be* interested in and benefit from the work your organization does to pledge allegiance to your organization by making a contribution and joining. This chapter provides an overview of the theory and practice of recruiting new members (also called prospecting) and suggests a framework for strategizing your organization's efforts. The next several chapters go into more detail about how to use the various techniques introduced here.

If you have been doing the exercises in the *Toolkit* thus far, you have already established the following critical building blocks for recruitment success:

1. *Partnership with your members.* The exercises in Chapter One helped you establish the strategic partnership between your organization's program objectives and mission and the role members play in your blueprint for success. Your new-member recruitment priorities should reflect these strategic priorities.

2. *An understanding of what motivates your members to join.* The information in Chapter Two described the basic reasons people join organizations like yours. The results of your member survey described in that chapter provide you with the specific words and phrases that your members use when they talk about the importance of your group to their life and future.

3. *A system for taking care of members once you have them.* Chapters Four and Five have covered putting together welcome packets for new and renewing members, establishing a procedure for developing renewals and special appeals, how to integrate your membership database and your accounting deposits, and how to set up a source code program for recording and tracking your campaigns and member-giving history.

4. *An idea of which of your programs are most compelling.* From your member survey, you should also have learned which of your programs your members value most. You have developed an elevator statement (discussed in Chapter Two) that communicates clearly and consistently why your organization makes a difference in people's lives. Your special appeals have helped you test messages and methods for talking about these programs in ways that are compelling.

These building blocks are the foundation of your membership program. Once they are in place, you can expand your reach beyond current members and friends to attract new members and extend your organization's influence and effectiveness.

What makes a likely prospect?

First, a note about terminology. The terms *prospect* and *in-house prospect* are used here and elsewhere throughout the *Toolkit* to describe someone who is not yet a member of your organization but whom you feel should be interested and someone you can engage in your work. An in-house prospect is someone who has already identified himself or herself to you by attending an event, signing a petition, visiting your Web site, or taking some other action. These folks are "in-house" because you already "own" their name and contact information. Other prospect names are provided by rent, exchange, or gift from an outside source.

Someone can be considered a prospect for a variety of reasons, including geographic location, personal experience, economic interest, need for services or information, or knowledge that this issue is something too big for her or him to tackle alone. The last factor is probably the most universally convincing.

Taking the plunge to become a member of a group is a two-step process. First, the individual must believe that he can accomplish whatever benefit or change he is hoping for more readily through an organization than on his own. This belief in the power of people working together is fundamental to deciding to join an organization. It's also the reason that your most likely members are probably already members of other organizations. If a prospect has had an earlier positive experience being a member of another group, he is more likely to be willing to join yours. *Giving USA 2002* cites four studies that indicate that 78–87 percent of Americans give to charity.

Not surprisingly, then, members of groups working on issues similar to yours should be good prospects for your next members. For example, members of the national organization The Nature Conservancy are usually hot prospects for local land trusts, since both these organizations work to protect landscapes by using similar tools. Similarly, members of a statewide economic justice group should be good prospects for other statewide social change organizations.

Dozens of different audiences believe in the effectiveness of joint action and belong to organizations similar to yours. The more characteristics a specific audience has in common with your existing membership, the more likely its members are to respond to your new-member appeal.

Identifying and finding your responsive audiences

The term *audience* refers to a carefully defined group of prospects who share specific characteristics, such as geography, interests, lifestyle, or experience. The more tightly you can define your targeted audiences, the more successful your strategy and choice of technique will be in motivating them to join.

Identifying key prospect audiences gives you the chance to coordinate your membership efforts with your programmatic goals. Here are some examples:

• A national gun-control organization, seeking congressional action on a specific bill to achieve its goals, may identify as targeted audiences voters in the states and congressional districts of swing or undecided senators and representatives.

• A state wilderness protection organization may find itself with a preponderance of members from urban areas. In order to confirm political support from the rural counties that include wilderness-quality public lands, it may choose to target people in rural districts.

• A local food bank may have learned from the 2000 census that its community's Hispanic population tripled in the last ten years and that that population includes a disproportionate number of families below the poverty level. Their membership plan may target Hispanic families in order to reinforce the group's credibility in the Latino community and assure access to a cadre of Spanish-speaking volunteers.

Technique identifies the most effective method you can use to motivate a particular audience to join your organization. As you can see on Worksheet 7.1, there are at least thirteen techniques to choose from; the most appropriate technique for any audience will require considering cost, energy, learning curve, other demands on your time and that of your colleagues, and strategic importance of this audience to your organization. Worksheet 7.1 shows how the Alaska Marine Conservation Council used its programmatic strategy to guide its membership plan (see Chapter Thirteen for AMCC's complete membership plan).

Matching Audience to Technique

Use this worksheet at this point merely to identify and prioritize your potential membership audiences as they relate to specific programmatic goals. It will be easier to identify the matching techniques after you have completed the rest of the chapters in this part of the Toolkit. (In Chapter 13, this worksheet will serve as a building block for your membership plan.) This page shows a filled-in example; the facing page shows the blank worksheet.

Priority/Strategy*	Audience	Personal Visit: In-Person Contact with Leadership or Known Contact	Special Event: Attending Event with Leadership or Known Contact	Telephone Call with Leadership or Known Contact	Personalized Letter from Someone Known	Personalized E-Mail from Someone Known	Field Canvass ("doorbelling")	Telephone Canvass	Personalized Mail (unknown prospect)	Personalized E-Mail (unknown prospect)	Direct Mail	Lead Generation	Web Site	Display Ad
A	Lapsed members			X	X	X								
B	Commercial fishing permit holders										X		X	
B	Exxon Valdez plaintiffs			X						X				
B	Homer residents		X											
C	List exchange with other groups		X								X			

*Priorities/Strategies:

A = Retain existing members

B = Recruit coastal residents

C = Recruit recognized environmentalists

Priority/Strategy	Audience	Technique												
		Personal Visit: In-Person Contact with Leadership or Known Contact	Special Event: Attending Event with Leadership or Known Contact	Telephone Call with Leadership or Known Contact	Personalized Letter from Someone Known	Personalized E-Mail from Someone Known	Field Canvass ("doorbelling")	Telephone Canvass	Personalized Mail (unknown prospect)	Personalized E-Mail (unknown prospect)	Direct Mail	Lead Generation	Web Site	Display Ad

Identifying potential audiences is a task that could benefit from input from your executive director and program director. Learning your leadership's latest strategic thinking on how to accomplish your organization's goals and current programs will help to pinpoint the characteristics of individuals who are most needed as members. Involving your colleagues here will help coordinate their actions and communications with your, while also reinforcing the value of your membership partnership to their work.

Defining critical mass

Your executive director and program staff will also be helpful in specifying numeric goals for each targeted audience, or what constitutes "critical mass" for your success.

Particularly for advocacy groups, critical mass is often determined by proportional representation. For example, if your group is seeking to influence your state legislature, it may be important to have a significant number of supporters in the districts represented by key committee chairs and committee members in the statehouse. For many states, where legislators from rural districts hold these powerful positions, recruiting as few as thirty or forty members in these rural districts may give your group significant influence, whereas thirty or forty members in an urban area may be almost invisible.

Conversely, you may find that just having ample numbers of members—especially ones that take action or send contributions—is more important than any other characteristic, regardless of where these members live. In that case, you can focus on the most likely recruits and those you can contact most cost effectively rather than developing time-intensive "boutique" campaigns for specific, strategic micropopulations.

The easiest way to know whether your group's membership is representative of your area, state, or the nation as a whole is to compare the demographic characteristics of your members with those of the public as a whole. In the United States, you can get information by zip code from the U.S. Census or invest in a copy of the *United States Zip Code Atlas,* which also provides demographic data (see Resource A). Advocacy organizations, particularly environmental groups, may also be able to get more enhanced comparison data for state or national legislative districts from a local League of Conservation Voters affiliate or similar organization.

Not every prospect can be a member

In discussions with your colleagues about strategically important audiences, you will undoubtedly touch on the importance of elected and appointed officials and media representatives to your success. These individuals rarely, if ever, join organizations, especially advocacy groups. Most elected and appointed officials, reporters, and other media personnel put a high priority on being perceived by the public as independent and unbiased; being a member of your group may well be out of the question. Although you can and should develop methods to secure their support in other ways, it would probably not be useful to add them to your priority list of targeted audiences for membership. Alternatively, seek to identify audiences that influence these opinion-setters. (See Worksheet 1.1 in Chapter One.)

"The Rule of 27"

Once you have identified your target audiences, it is time to explore techniques for recruiting them. The most common reason that a prospect has not yet become one of your members is that you have not yet provided him with a compelling and convenient opportunity to do so. In his books, especially *Guerrilla Marketing* and *Guerrilla Marketing Attack,* J. Conrad Levinson describes how many times you must reach a prospect before they may notice your messages and then decide to act on them. He calls this "The Rule of 27":

> A marketing message must penetrate the mind of a prospect a total of nine times before that prospect becomes a customer, and your message gets missed or ignored two out of three times.

This means that, despite your very best work in getting your message out, people miss two out of every three messages you put out. They were running late for work and so missed your radio spot; they were on vacation when your op-ed piece ran in the local newspaper or your direct mail package arrived; the in-laws came to visit so they didn't make it to the street fair where you were tabling.

The Rule of 27 is daunting, but it also provides hope. On the hopeful side, once you realize that you need to reach out to a specific prospect twenty-seven times in order to reasonably expect them to respond it is easy to understand why all those people who should be interested in your organization haven't joined: they probably don't know about you—yet.

The daunting part is that providing twenty-seven compelling, convenient opportunities for someone to join is a significant undertaking, to put it mildly. The good news is that all kinds of media can be used to deliver your marketing message. Exhibit 7.1 lists the variety of recruitment and contact techniques available to get your marketing message out, along with their approximate effectiveness. Note that the response rates estimated are for membership-level donations, contributions of less than (and often significantly less than) $100. Membership gifts can usually be made from a prospect's cash flow rather than their assets and frequently require only one decision maker, so they are relatively spontaneous. These rates will be different for major donor gifts, especially ones that require liquidating assets.

	In-person one-to-one contact with leadership or known contact	40–50%
	Attending event with leadership or known contact	15–30%
	Telephone contact with leadership or known contact	15–25%
↑ Building on Relationships	Personalized letter or e-mail from someone known	10–20%
	Field canvass ("doorbelling")	10–15%
	Telephone canvass	4–7%
	Personalized mail or e-mail	2–6%
↑ Targeted Contact	Direct mail or e-mail	0.5–1.5%
↑ Ease of Response	Prospect generation	0.1%
↑ Awareness Building	Display ad or Web site	0.01%

EXHIBIT 7.1.
Relative Effectiveness of New-Member Recruitment Techniques

Use this list to estimate the percentage of contacts who will join your organization when solicited by the listed technique.

As Exhibit 7.1 shows, you have countless options for delivering those twenty-seven messages to your targeted audiences. Some will be suitable for your group and others will not be. Most growing organizations use more than one recruitment technique to reach their prospects; hardly any group uses every technique. Note that at the top of the list the most powerful recruitment technique by far is direct contact between a prospect and someone she knows, a technique available to every organization regardless of size or staffing levels.

The rest of this chapter describes the most common techniques, starting from the bottom of the "Relative Effectiveness" ladder. Later chapters cover the more effective techniques in depth. Chapter Thirteen helps you choose the right techniques for your group, match them with your key audiences, and create a comprehensive membership plan.

Awareness-building techniques

Awareness-building could also be called "getting your name out." Awareness-building techniques include display ads and editorial and op-ed features in newspapers and magazines, articles by a local reporter, billboards, and your Web site. Because these techniques by themselves do not offer convenient ways for prospects to join your organization, their effectiveness as recruitment techniques is quite low: approximately 0.01 percent of prospects will be compelled to join from a simple awareness-building technique.

Nonetheless, each time someone hears your radio sponsorship of "All Things Considered," reads your name in the newspaper, or has your Web site pop up on their search engine, they become more aware of your organization and more likely to take a joining action in the future. Awareness building works because you can use these techniques to reach large numbers of people relatively inexpensively. One of the most cost-effective ways of building awareness is through public service announcements (PSAs). These can be print, audio, or video messages. You develop standard announcements about your group in a variety of sizes (for magazines and newspapers) and lengths (for radio and television) and submit them to as many media outlets as you can. Media often use PSAs to fill extra space in print or a few seconds of on-air time as part of their community service. If your PSA is well produced and the cause is compelling, it can pay off. Weekly papers almost always include one or more spots about community organizations, especially if they include useful information or helpful facts, and weekly, community, or neighborhood newspapers have some of the highest readership levels. See Exhibit 7.2 for an example of a clever and informative PSA.

Prospect generation

The technique of generating prospect names moves up the effectiveness scale an important rung beyond awareness-building by providing someone interested in your mission with an easy way to identify themselves to you. Generating prospect names is often a two-step process. First, the initial technique—such as a clip-out coupon in a neighborhood newspaper, an 800-number on your radio sponsorship, a request to sign a statement of support or petition at a local farmers' market, or an invitation to receive an e-mail alert or newsletter on your Web site—encourages individuals who have some interest in your programs or causes to identify themselves. In the second step, you follow up on their initial contact by providing them with more information and an invitation to join.

Prospect generation on its own can be expected to return, at best, about a 0.1 percent response: no more than one out of every thousand folks contacted by your prospect generation campaign will actually join your organization based on that contact. When combined with a compelling message and vast visibility, however, prospect generation can be a powerful tool. For example, over a period of twenty years Save the Manatee Club built its membership to more than thirty thousand people almost exclusively through printed PSAs inviting readers of neighborhood

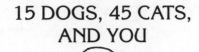

15 DOGS, 45 CATS, AND YOU

FOR EVERY PERSON THAT IS BORN,

FIFTEEN DOGS

AND FORTY-FIVE CATS ARE ALSO BORN.

Pet overpopulation is a BIG PROBLEM as these statistics show. In order to keep up with the current flood of puppies and kittens, every person would have to own two dogs and six cats during their entire lifetime (assuming that people live for 75 years, and dogs and cats for 10). A household of five would have to harbor ten dogs and thirty cats! Adoption alone is obviously not the answer; altering is.

PLEASE SPAY OR NEUTER YOUR DOGS AND CATS

"There aren't enough homes for them all.
Please spay or neuter"
Call Your Local Vet Or Humane Society

EXHIBIT 7.2.
Print Public Service Announcement

Clever graphics and a clear public service message increase the chance that your PSA will be printed.

newspapers, weekly shopper publications, and friendly magazines to "Adopt A Manatee" by calling their 800-number. The key to effective prospect generation is speedy and repeated follow-up (see Chapter Eight).

Targeted contact

Targeted contact builds on the techniques of awareness-building and prospect generation by bringing awareness and ease of response to an audience even more likely to be interested in your issues and work. Whereas the first two techniques can be compared to casting a wide net in hope of catching some choice fish from a sea of very general prospects, targeted contact is more like long-line fishing, where you cast your best bait in a location known to be home to the fish you're trying to catch. Targeted contact delivers your compelling message to prospects you've identified as likely to be interested in your organization, along with an easy way to respond. There are a number of methods for targeted contact, with increasing success rates as you move up the effectiveness ladder.

Direct mail

Direct mail is probably the most widespread and predictable of the targeted techniques. Direct mail refers to any campaign that sends a stand-alone version of your message, along with a response device, to people you think should be interested in your organization even if they may never have heard of you before. The classic direct mail membership recruitment package includes an unpersonalized letter, perhaps an insert, and a response form and return envelope, all usually mailed at bulk rate in a window or labeled outside envelope.

Why is direct mail such a reliable powerhouse? Consider for a moment your personal shopping habits. Do you make a habit of patronizing neighborhood stores? Have you ever purchased over the Internet? Have you ever bought from a catalog, responded to a telephone solicitation or television infomercial? Do you patronize a mall or outlet center? Have you ever responded to a direct mail package?

Chances are you have responded to some of the shopping options listed in the preceding paragraph but not all of them. Our willingness to respond once to a marketing method is a good indicator of our willingness to respond to that method again, although it does not necessarily predict how we will respond to a different marketing technique.

Now, think about how your organization communicates with your members: Do you mail members a newsletter? Renewals? Special appeals? Action alerts or updates? Most groups communicate with their members through the mail. This is one reason that direct mail continues to be such a powerful tool for membership recruitment. Therefore, if you are going to follow up with your members by mailing them written materials, it makes sense to attract people who enjoy receiving information through the mail and who respond to that information.

There are three primary reasons that direct mail remains the workhorse of nonprofit fundraising and probably will remain so for the foreseeable future:

1. *Lists of people who buy or join by mail are readily available.* Fortunately, thousands of lists of people responsive to joining and buying through direct mail are available. On the theory that there are similarities among all members of a single organization, or purchasers from a certain catalog, or subscribers to a specific magazine, with direct mail you use these lists (or more often a collection of these lists) to target and distribute your message to likely prospects.

2. *Direct mail primarily reaches prospects at home.* Unless you are a professional or trade association or some other membership group that provides services directly related to a prospect's workplace, you're much more likely to get a response to your direct mail package when you reach people at their home address. Consider for a moment your own situation: when you are at work your brain and, perhaps even more important, your heart are focused on the tasks and obligations of

your job. When you're at home, however, you are more likely to be interested in and available to consider issues of community concern and personal passion. In addition, many workplaces screen what mail arrives on workers' desks; direct mail is often discarded in the mailroom. Whenever possible, then, try to have your message arrive at the prospect's home address.

3. *Direct mail allows your organization to speak directly to the prospect.* A letter can deliver background information, educational material, and other key messages about your organization in your own words. Unlike a news release from your organization, which may or may not result in a story that covers the key points you had in mind, direct mail delivers your information at some length, without the filters placed by reporters, other interpreters, or even the occasional mixed messages that come from well-meaning volunteers or board members. Better yet, you're delivering your message directly into the hands of the audience you are most interested in reaching, at a location where it is comfortable to read.

On the down side, as direct mail experiences increasing competition in the mailbox from other marketers (including nonprofit marketers), a healthy rate of response of people joining your organization from a direct mail campaign is only about 0.8 percent. That rate will vary based on the number of people you mail to, the immediacy of the issue, the external visibility of your issue, and the content of your campaign. (Direct mail techniques are covered in depth in Chapter Ten.)

Direct response e-mail

Direct response e-mail, an electronic version of direct mail, is just beginning to be used for membership recruitment. The benefits of e-mail communication are that it is relatively inexpensive and carries the environmental advantage of being "paper free." There are, however, several challenges of e-mail direct mail:

- There is a shortage of reliable, tested lists. Privacy and "spam" sensitivities have made many e-mail list owners hesitant to share their addresses.

- It is virtually impossible to target e-mails geographically, as e-mail addresses do not indicate where the addressee actually lives or works.

- Even today, most e-mail goes to people at their office rather than home.

- There is a practical limit on the length of a message that you can expect a prospect to read in an e-mail.

Because of these limitations, bulk direct e-mail campaigns to folks you have not already had contact with are not productive for most nonprofit organizations. Later in this chapter and in Chapter Eleven we discuss where e-mail can be most effective.

Personalized mail

Personalized mail takes the advantages of targeted communication and makes it more likely to be read and responded to than unpersonalized direct mail. The goal of personalized postal mail is for a letter to look as much like a personal letter directed specifically to the individual addressee as possible. This impression is accomplished by using a close-faced envelope (one without a window), hand-writing or imprinting the outer address, using a real ("live") bulk or first class stamp or postal meter rather than a pre-printed imprint, and perhaps using a personal address and greeting in the letter itself. These types of personalization are usually more expensive and often more time-consuming than classic direct mail. However, they can increase your response from two to six times over standard direct mail approaches. Personalized mail especially pays off when you are trying to get the greatest response from a relatively small list, a list you have only one-time access to, or a list that has been especially powerful in the past.

A note on the power of hand-addressing: if you have a short list of prospect names from which you want to boost the response, consider hand-addressing the envelopes. Glenn Marangelo of Wilderness Watch tested four lists ranging in size from seven hundred to eighteen hundred names by hand-addressing half the envelopes for each list and using self-adhesive labels on the rest. In all cases, the hand-addressed mailings attracted a stronger response, from a 26 percent increase over the labeled envelopes to a 141 percent greater response! Glenn cautions, though, that the amount of time this takes is only worth it with your most promising lists; a similar test with five thousand names from a general publication list resulted in a difference of only 0.02 percent, which was certainly not worth the effort. To get help with hand-addressing the envelopes, Glenn recruited volunteers from the local Retired Senior Volunteer Program (RSVP). (Check with your United Way to find out how to reach RSVP in your community.)

Personalized e-mail

Personalized e-mail follows a similar route, usually including the recipient's name in the first-line greeting of the e-mail address. Note that these techniques are still using lists of prospects who are not known to the letter-writer.

Telephone canvassing

Telephone canvassing, or telemarketing, involves telephoning an unknown prospect, telling them about your organization, and inviting them to make a donation. On this rung of the recruitment ladder, telephone canvassing involves hired telemarketers calling lists of likely prospects, similar to those identified for direct mail contact. The advantages of a telephone canvas are that it is a "closer" contact with the prospect: it's much more difficult to say "No" to a real, live person, even at the end of a telephone line, than it is to say "No" to a piece of paper or e-mail that arrives in the mailbox.

The challenge of telephone canvassing is that, with technologies that can screen calls using caller ID and answering machines, combined with people's busy schedules, actually making contact with an individual by phone is often difficult. As a result, fewer than 10 percent of the people you hope to call will actually join. True to expectation, those recruited by phone are more likely to respond by phone to appeals for renewals, special projects, and upgrades, which adds an extra follow-up burden on your organization.

Field canvassing

Field canvassing, or "doorbelling," sends hired canvassers door-to-door in specific neighborhoods to recruit new members. Door-to-door canvassing enjoys one of the highest response rates for targeted recruitment, in large part because it is so difficult for individuals to say "No" to an energetic, dedicated individual standing on their doorstep. Door-to-door canvassing is most effective when combined with the need for timely political action, such as signing a letter to the governor or legislature or endorsing a statement of support to the city council. Door-to-door canvassing can also be especially effective in reaching key communities where your organization needs representation quickly. The person-to-person aspects of door-to-door canvassing can build trust among new audiences by demonstrating that your group includes people the prospect can feel comfortable with.

Unfortunately, door-to-door canvassing is also rife with challenges. First is the issue of message control. Canvassers are often young people working for you on a summer job, not permanent staff, so the visual image of your canvasser may not reflect the general culture of your group.

Second, canvassers are traditionally compensated on the basis of contributions they raise. As a result, canvassers may tweak or massage your message in order to ensure the greatest response from the prospect.

Third, compensating canvassers on the basis of how much money they raise means that they often prefer to work in neighborhoods where they will get the most contributions, not necessarily those areas where you strategically need representation.

Fourth, supporting a field canvas is expensive, involving the costs of insurance, transportation, supervision, and so on. Such expenses are usually only justified by a team of at least six to ten canvassers. If they are successful, you will have hundreds of new members to process every week and you will need to have the capacity to service these new members promptly.

Finally, sustaining members recruited through a canvas is most successful if your follow-up appeals for renewals or other funds are also made in person, at the door. This requirement adds a further level of complexity and expense.

Building on relationships

Relationship-building takes your recruitment one important step forward by involving directly in the recruitment an individual known to the prospect or in a leadership position with the organization. Not surprisingly, the power of association with a known, trusted contact significantly boosts the response to your recruitment request.

Contact between a prospect and someone he or she knows works well because it builds on a level of trust already established between the prospect and the recruiter. A personal ask from a friend or colleague—by letter, telephone, or in person—serves as an endorsement; the recruiter is implicitly saying, "I trust this organization to do what it says it will and be an asset to our community. You can, too."

This kind of personal request is also a way of honoring and showing respect for the prospect. By taking the time to make the request, the recruiter demonstrates that he or she has a level of respect for the prospect that merits and deserves a response.

Since your staff, board, and other knowledgeable, dedicated members, have limited time and ability to dedicate to membership recruitment, you need ways to get the most out of these techniques. Following are some ideas. (See Chapter Nine for more on using these techniques.)

• *A personalized letter or e-mail* from someone known to the prospect can result in a 10 to 20 percent response or even higher. This is a classic technique that every board member is familiar with: you bring your address book to a board meeting and you and your colleagues spend time addressing envelopes, personalizing, and adding notes to standard letters to friends, family members, and colleagues asking them to join the organization.

Board members and others who participate in these kinds of asks need to be reminded that a 10 percent response is a strong return and a great return is a 20 percent response. With this in mind, few solicitors are disappointed when only one or two out of ten friends they write to actually join. When launching a program like this, review the recruitment ladder in Exhibit 7.1 with participants as a way to manage expectations.

• *Telephone contact* with someone known to the prospect or a leader of your organization can be even more powerful, creating a positive response as much as 25 percent of the time. This approach, like telephoning and field canvassing, is so powerful because people have difficulty turning down a live individual on the phone, especially someone they know or respect because of their position with the organization (board member, staff, executive director, or dedicated volunteer). The reason this rate isn't higher reflects the difficulty of actually getting to talk to someone on the phone. You can boost this response by leaving a message and then following up by mail. The message might be something like, "I've tried to reach you several times, with no luck, so I'm sending you an invitation to join me as a member of [name of organization]. I hope you will say 'Yes.' Thank you." Within a day or two, send a personalized letter to the prospect.

• *Attending an event* with a known contact or leadership person from your organization can be another powerful recruitment technique because it combines the impact of face-to-face contact with the fun and learning opportunity of a meeting or event. To make sure your organization maximizes the membership recruitment potential of slide shows, presentations, and other meetings or special events, apply the three requirements of this technique:

1. Ask attendees directly for their support.

2. Provide attendees with a convenient method for joining right then (remember those remits).

3. Create a short "quiet time" at the event during which attendees will be expected to join.

Chapter Eight provides some valuable tips on how to gain double-duty impact from the presentations and events that your organization is already making and turn them into a membership gold mine.

• *A one-to-one, in-person meeting* between a prospect and a known contact or leader with your organization remains the most powerful recruitment technique available. The intensity of the one-to-one, face-to-face ask increases the likelihood of a "Yes" over attending an event or other group contact. The immediacy of speaking in person, without the distance imposed by a telephone or letter, also increases the probability of success by building on the elements of trust and respect. That's why this technique generates a positive response from as many as half of those asked.

Most advantageous is that these kinds of one-to-one recruitment opportunities actually occur every day. Unlike a major donor visit or similar request for a sizeable gift, a membership ask, which generally seeks less than $100, does not involve a significant financial commitment. Instead, acceptance is dependent upon the prospect agreeing that your organization's mission and programs are important to his quality of life and that of his loved ones. To that end, each of your board members and staff as well as your most involved and dedicated volunteers have the opportunity to be daily ambassadors for your membership program.

The next several chapters recommend a variety of ways you can use this recruitment ladder efficiently and strategically to build your membership.

Converting In-House Prospects to Members

The term *in-house prospect* refers to someone who has had some contact with your organization and registered an interest in it but has not yet joined. *In-house prospects are your very best source of new members.* This chapter will help you establish systems for capturing the names of these people and convincing them to take that important next step of joining your organization.

In-house prospects may have attended an event or taken an action on your behalf. They may have responded to one of your outreach or prospect generation efforts, as discussed in Chapter Seven. Better yet, they have identified themselves as interested in something your group has to offer. Furthermore, they know your group's name! That in itself gets them well along the road to that total of twenty-seven impressions needed to take action (see "The Rule of 27" in Chapter Seven). Your job now is to convince these in-house prospects that they made the right decision in connecting with you and provide them ample reasons and opportunities to join.

Understanding in-house prospects

Imagine this scenario: You are getting ready for work. You're juggling getting dressed, feeding the dog, making lunches for yourself and the kids, and listening to the radio in the background. Suddenly you're engaged by a story on the radio about a new project a local organization in your community is doing. Sounds like just the thing you've been looking for. You grab a pencil and on the back of an envelope jot down the name (or what you think is the name) of the group, then get on with your morning chores. That weekend you come across your note again and remember you wanted to get in touch with those people to get more information. You pull out the phone book to look them up and, if the group you are contacting is well prepared, take the first step toward becoming a member.

If your organization's message has risen above the noise to capture the attention of an interested prospect and motivate her to want to reach your organization, you want to make sure that, first, this eager prospect can reach your group quickly and easily and, second, you are prepared to jump on that interest and respond to it as speedily and completely as possible. A person who contacts you "out of the blue" in this way is one of your best prospects for joining.

Given this fact, it's surprising how few organizations take advantage of these prospects. A few years ago, my then-assistant Lisa Black, cleverly disguising herself as Maria Black, conducted a test to find out how other nonprofits responded to inquiries. She hand-addressed and hand-wrote a postcard to fifty-five nonprofit organizations of all kinds asking for additional information about their group. Here are the returns:

- Responded within one week: 38 percent

- Responded within three weeks: 73 percent

- Never responded at all: 16 percent

- Response came as a packet in a 9" x 12" envelope requiring at least $2.00 in postage: about 50 percent

- Included a cover letter explaining the materials in the packet: 44 percent

- Wrote on the envelope that this was information the recipient had requested: None

- Included a direct ask to join the organization: 9 percent

- Followed up with additional requests to join after the first contact: 7 percent

These are disheartening statistics. While most organizations sent at least a current copy of their newsletter (and sometimes back copies as well), an annual report, a brochure, perhaps a cover letter, sometimes an events list, only five of them specifically asked "Maria" to join their organization as part of their packet and directed her to the appropriate materials for joining and returning a contribution. And even fewer followed up with a further ask.

Responding to in-house prospects

Of those who did include an asking letter in their response packets to "Maria," two had especially noteworthy requests. The first was Idaho Rural Council, then a small group of 250 to 300 members working to help protect family farms in rural Idaho.

At that size and with their mission, every member was especially valuable and extraordinarily difficult to identify and recruit. In her quest to enroll every possible member, membership director Angie Janquart included a personalized cover letter with the materials she sent in response to Lisa's postcard.

The personalization in Angie's letter went beyond the inside address and greeting to refer in the first paragraph to the friendly postcard that Maria had mailed. The rest of the letter was boilerplate that could be used to describe the organization and its mission to just about any new prospect. It discussed the organization's mission and goals, how it was governed, whom it served, and what activities it promoted, and listed several of its accomplishments and current program priorities.

The next-to-last paragraph directed the reader to the materials in the information packet: a brochure and a copy of the most recent newsletter. The final paragraph invited Maria to join Idaho Rural Council and "help us make Idaho voices strong." It directed Maria to "the enclosed contributor's card and return envelope for you to use." This specific reference and direction let the prospect know exactly what Angie wanted her to do.

Angie also invited Maria to take one more step in getting involved with Idaho Rural Council: "I am also curious as to how you heard about IRC. If you would drop me a line about how you found out about us in the return envelope, I'd really appreciate it. It will help me with further outreach in the future. I look forward to hearing from you!" Angie ended the letter by telling Maria how her participation in the organization could make a difference.

The other model letter came from Northwest Environment Watch, a research and communication center that attracts thousands of inquiries a year through its books, reports, op-ed pieces, speaking engagements, and other very visible policy outreach. In order to respond to these inquiries promptly, the group uses a standard "Dear Friend" letter.

In the first paragraph the reader is reminded of why she is receiving this information: "Thank you for your interest in Northwest Environment Watch. Enclosed is the information you requested." Even if you mail your packet the day after you received the request for information, chances are that it will not arrive any sooner than four or five days after the prospect made the request. During that time, your prospect has continued on with her busy life and perhaps forgotten why she contacted you in the first place. The more you can do to remind your prospect of the experience that initiated that contact, the more likely you are to be able to return her to the moment that originally attracted her interest. That's the purpose of this introduction to the letter. Another useful technique to ensure that the prospect will open your letter quickly is to stamp a message on the envelope such as, "Here is the information you requested."

Like the letter from Idaho Rural Council, the Northwest Environment Watch letter describes the organization, what it does, its current issues and past accomplishments, and the benefits that members receive. Better yet, this letter asks the prospect to join a total of four times:

- In the first paragraph: "Now I'd like to invite you to take another step towards protecting the environment: please join Northwest Environment Watch today."

- Midway through the letter: "Becoming a member of Northwest Environment Watch means adding your voice to this dedicated group of informational activists. Together, as a community, we are creating hope and making a difference in crafting a sustainable way of life in the Northwest. Won't you join us?"

- In the close: "Help us continue to spread the word and to lead the way by becoming a Northwest Environment Watch member today."

- In the P.S.: "Please join us today."

This letter provides compelling reasons for joining, explains the benefits, elaborates on how each member makes a difference, and specifically instructs the reader how to join: "Just return your gift with the enclosed pre-paid response card."

Collecting e-inquiries

The World Wide Web adds another challenge to tracking people who are interested in your organization and encouraging them to join. Northwest Coalition for Alternatives to Pesticides (NCAP) has worked out a system for efficiently distributing information through their Web site and collecting mailing addresses to use in new-member recruitment.

When public education coordinator Megan Kemple receives a telephone or e-mail inquiry, she lets the prospect know that the Coalition has some great information she can mail to them if they like, and gets their name and address. At that point (and not before), she asks if the caller or e-mailer has Web access. If so, she directs them to the group's Web site for free information as an alternative to mailing the information for a fee.

Once Megan has the address, she hand-writes a half-sheet note that thanks the person for getting in touch and asks them to join. She includes a membership response form, return envelope, and two brochures describing NCAP's publications and services. Keeping track over nine months, Megan sent out 106 of these letters from which she received eleven memberships; thirty-four other memberships were generated directly from the group's Web site. Development director Becky Long writes, "In 2001, our Web site hosted 112,000 sessions, and we generated thirteen memberships for $335. For the first ten months of 2002, we hosted

145,000 sessions and through December 2 generated thirty-four memberships for $1,070. In December 2001, we made it possible for people to use a credit card to join from our Web site. I believe that's what accounts for the increase in memberships from 2001 to 2002." For more on how to use e-mail and your Web site to increase membership, see Chapter Eleven.

Make sure prospects can find you

There are two key places that prospects who want to find you will look: the telephone book and the Web. Going back to the scenario at the beginning of this chapter, if this prospect tried to find your organization in her local telephone book, would she? When I lived in Seattle, for example, three different local telephone service providers covered King County alone. That meant that, if an organization wanted to be accessible to the entire Seattle metropolitan area, it needed to list the organization in all three of those phone books, along with ones for neighboring counties. (And perhaps in the small, local community phone books printed for rural districts.) If you are a statewide organization, you will want to be listed in the phone books for each major metropolitan area at least.

Fortunately, the cost of additional listings is as low as $1 a month. At this rate, you may want to list your organization under every name it may be known by, as well as any name people often mistakenly associate with you. For example, Northwest Coalition for Alternatives to Pesticides may increase the probability that people will find them by also listing as "Pesticides, Northwest Coalition for Alternatives to." If your organization has recently changed its name, remain listed by both names for a year or two so folks who are just now getting their quota of twenty-seven messages can still find you. Once someone does find you by phone, be sure they can leave a message for you twenty-four hours a day. Then, close the loop by establishing a reliable system for retrieving those messages daily and responding to them promptly.

Your organization's location in cyberspace is increasingly important. To maximize your contact with potential prospects, make sure your group can be found by the top search engines and list with them the key words people may use when trying to find you. Those can sometimes be surprising. Alaska Wilderness League, for example, discovered that the second most frequently used keyword people tried was "Artic," a misspelling of "Arctic." The written responses to your membership survey will also give you cues about the words your members use when referring to your organization.

Many organizations have a button on their Web site that allows visitors to send a message directly to the organization. These buttons may read, "Ask us a question" or "Get in touch with us." These messages need to be responded to at least daily, perhaps several times a day, given the expectations of speed among e-mail communicators.

Once you've set up these response systems, mark your calendar to test them regularly—at least once a month. Horror stories of telephone messages languishing on an answering machine for weeks or e-mail messages being misdirected to a vacant in-house address are far from rare. Treat every contact as the potential member that they are.

Capture every contact

Another source of in-house prospects are people your organization and the people associated with it connect with in your community. If the names and contact information for those prospects are captured at every step, you'll be able to invite them to become members. Here are a few options to consider:

- *Telephone inquiries.* One of my most memorable learning experiences involves an enthusiastic new secretary who, on joining the staff of a whistle-blower organization, was instructed to respond quickly to people who requested information by sending them a copy of the latest newsletter. A few months later, when we noticed that the size of the in-house prospect file was exactly the same size as before, we realized that her very efficient method was to grab a newsletter while the person was still on the phone, write their name and address in the address block, and drop it in the mail. Unfortunately, those names and addresses were never seen again and never captured in the in-house prospect database.

This simple example illustrates how easy it is for even your most well-meaning colleagues or volunteers to misunderstand the importance of collecting prospect names. To eliminate these kinds of errors, establish a central system for fulfilling inquiry requests and a routine process for collecting information. If your organization relies on a voicemail system to direct calls, have it forward requests for more information to a single mailbox that you have responsibility for servicing. Moreover, train other members of your staff and volunteers to direct such inquiries to you.

- *Contact record forms.* Exhibit 8.1 shows a form to help systematize the information that you and your colleagues collect about each new prospect. This form should gather all the information you need, in the order your need it, for processing a new inquiry and retaining contact information in your database. Have your local copy shop print these up, two-sided, on brightly colored paper, and padded into small tablets. Give everyone on your staff as well as your board members and key volunteers a couple of these pads and emphasize the importance of completing this form for each new contact and delivering it to you for fulfillment.

Contact Record

Title: Mr. Mrs. Ms. Miss Dr. Other _____

First Name: _____

Last Name: _____

Street or P.O.: _____

City: _____ St/Prov: _____

Zip: _____ Fax: _____

Tel: _____ (day) _____ (eve)

E-Mail: _____

Source: _____

Notes: _____

Action Required: _____

☐ New ☐ Update ☐ Action Req. Date _____ By _____

Contact Record Form Directions

This form will help us retain accurate information about members and others interested in our organization. Please complete one of these forms for every phone or personal contact you make. If easier, simply staple the business card or meeting sign-up sheet to this form, complete the bottom half, and send it along. Thanks!

Title: Please circle appropriate title.

First Name: Fill in first name or names. List any initials here.

Last Name: Fill in last name. If a couple with different last names, put one in "First Name" and one in "Last Name".

Street or P.O.: Enter complete mailing address.

City: Enter full city name. **St/Prov:** Use appropriate two capital letters.

Zip: Enter zip or postal code. **Fax:** List area code and number.

Tel: Include area code and number; circle any calling preference.

E-Mail: Pay special attention to capitalization.

Source: List how the person found you, what meeting or event they attended, or otherwise how this initial contact was made.

Notes: Include any special information we should be aware of about this person. Is their job connected with our work? Did they offer assistance?

Action Required: Specify any follow-up needed and by whom. If action is to be completed by another, please designate whom and check box below.

☐ New ☐ Update ☐ Action Req. Date _____ By _____

If you know the contact's status (New or Update), check the box. Check if action is required. Indicate the date of your contact and initial the "By" box.

Please forward this form to: _____

Thank you!

EXHIBIT 8.1.
Contact Record Form

Print up pads of a form like this one and distribute them throughout your organization for colleagues to use in collecting prospect names. Completed forms should be returned to the membership department in order to fulfill requests for information and enter the names into the in-house prospect database.

How to get more members from your presentations

Despite the astounding number of obligations people squeeze onto their calendar, many of them also make the time to come to your organization's slide shows and other presentations. While there, they hear helpful and valuable information and have an opportunity to see, hear from, ask questions of, and perhaps even shake hands with an official representative of your organization.

Why don't these people join your organization? The answer is most likely that they were not asked in a compelling manner nor were they provided a convenient way to respond at the moment. With a little advance preparation and training of colleagues and volunteers, you can make your organization's routine presentations into a powerful membership recruitment opportunity. Here's how.

First, put together a membership information kit and make sure your presenters bring it to each scheduled presentation. This kit should include a couple of clipboards, several of your standard sign-up sheets, pencils or pens, enough remit envelopes (see Chapter Six) or brochures with return envelopes for every expected attendee, about a dozen copies of your most recent newsletter, and a table tent card or display inviting participants to join. (There's a story about the world-traveling executive whose secretary prepared five briefcases, each stocked identically right down to his favorite candy bar. As he headed out the door to his next flight, he dropped off the used one and picked up a new one, so he always had the supplies he wanted on hand. Consider pre-assembling several of your prospecting kits in look-alike containers, so that your speakers will always have one handy, perhaps even including a candy bar or other treat to thank them for their help!)

Next, give your presenters the following instructions (and include a sheet with these instructions in the kit):

- Place a remit envelope or a copy of your brochure with return envelope on every chair (invite a volunteer or early arrival to help with this task).

- Stack any extras on a table in the back of the room, along with your spare newsletters and your "invitation to join" sign.

- Moments before the presentation begins, ask a volunteer to begin circulating the clipboards with sign-up sheets, beginning at the front of the room.

- Use the moments after the formal presentation but before the question period to ask for memberships.

Your speaker can take advantage of the fact that attendees have received valuable, engaging information, usually for free, and will stay seated for at least some length of time for the question-and-answer session.

Include a draft script that speakers can use to make a membership ask, such as the following:

That concludes my formal presentation for this evening. I appreciate the opportunity to speak with you. I suspect you have questions, and I look forward to responding to them in just a minute.

Before we begin, however, I'd like to remind you that I am here tonight because of the generosity of members of [organization name]. Working on your behalf in our community for more than _____ years, [organization]'s successes and programs have been possible thanks to the support of more than [number of] members—people like you who also care about the issues we discussed tonight and the future of our community.

On your chair when you came in tonight was a copy of an [envelope or brochure] like this one. [Hold up remit or brochure.] I hope you will take a moment to also become a member of [organization]. Your support now will truly make a difference. Simply complete the form and drop in your check, cash, or fill in your credit card information. If you hand them to the volunteer at the back of the room tonight, I'll make sure they get to our membership director tomorrow morning to put you on our roster right away. (Thanks for your help, [name of volunteer].)

Thank you again for coming tonight and thank you in advance for your support. Now, who has the first question?

This kind of request takes less than a minute to deliver, yet makes the important connection between the presentation that attendees just heard and membership in your organization. By working with your presenters to help them become comfortable with delivering this ask, you will significantly increase the number of memberships received from such presentations.

To boost effectiveness even more, consider offering speakers an incentive. Here's an example: for several years, Alaska Wilderness League coordinated a speaking tour about the Arctic National Wildlife Refuge, and one speaker presented dozens of slide shows across the country. Although he successfully secured thousands of passionate letters to key congressional delegates opposing drilling in the Refuge, he had recruited only a handful of new members.

Before launching the 2001–2002 slide show series, executive director Cindy Shogun and development director Corinne Ribble sat down with their slide show host and discussed ways to boost the effectiveness of the slide show program as a membership recruitment tool. In that conversation they learned that their presenter had always wanted to visit Ireland. They struck a deal: If he could bring in two hundred new members from the slide show series, Alaska Wilderness League would provide him with a round-trip ticket to Ireland. That year, Alaska Wilderness League recruited more than ten times as many new members from the slide show program as in the past, there was no fall-off in the number of letters written during the slide show programs, and the presenter had a great time in Ireland.

You can use another form of incentive to recruit members at paid events. Earth Charter of Sanibel launched its formation with a literary reading by award-winning authors Peter Matthiessen and Janise Ray. Tickets cost $10. The evening's printed program and an announcement by ECOSanibel's chair at the close of the readings (but before the question-and-answer period) invited the attendees to join the new organization and apply the price of their ticket to the membership rate. About 15 percent of the hundreds of people who attended took advantage of that special offer and joined that night; the organization also received several memberships on forms from the program by mail.

Piggybacking on other communications

You can significantly improve the efficiency of your membership program by working with your colleagues to help other existing outreach activities also do double duty. Once everyone begins to view every communication as a potential membership recruitment opportunity, you'll see countless simple ways to capitalize on existing efforts. Here are some examples:

- *News releases.* Craft a standard descriptive paragraph to be included at the end of each of your news releases that describes your organization and invites inquiries. Incorporate the elevator or positioning statement you developed in Chapter Two, your phone number, and your Web site address. Consider inviting readers to sign up by e-mail for an e-mail newsletter that has more information about the news release topic. Although most large newspapers will not include all the information you give them, local weeklies and neighborhood shoppers—publications with a very high cover-to-cover readership rate—will frequently print your entire news release verbatim.

- *Op-eds and letters to the editor.* In most newspapers, the editorial and opinion pages are among the most-read sections. When someone in your organization submits an editorial or opinion piece, be sure they know to include a paragraph similar to the one described in the previous item on news releases that describes the purposes and benefits of your organization and how readers can contact you. Similar information should be included with magazine articles. Finally, whenever someone from your organization submits a letter to the editor, they should also include the organization's phone number and Web site address in their identifying information.

- *E-mail signatures.* Every e-mail message sent by someone on your staff or board offers another potential impression toward The Rule of 27. Work with your leadership to create a standard e-mail closing that includes your elevator statement and an invitation to join the organization. Make sure everyone on staff uses it. Here's what one group uses:

Not a member of Chicagoland Bicycle Federation? Join today and add your voice to the thousands of local bicyclists who already look to CBF to protect their rights and promote their dreams of making Chicagoland a safer and more enjoyable place to ride: http://www.biketraffic.org.

- *Action alerts.* Include a standard description of your organization and a reminder of the number of members and communities you represent with each action alert. That way, you not only provide reinforcement of a common message to activists who are receiving your action alert, you also reaffirm the importance of their participation as a member—or give those who aren't another nudge to join.

- *Voicemail.* Beyond clearly identifying on your organization's main voicemail system an option for getting more information about your organization and joining your group, consider recording some motivational membership messages for people to hear while they are on hold. Save the Manatee Club's hold system features co-founder Jimmy Buffett giving informational and membership messages. The Club also uses an easy-to-remember toll-free number: 1-800-432-JOIN.

Managing your in-house prospect file

Once you start collecting all these in-house prospects, you need a system for what to do with all the data. One approach is to include all of your in-house prospects in one database with your membership list. The advantage of combining all your in-house files is that you can minimize duplicates and eliminate confusion about who is a member and who is a prospect. Your database also allows you to record additional information about a prospect, including how they found you (noted in their origination source code) and when the initial contact was made. (See Resource C on source codes.) This system ensures that when a prospect eventually becomes a member, you will know what originally brought your organization to his or her attention, enabling you to focus outreach efforts on those that are most likely to produce prospects who convert to members.

As you attract more and more prospects, knowing the original contact date and source code for each will be helpful in managing your follow-up contacts. For example, if you are preparing a special appeal around a clean-water protection theme, you could reasonably expect this letter to be of interest to people who signed your petition on this subject. If all your prospects are also in your master database, you can extract a file of everyone with the clean-water petition source code, between the dates of X and Y, who have contributed zero dollars. Your source code system can also help you reduce the number of prospects in your active database. If you get to the point where the number of prospects overloads your system, you can archive information for less current prospects in a file outside your database, sorted by the date and source code information you have collected.

Rather than purging these or any other data, store them in a way that you can retrieve such deactivated files when you have a hot campaign that is bringing in people you haven't heard from for a long time. You can update addresses for these files by using the post office's national change of address system (NCOA) (see Data Direct in Resource A), then contact those older prospects for support as well. For example, NARAL is successfully reactivating in-house prospect names and long-lapsed members from the early 1990s to respond to new threats to reproductive rights.

The many ways of capturing in-house prospects are summarized in a checklist in Worksheet 8.1. Use this checklist to review whether you are using all possible ways to collect in-house prospect information.

Create an inquiry follow-up routine

As we know from The Rule of 27 discussed in Chapter Seven, it's probably going to take more than a single inquiry response packet to turn in-house prospects into new members. Worksheet 8.2 will help you formalize a procedure for managing inquiries and follow-up. In the interest of allowing as many of your projects as possible to do double or even triple duty, the follow-up calendar suggests contacting prospects using your established communications programs, such as special appeals and new-member prospecting campaigns. As with similar worksheets in this manual, you may want to revise and improve this one to fit your specific circumstances.

Converting individuals who have shown interest in your work into members can be exponentially more successful than cold prospecting. One big reason for this difference is that a request for membership in response to an individual's inquiry is usually perceived as professional and appropriate, whereas a cold approach—by letter, phone, doorbelling, or e-mail—can be perceived as intrusive or never make it into the prospect's awareness at all. The more you can encourage and efficiently cultivate in-house prospects, the more likely you are to turn them into members who support your organization and work for your cause.

Capturing In-House Prospects: A Checklist

Use this checklist to make sure you are maximizing your opportunities to collect contact information from everyone who shows interest in your group.

- [ ] 1. In-house prospect processing system established. Goal = response in 72 hours maximum
  - [ ] Inquiry systems checked monthly
- [ ] 2. Database is functioning
  - [ ] Capturing name, address, phone, e-mail, source, and date
  - [ ] "Do not mail" file
- [ ] 3. Standard prospect response letter prepared and packets assembled
- [ ] 4. Web site sign-up (e-newsletter, guest book, survey, contest, etc.)
- [ ] 5. Logical, comprehensive phone book listings
  - [ ] All logical names
  - [ ] All logical locations
  - [ ] White & Yellow Pages
- [ ] 6. Web site found by top search engines (update monthly or quarterly)
- [ ] 7. After-hours answering system in place; system for collecting messages
- [ ] 8. Contact record forms printed and distributed
  - [ ] Reception/phone answerer
  - [ ] Program staff
  - [ ] Outreach staff
  - [ ] Board and other key volunteers
  - [ ] Other: _____
- [ ] 9. Speakers collecting attendees' names; sample sign-up sheet; membership kits
- [ ] 10. Remit envelopes in:
  - [ ] Newsletters
  - [ ] Thank-you notes
  - [ ] Annual report
  - [ ] Information packets
  - [ ] Other: _____
- [ ] 11. Standard closings adopted for communications
  - [ ] News releases
  - [ ] Op-eds and letters to the editor
  - [ ] E-mail signatures
  - [ ] Action alerts

In-House Prospect Processing Procedure

This worksheet helps you decide how you will process inquiries, who is responsible, and the appropriate timeframe so that you can ensure an integrated, manageable routine.

Coordinator: _____

	Responsible Parties	Timing/ Frequency
Meet to review inquiry collection/response procedures	_____	_____
Formalize inquiry processing procedure	_____	_____
Develop and distribute contact record forms	_____	_____
Upon initial contact, collect following information:	All	Daily

☐ Name

☐ Mailing address

☐ Telephone (day? evenings?)

☐ E-mail

☐ Source of contact (see source code log)

☐ Date of contact

☐ Special request/interest

Deliver contact record forms for processing	All	Daily
Enter contact information into database	_____	_____
Prepare inquiry response packets	_____	_____

Contents:

☐ Welcome message

☐ Response device with envelope

☐ Newsletter

☐ Outer/carrier envelope

☐ _____

☐ _____

☐ _____

Address and mail inquiry response packets	_____	_____

	Responsible Parties	Timing/ Frequency
Review inquiry response program and effectiveness:	_____	_____

- ☐ Evaluate response to inquiry mailings
- ☐ Summarize sources of inquiries and relative response
- ☐ Review inquiry response packet materials
- ☐ Revise/reorder materials
- ☐ Other: _____

Follow-up:

☐ Include in-house prospects in membership recruitment direct mail	_____	_____
☐ Mail special appeal to in-house prospects	_____	_____
☐ _____	_____	_____

CHAPTER 9

Inviting Membership One-on-One

As mentioned in earlier chapters, there is simply no more powerful fundraising technique than the one-on-one request—and this is true for recruiting members as well. Yet many organizations do not use this tried-and-true strategy as effectively as they could. This chapter outlines how you can overcome the perceived barriers to one-on-one asking and incorporate this powerful tool in your membership program. This chapter also describes the reasons this technique is so effective and suggests some specific ways you can put it to work to build your membership immediately, regardless of the size, scope, or sophistication of your organization.

The benefits of asking one-on-one

There are several reasons that a one-on-one request is so powerful:

- A request to someone you know *builds on the levels of trust and accountability* already existing in the relationship between the asker and the prospect.

- A solicitor's *knowledge of the prospect* creates a context that reinforces the enthusiasm, sincerity, and credibility of the request.

- A one-on-one ask from someone the prospect knows, whether by mail, e-mail, telephone, or in person, *puts a personal, familiar face on your organization* and its services, effectively bringing it into the life and community of the prospect.

- One-on-one asks provide both parties with a *convenient, unintimidating option for follow-up.* The asker can be reasonably assured that he or she will be able to see and talk to the prospect in the near future, allowing a comfortable chance to reaffirm the value of the prospect's participation. Similarly, the prospect can easily re-contact their friend, colleague, or co-worker, and ask for additional information about your organization.

In addition to being a low-cost method to reach prospects, training members of your organization to ask one-on-one creates organizational benefits. First, preparing to conduct a one-on-one membership recruitment campaign requires board and staff to review and recommit to the reasons membership is important to your organization.

Second, such activities help to hone your leadership's vocabulary around the importance of membership and increase their overall asking skills. Since most people find it difficult to ask for money, by discussing the art of asking, practicing making requests, doing some group role plays, and sharing the specifics of successes, your board, staff, and key volunteers will feel more comfortable seeking support for your membership program.

A third benefit of a one-on-one membership recruitment campaign is that the training it provides for your team can later be applied to other campaigns. Most membership-level asks of $50, $25, or even less as a starting point are so low that they practically eliminate the barrier of financial ability to respond. When you build confidence among your team in asking for membership support, you also increase their comfort level with eventually asking for larger gifts. This can be very helpful when you launch a major donor campaign (see Chapter Twelve).

The end result can be a spectacularly increased membership. For example, Alaska Wilderness League and Natural Resources Council of Maine each recruited more than two hundred new members when they launched a one-on-one recruitment campaign.

The gift of asking

Think about one of your close friends, social acquaintances, or family members—someone who may have heard you talk enthusiastically about your group's new projects, rail against the opposition, and share your frustrations. She may even have mentioned that she is impressed with the work your group has done, making such comments as, "I never knew that was a problem. I'm so glad you folks are working on that," or, "I'm amazed. I can't imagine accomplishing that by myself," or, "I love to hear you talk about your organization. You always get such a charge out of its work." Have you invited this friend, acquaintance, or family member to become a member of your organization? Maybe you've talked around it some but have not yet asked directly. Let's look at why not.

Perhaps you felt, "I couldn't impose on our friendship," or, "If she's really interested, she would have joined already." Now look at this interaction from the perspective of your friend. Since you have yet to ask for her support, your friend may reasonably assume that either you don't need her support or that she somehow would not fit into your group.

It's time to get yourself out of this situation and directly ask those friends, colleagues, and family members to join you in supporting your organization. The next few sections will tell you how.

Focus on the benefits you are offering

The beauty of one-to-one recruitment is that it can and in fact should be informal rather than formal. It should also rely heavily on the power of the asker's personal experience with the organization and the asker's connection with the prospect. This means that every one of your askers already has the information at hand that they need to be an effective recruiter for your membership program. Often they just need to be made comfortable with having the conversation. Schedule about half an hour at your next board or staff meeting to discuss membership.

Start by asking each participant to talk about his or her personal relationship with the organization, focusing on questions such as, What brought you to the organization? Why are you still involved? Invite each participant to share a favorite story that illustrates the importance of your organization to his or her life. Capture the essence of these stories on a flip chart and post the sheet where everyone can see it. Identify themes and common priorities; these are your most compelling benefits.

Identify personal prospects

Keeping in mind this list of organizational benefits and ways your group has positively touched people's lives, have the group brainstorm a list of the kinds of people the participants know who could also benefit from or find value in your group's programs, opportunities, and services. People's lists may include high school and college classmates, fellow sports team members, other parents at their child's preschool, vendors and service providers to their business, and countless others. Again, capture these types of contacts on a flip chart and post the list so everyone can see.

Learn how to ask

Membership recruiters need only four attributes to make their one-on-one campaign a success:

1. Sincere, heartfelt enthusiasm about the value of the organization

2. The personal conviction that membership in your organization truly provides a valuable benefit to the prospect

3. A reasonable expectation of success, with the awareness that not everyone will say "Yes"

4. A comfortable way to accept a negative response so that both the recruiter and the prospect are honored

One reminder that helps achieve all four of the above requirements is the firm understanding that a membership request is an invitation to support a dynamic and successful organization that is making a difference in the future of your community. It is *not* asking for money for yourself; rather, it is inviting your associates to benefit from a successful investment opportunity that you have discovered.

Think back over conversations with friends during the past several months. They may have included discussions of retirement planning, stock market ups and downs, and the future of the economy. Some friends may have had an idea about a worthwhile investment for the future. Consider putting the work of your organization in that same context. What other investment can guarantee better returns on their money—in terms of community improvement, personal services, information and education, social opportunities, and more—than a membership in your organization?

The very best way to become a successful one-on-one membership recruiter is to practice. However, no manual like this would be complete without a suggestion on how to craft your ask in a comfortable way. Here's something simple and easy to remember: use the mnemonic INSIDER. INSIDER suggests an outline for telling friends and relations the story of your connection with your organization and asking for their support. It's a way to convert a prospect—an outsider—to a new member of your organization—an insider.

The INSIDER ask technique can be used comfortably in a one-on-one personal conversation or telephone call. It can also serve as an informal outline for writing a membership invitation letter or e-mail. It begins with the fact that you have reason to believe that, because the individual you are talking with lives in your community, has shared concerns with you in the past about an issue your group is dealing with, or otherwise can be expected to benefit from your group's services, she or he would be a good prospect for your organization. Here's what the INSIDER acronym stands for.

• **INvite with a question.** A question is a great way to start a conversation about your organization. It lets your friend know that you honor her opinion and are interested in what she has to say. Such a question may be, "Did you see the article in yesterday's paper about [an issue that your organization is dealing with]?" or, "How long have you lived in our community? Isn't it amazing how [bad traffic has gotten, polluted the river has become, many more homeless people there are] today compared to when you and I first came here?"

• **Share common experience.** The opening question allows you and your prospect to discuss common experiences and concerns around the issues your organization is working with. This helps establish that your prospect recognizes personal or community needs that are being addressed by your organization's programs and services.

• **Inform about how your group makes a difference.** Now that you and your prospect have recognized a mutually agreed-upon need in your community, you can introduce your organization and what it is doing to affect this issue. Emphasize your personal involvement and support for your group by beginning this part of your conversation with something like, "It's just this kind of situation that led me to get involved with [group's name]," or, "The kind of concerns that you and I have just discussed underscore the importance of [group]." Continue by giving a short description of your group's mission and programs. (Use the elevator statement you developed in Chapter Two.)

• **Describe the threat or urgency.** Here's your opportunity to reconnect what your organization does with the common experience and concerns that you shared earlier with your prospect. At this point, you can describe the challenges to your group's success. These could include general misunderstanding of your issue, apathy, financial challenges such as government budget cuts or increased demand, or the techniques of the opposition. Consider reinforcing your points with a sticky stat (see Chapter Two).

Be sure to introduce the need for urgent action at this point. Give your prospect every reason to respond immediately.

• **Explain how the prospect can help.** Certainly, many of the classic reasons to compel your prospect's participation apply at this time: "Every voice speaking out in favor of these issues right now really will make a difference," or, "With the county commission vote just three weeks away, every new member reinforces the importance of this issue to the commissioners," or, "In an effort to really show community support for these concerns, our board and staff are conducting a campaign right now to attract as many new members as we can," or "Your membership donation today will truly help provide much-needed services during this critical emergency."

A great advantage of a one-on-one ask, and one of the reasons for its success, is that you can tailor your request to the specific talents, skills, and interests of your prospect. For example, this would be the place to say, "As a parent of school-aged children, your support will really make a difference," or, "I know you share my concerns about this; since you are a business owner and our opposition is claiming that these kinds of solutions will undermine the area's economy, your support will have a real impact." You might also want to list the kinds of things that individuals can do to help out in addition to joining: write a letter to the editor, come to an organizing meeting, take part in a special event, attend a public hearing, volunteer time at the office or clinic.

• *Request support.* At this point you wrap up and secure that new membership. A logical transition would include a statement such as, "In addition to these kinds of direct actions, perhaps the simplest yet most important way you can support our organization is to become a new member. I've been a member myself for five years and can assure you this is one of the best investments you'll ever make. I'm constantly amazed at how this talented group of individuals can have such a big effect in our community so cost-effectively. Less than .15 percent of our organization's budget goes to administrative and fundraising expenses. The vast majority goes for providing the kind of services we've just been talking about. Basic membership begins at $25, although many people join with a gift of $35, $50, or $100. Can I count on you to join us? It would sure make a difference to me to have you on our team. And I know it would be a real benefit to you and your family." At this point you hand them a remit envelope (see Chapter Six) and give them a way to say "Yes."

Wrap up your board and staff discussion of membership with a practice session. Give everyone five minutes to jot down some notes to themselves about how they would make an INSIDER ask. Then, divide your team into pairs, with each member taking five minutes to ask the other member of the pair to join. In about fifteen minutes, each of your team will have had the chance to experience a one-on-one ask, both as an asker and as a prospect. Conclude your meeting by bringing the group back together and sharing reactions and success.

Board and staff get-a-member campaign

Now that your team is trained and ready to go on membership recruitment, give them a reason to put that energy to work immediately. One way is through a board and staff get-a-member campaign. Please note that this is not a put-a-notice-in-the-newsletter-inviting-each-of-your-members-to-get-a-new-member campaign. Those kinds of programs almost always have disappointing results, primarily because there is little or no energy behind them and, as discussed in Chapter Six on publications, a newsletter is not a particularly effective action device. Rather, this campaign uses the contacts, skills, time, and energy of your entire board, other key volunteers, and staff. Worksheet 9.1 shows the elements of how it works.

- *Team captains.* This campaign incorporates the fun of a low-key competition within your organization. Because you are asking for gifts of less than $100, virtually everyone has access to potential new members. Team captains help keep the enthusiasm going. Work with your board chair and executive director to identify team captains. Consider choosing your newest board members for this role, which will give them an opportunity to contribute immediately in a tangible way, regardless of their specific skills and backgrounds. It also lets you see how well they can motivate fellow team members and organize for success. Using new board members as team captains can inspire the rest of your board and staff, who want new board members to succeed and who may therefore give them extra latitude. The board chair should personally ask the team captains to take on the job; this will reinforce the importance of this task to the team captain candidates and the board as a whole. Once confirmed, the team captains can work with you in planning and setting a time schedule, goals, and incentives, as outlined below.

- *Team participants.* Consider designating two or three teams along lines that enhance other goals of your organization. For example, if you are looking to strengthen ties between board and staff, you may want to include a cross-section of board and staff members on each team. Perhaps you have a friendly rivalry already going between urban board members and rural board members, or east side and west side. You can create a team to take advantage of that natural competition or you can seek to minimize it by including both camps on every team. Alaska Wilderness League took advantage of the assistance of a team of Green Corps interns to organize a board and staff get-a-member campaign, with the team of Green Corps interns competing against two mixed teams of board and staff members. They chose names of favorite Arctic wildlife to designate the teams: Polar Bears, Tundra Swans, and Musk Oxen.

- *Timing.* Launch and conclude your get-a-member campaign when all participants can be together. As shown on the calendar section at the bottom of Worksheet 9.1, limit the duration of the recruitment campaign to about two months. This will help to sustain the level of energy and productivity. Because you want board and staff to be able to concentrate on the demands of the campaign, schedule it during a period when other board and staff obligations are minimal. The greatest energy for the campaign will be at the beginning and during the wrap-up week. Ask your team captains to keep participants energized and focused by providing weekly e-mail updates of success stories and accomplishments to date.

- *Theme.* Although it's not necessary, a theme may help motivate participants and enhance their INSIDER ask. Themes could reflect your timing schedule ("Help us recruit a hundred new members before the legislative session begins"), reinforce a current program objective ("Fifty new members would allow us to feed

Board and Staff Get-a-Member Campaign

This worksheet will help you and your team captains orchestrate a successful board and staff get-a-member campaign.

Team Captains:

1: _____ 2: _____ 3: _____

Teams/Participants:

_____ _____ _____
_____ _____ _____
_____ _____ _____
_____ _____ _____
_____ _____ _____
_____ _____ _____

Timing: _____

Theme: _____

Goals:

Campaign: _____

Individual: _____

Team: _____

Incentives:

Top Team: _____

Top Individual: _____

First to Goal: _____

Other: _____

Calendar (weeks out):

-9 Campaign plan drafted

-8 Executive director and board chair approve campaign

Team captains identified

-6 Team captains confirmed

Theme and goals identified

Incentives recruited

-5 Meet with team captains:

Identify materials needed (remit envelopes, brochures, and so on)

Confirm timing, theme, teams, training, incentives

-3 Invite participants to launch meeting

0 Launch campaign (teams confirmed, materials distributed, training)

2, 4, 6 Provide biweekly update to team captains

Team captains contact participants, replenish materials as needed

8 Celebrate success!

five hundred more families for a week"), or build on seasonal competitions such as the World Series or basketball playoffs ("Here's a playoff where everybody wins: your membership helps [group]'s great work and helps my team win!").

• *Goals.* Establish goals for the campaign as a whole, for each team, and for each participant. Make sure that your goals are reasonable and do-able; most of all, you want every participant to feel as though the campaign was a success. A reasonable goal for individuals is to recruit five new members. Almost everyone can reach this goal without an inordinate amount of effort, and several people will exceed the goal (which will make them feel fabulous about the program and maybe even willing to do it again). You could also choose goals that reinforce your membership or fundraising objectives. For example, you could choose to put a priority on or give "extra credit" for members recruited from special targeted communities, or with specific skills or abilities that your organization is seeking. Alaska Wilderness League's second board and staff get-a-member campaign offered extra points for recruiting monthly donors.

• *Incentives.* Invite your team captains to help identify fun premiums or gifts to further motivate campaign participants. For example, Idaho Conservation League timed the end of their campaign to coincide with their annual retreat for board and staff in a rustic setting. Knowing that the winning team would be exempt from all dishwashing and other housekeeping chores throughout the weekend was a big incentive to the teams to bring in more members. Another organization required the losing team to host a dinner for the winning team. At the resulting soirée, tuxedo-dressed losers waited on the winners, with all having a great time.

• *Cheerleading and measuring success.* As membership staff for your organization, you should limit your responsibility for the get-a-member campaign to providing materials, coordinating and confirming new-member returns, and cheerleading. Upon campaign launch, provide each participant with an ample supply of remit envelopes or brochures with return envelopes and sample recruitment letters and e-mails. Review the chart on relative effectiveness of recruitment techniques in Exhibit 7.1 with your participants so they have realistic expectations of the response they can expect from each of their efforts.

To those who protest, "Everybody I know is already a member," suggest they put together their own prospect list and review it against your active membership base. The overlap is likely to be less than anticipated.

Another question that will arise is, "What happens if three of us all ask the same person?" Terrific! What better way to reinforce the value and importance of your organization than to have three associates of an individual all asking for support. In this case, the first individual to recruit the membership wins.

To assure appropriate credit, ask each team member to write their name or initials on the brochure response forms or the remit envelopes they use for recruitment. Each week or two, whoever manages your database should send an e-mail summary to each team member listing new members' names and who is credited with recruiting them. This will help keep the campaign in the forefront of participants' minds, while providing valuable information for follow-up for folks whose prospects agreed to join but haven't sent a membership contribution yet.

The cost-effectiveness of this campaign in new membership contributions, awareness of the organization, and goodwill recruited is hard to beat. Regardless of how old your organization is, a get-a-member campaign will bring in a significant number of new members.

Natural Resources Council of Maine celebrated its fortieth anniversary in 1999. Although its membership tops five thousand—an especially impressive number for a state the size of Maine—board members brought in 244 new members through their anniversary get-a-member campaign. Recruiters averaged ten new members each, with one recruiter bringing in a whopping forty new members. The average gift was more than $55, raising more than $13,600 for the organization, with negligible expenses. WOW!

At Alaska Wilderness League, thirty-two board members, staff members, interns, and consultants made up three teams of individuals scattered across the country. Their campaign recruited 234 members and $14,834!

A board and staff get-a-member campaign is a low-cost, high-return, and fun way to build camaraderie and membership. It can work for new groups and long-established groups; local, state, and national groups; groups with staff and groups without. Perhaps the greatest bonus is that it gives every participant a chance to feel great about your organization and get some training for bigger asks down the road.

CHAPTER 10

Recruiting Members by Mail

When it comes to efficiency and reliability, it's hard to beat the benefits of direct mail membership recruitment. Whether your cause and target audiences encompass an area as small as a major metropolitan community or as large as the nation or even extend internationally, direct mail offers your organization an effective and efficient way to attract hundreds of new members with a moderate investment of staff time.

This chapter uses examples of statewide, community, and national campaigns to illustrate the many aspects of a direct mail campaign and help you create and manage one of your own. Direct mail may not be right for you now if you are a very small organization, but if you hope to grow, it probably will become an important tool in the near future.

The advantages of direct mail

As access to cyberspace and other high-tech communications grows, it may be easy to view direct mail membership recruitment as ineffective or old-fashioned. Yet this technique remains the workhorse for nonprofit membership development for a number of reasons:

• *Direct mail reaches your targeted audience.* By exchanging mailing lists with other organizations and renting lists compiled by list brokers, you can be confident that your direct mail package will arrive in the mailboxes of thousands of people who are interested in issues like yours. These prospects have registered that interest by joining similar organizations, subscribing to related publications, or purchasing products that indicate a lifestyle or hobby that complements your programs.

- ***Direct mail delivers your message personally and unfiltered.*** The letter style of a direct mail package allows your organization to make your case to a prospect in your own words, using your own examples and measures of accomplishments, in a way that builds the reader's enthusiasm for making the commitment to join. We know from returns of interactive devices like signed statements of support or petitions that a minimum of two to three times as many people read your direct mail package as will join from it. Thus, every direct mail campaign has the added value of getting your name out there and increasing your visibility while improving understanding and the perceived value of your organization.

- ***Direct mail provides convenience and privacy.*** When respondents are asked why they like direct mail, convenience and privacy are the two top reasons they give. Direct mail is convenient for the prospect: it allows the recipient to learn about your organization on their own time, in the comfort of their own home. Direct mail is also non-intrusive. No one is calling during dinner or knocking on the door.

- ***Direct mail is easy to respond to.*** Direct mail packages invariably include a response form and business reply envelope (BRE) or courtesy reply envelope (CRE). (BREs require a permit from the post office, and the organization pays the postage; with a CRE, the prospect pays the return postage.) If you include additional response options, such as a toll-free telephone number, fax-back number for paying with a credit card, and a reference to your Web site, a prospect can respond to your direct mail campaign by choosing their favorite method.

- ***Direct mail uses your time efficiently.*** It takes almost as much of your time to prepare and coordinate a direct mail campaign of five thousand pieces as it does for one of fifty thousand or even five hundred thousand. Once you have established your direct mail distribution system, each new campaign should require less and less of your hands-on attention. (By the same token, do not plan to do direct mail as a one-time-only strategy. The time and cost of the systems it takes to prepare your first direct mail campaign are worth it only when they can be amortized over a series of campaigns.)

- ***Direct mail is measurable and accountable.*** By following the procedures discussed in this *Toolkit,* you can reliably measure the level of response to each segment of your direct mail campaigns. This feature makes it easy to predict future responses, identify trends, target productive new lists, and otherwise build on your success while managing your potential risk.

- ***Direct mail uses resources efficiently.*** The myth of the "wastefulness" of direct mail has probably created the greatest controversy over this technique. Yet, by carefully targeting your lists and merging them using a rigorous program to eliminate duplicates, you can make sure that only one mailer goes to each prospect. Direct mail is also energy-efficient because it uses an existing distribution method—the postal system—so no additional fossil fuels or other resources are needed for delivery. By using 100 percent recycled paper, working with your printer to maximize efficient use of that paper, using soy-based inks, and avoiding non-recyclable materials, you can responsibly produce an environmentally friendly and effective direct mail package.

Several excellent books cover the specifics of how to write successful direct mail letters (see Resource A). This chapter summarizes the key techniques direct mail letters use and focuses on the strategies involved in tackling a direct mail campaign, the steps in getting your project out the door, and some examples that have worked well for other groups. The Bicycle Alliance of Washington's first campaign serves as a case study to help walk through how to think about and prepare for your direct mail campaign.

Setting your strategy

When Barbara Culp, executive director of the Bicycle Alliance of Washington, first approached me to prepare a direct mail membership recruitment campaign, we discussed the organization's objectives and its current program priorities and concerns. After considering several possible themes for this campaign, we decided on one suggested by the powerful quotation that you see at the top of the letter in Exhibit 10.1.

For many organizations, a strong discrediting by an official as respected as a mayor would be a death knell. For bicyclists, however, who often perceive themselves as the underdog at the mercy of automobile drivers and the transportation bureaucracy, it was a source of some pride to be referred to as having "raw political power." The quotation established the effectiveness and credibility of the Bicycle Alliance as an organization in the forefront of an important fight. The first page of this letter also demonstrates three of Barbara's other strategic objectives:

1. *Establish continuity and credibility.* Shortly before this letter was distributed, the Bicycle Alliance changed its name and broadened its scope to include the entire state of Washington rather than just the Puget Sound region. To reinforce the group's history and longevity, we added the tag line at the bottom of the first page: "Founded in 1987 as the Northwest Bicycle Foundation (NOWBike)."

2. *Welcome all cyclists.* The Bicycle Alliance had heard that some prospects assumed that one needed to be a racer or super-cyclist to qualify as a member. To counter that misunderstanding of exclusivity, the letter listed the Alliance's board of directors—a classic addition to many direct mail letters and a potential way for establishing credibility within your community—to emphasize the breadth of experience on the board both professionally and regarding cycling. The use of descriptors

Bicycle Alliance of Washington

PO Box 2904 • Seattle • WA 98111
bikeinfo@bicyclealliance.org
www.bicyclealliance.org
206.224.9252

"The raw political power of bicycle clubs."

City of Sammamish Mayor, Phil Dyer
In the Eastside Journal
August 6, 1999

Dear Friend of Bicycling,

When Mayor Phil Dyer of Sammamish accused King County Executive Ron Sims recently of bowing to "the raw political power of bicycle clubs", he was referring to the debate surrounding the proposed East Lake Sammamish Trail for pedestrians and bicyclists...a trail that has been in the county's plan for more than 25 years.

Since 1996, the Bicycle Alliance of Washington has cultivated broad public support for this trail. The Alliance has gathered thousands of signatures in support of the trail, helped organize Friends of the East Lake Sammamish Trail, and applied public pressure on King County Council to acquire the right-of-way to develop the trail.

Who could imagine that an Alliance of clubs, trail supporters, and citizens who walk and bicycle could wield so much "raw political power"? Mayor Dyer gives advocates a lot of credit and the Bicycle Alliance is happy to take it. But creating the political will for this trail requires constant diligence. The Bicycle Alliance holds weekly meetings with supporters; sends letters, postcards, and emails to the King County Council; gathers signatures on trails; gathers signatures at meetings; and sends action alerts to supporters. This is "raw political power" working to give more people a safe place to ride.

Why should you care about eleven miles of trail between two communities in King County? The East Lake Sammamish Trail is a trail of statewide significance, ultimately connecting across the Cascades to the John Wayne Trail and beyond to Spokane. The battle lines drawn along East Lake Sammamish could happen anywhere in Washington unless bicyclists and advocates rally together. If adjacent property owners stop the

Founded in 1987 as the Northwest Bicycle Foundation (NowBike).

EXHIBIT 10.1.
Bicycle Alliance of Washington Recruitment Letter

This powerful letter (and updated versions of it) has recruited more than one thousand new members for the Bicycle Alliance of Washington.

East Lake Sammamish Trail, the entire state will lose a scenic treasure, and a dangerous precedent will be set, potentially jeopardizing every other trail planned for the state.

Without strong bicycle advocates, this same kind of willful opposition can happen in *your* **community. Here are a few examples:**

- The Cascade Trail in Skagit County and the Columbia Plateau Trail in eastern Washington join the East Lake Sammamish Trail in King County as trails of regional significance facing organized opposition from adjacent property owners.

- Tacoma and other jurisdictions resist putting signs on bike routes because they fear increased liability.

- A major bike lane project in Wenatchee faces opposition from vocal residents because the lanes would remove on-street parking.

- Many Washington communities have bicycle plans that identify planned trails, bike lanes, and bike routes. Most of these planned improvements remain on the drawing board due to a lack of funds or lack of political will.

The Bicycle Alliance represents *you and your fellow* **Washington bicyclists statewide in city councils, county commissions, and the State House and Senate.**

- Working in Olympia, the Bicycle Alliance stopped anti-trails bills in the State Legislature.

- The Bicycle Alliance helped pass a major bicycle safety education bill to increase protection for bicyclists in collisions, and create a safety education coordinator position at the state level.

- The Bicycle Alliance helped establish bicycle advisory boards in Vancouver, Bellingham, Wenatchee, and Pullman to develop bicycle transportation plans for their

EXHIBIT 10.1. (continued)

communities and make sure bicyclists are represented before their city councils.

 The Alliance provides advocacy advice and technical support to bicyclists and bicycle clubs from Clarkston to Port Townsend.

 Alliance members and staff serve on regional and state transportation boards, which grant funds to agencies for bicycle and pedestrian projects. (As a result, Washington has been one of the most successful states in the nation at obtaining funds for bicycle projects: more than $12 million in 1998 alone!)

> *When I have questions about bicycle issues, I call on the Bicycle Alliance. I rely on their expertise. There is no question in my mind, that without their assistance, the Cooper Jones Bicycle and Pedestrian Safety Act would not have become reality. Without their support, there would be no statewide voice for cyclists in Olympia.*
>
> *Representative Duane Sommers, Spokane, 6th District*

Why should you join the Bicycle Alliance? There are three answers: Recreation, Transportation, and Fitness. Bicycling provides close-to-home recreational opportunities for families, and the Bicycle Alliance works everyday to prevent trail opponents from stopping trails. Bicycling provides non-polluting solutions for commuting, and the Bicycle Alliance works everyday to help fund more bike lanes for safe urban riding. Bicycling provides fitness fun for all ages, and the Bicycle Alliance works everyday to make sure Washington roads are shared safely and fairly by all users.

> *The only way we're going to have any place to ride is if we organize, and advocate for good places to ride bicycles. The Bicycle Alliance is the single best voice working statewide to protect our interests as bicyclists.*
>
> *Teri Aldrich, Chair, Seattle Bicycle Advisory Board*

Today, the threats to better bicycling are real, and the opponents are vocal and well-organized. By joining the Bicycle Alliance now, you take an important stand for the

EXHIBIT 10.1. (continued)

future of bicycling. With your support, the Bicycle Alliance can create recreation and transportation options for future generations of cyclists. The Bicycle Alliance speaks out at hearings in favor of bicycle lanes; the Alliance speaks for the right to share the road, wherever that road may be. The Bicycle Alliance speaks for you and all cyclists in Olympia. Help preserve your right to ride by joining the Bicycle Alliance.

Please become a member of the Bicycle Alliance of Washington today to support strong local and statewide bicycle advocacy. Membership includes a monthly newsletter featuring statewide issues, action alerts about timely issues such as the budget hearings that affect trail construction, and invitations to conferences and workshops like the Footprints and Bike Tracks Conference this fall in Seattle. As a member, you will also be invited to meet with legislators and other statewide bicycle advocates at the annual Bicycle Lobby Day in Olympia.

Most importantly, your membership helps assure all Washington cyclists access to scenic trails, bike lanes, and safe roads to ride. Please join "the raw political power" of the Bicycle Alliance of Washington now. Return the enclosed form with your membership contribution today. Thank you.

Sincerely,

Barbara Culp

Barbara Culp
Executive Director

P.S. Your support **now** will truly make a difference. The future of the East Lake Sammamish Trail will be determined in the next few months by a vote of King County Council. At the same time, the Bicycle Alliance will be working with your state legislator preparing for the next Washington legislative session. Your membership contribution will go a long way to making these immediate campaigns a success. Your special donation of $100 now will really make a difference. I look forward to hearing from you soon.

EXHIBIT 10.1. (continued)

such as "Daily Commuter" and "New Parent, Riding Less" reinforced that the organization is fun, family-friendly, and approachable.

3. **_Establish statewide scope._** To reinforce the Alliance's new goal of representing bicyclists around the state, the letter mentions the organization's activities in other parts of the state to make sure every reader can find a close-to-home benefit.

Turning strategy into copy

The sequence of this letter follows somewhat traditional direct mail techniques that offer proven methods for success:

1. **_Grab the attention of the reader right away._** The Bicycle Alliance of Washington used a plain, "letterhead style" envelope for this mailing: a white window envelope with just the logo, organization name, and address printed on it. This straightforward approach was effective for two reasons. First, the group has a descriptive name. If you care about bicycles and you live in Washington, chances are you're going to be intrigued by this communication. Second, we wanted to communicate a cost-effective yet professional look. The entire package was printed in two colors, without flashy additions or expensive-looking graphics. My recent testing shows that packages with simpler envelopes like this one usually do better than packages with fancy graphics or teasers (text on the outside of the envelope). Inside, the letter leads with the quote in oversized type to catch the eye.

2. **_Establish a shared concern or need._** By emphasizing that the trail that is the subject of concern has been on the county's plan for more than twenty-five years, and that the Alliance has gathered thousands of signatures of support, the letter immediately identifies the group as a champion for the very people reading the letter—pedestrians and bicyclists. The third paragraph explains that creating political will for this trail requires constant diligence and gives specific examples of the kind of work that the Bicycle Alliance is conducting on the reader's behalf.

3. **_Establish why this issue makes a difference in the life of the reader and his loved ones._** The fourth paragraph addresses the value of the group's work specifically by asking, "Why should you care?" The second page of the letter expands local concern by itemizing similar locations around the state that are also being threatened.

4. **_Tell the reader what you're doing for her._** The second set of bullets, on pages two and three, itemizes specific accomplishments of the Bicycle Alliance. From current members' responses to the group's membership survey, the Alliance already knew that members prized the group's representation before the state legislature and other government bodies. That service led the list and is reiterated throughout the letter. Survey responses also confirmed that members gave high priority to trails, another theme of this letter.

5. *Tell the reader he can trust you.* One of the continuing wonders of membership development is that you can send out a thousand envelopes with a couple of pieces of paper, a response card, and a return envelope in them, and eight, ten, or twelve people will actually send back money! This level of response is especially heartening when you consider the competition for your readers' attention and the fact that most of them have never heard of you before. The Bicycle Alliance letter establishes trustworthiness by listing the board of directors on the first page, establishing that more than twenty fellow citizens (and fellow bicyclists) have taken responsibility for overseeing the success of the organization. The list of accomplishments later in the letter shows credibility, and the use of complimentary testimonials from recognized authorities—in this case an elected official and an appointed official—further affirms the legitimacy of the organization.

6. *Tell the reader why she should join.* The letter addresses this issue from a general viewpoint on page three and on a more personal level several more times on page four.

7. *Tell the reader what you want him to do.* You must be as specific as possible in instructing your prospects what action you want them to take. This letter repeats the invitation to join several times and states specifically, "Return the enclosed form with your membership contribution today."

8. *Use the P.S. as an executive summary.* Direct mail readers most frequently look at the initial paragraph first and then turn to the last page of the letter to see who signed it. As a result, the P.S., which appears just below the signature, is almost always read before the entire letter. The purpose of summarizing the letter in your P.S. is to intrigue the prospect to go back and read from the beginning, while reinforcing your request for membership. Use the P.S. to restate the theme of your letter, tell the reader how he can make a difference, and specify what you want him to do.

9. *Tell the reader why she needs to respond today.* The objective of each direct mail letter is to create a sense of understanding and mutual concern between your group and your reader; bring her to a peak of compassion, indignation, or outrage (or some other action-focused emotion); and turn that emotion into a joining gift. Ideally, your letter will be so compelling that the prospect will join immediately. By providing a reason for that immediate action, you minimize the probability that your letter will be put on a stack for attention later and perhaps get lost. The Bicycle Alliance letter emphasizes the sense of urgency at the beginning by talking about what could be lost if action is not taken immediately. The specifics of urgency are restated in the P.S. with the statement, "The future of the East Lake Sammamish Trail will be determined in the next few months by a vote of King County Council."

Translating copy into layout

As much as possible, you want to make your letter easy to read and understand and for it to feel like a personal communication. Printing on two sheets, collated and folded, instead of "booklet style" on one folded 11" x 17" sheet, adds to the personal feeling of the letter. Notice that the first line of each paragraph is indented, there's plenty of white space between the lines (called *leading* in designers' language), key points are called out with bullets or bold type, and endorsements are indented and put in italics.

To make your letter readable, use at least twelve-point type; if there's room use thirteen-point type. Also, a serif typeface like this one (your computer probably has Times New Roman or Courier) is much easier to read than a sans serif face. (Serifs are the little "feet" that balance the bottoms of letters in a serif typeface.)

The Bicycle Alliance's letter is also a good example of why four-page letters are frequently more effective than shorter ones. The only way you could deliver this amount—or even two-thirds of this amount—of information in a two-page letter would be to reduce the leading or type size, combine or eliminate bullets, lengthen paragraphs, and reduce the margins. All of these "fixes" would result in a letter that was harder to read, which would probably reduce your response rate.

The response form

The goal of every membership recruitment campaign is to inspire prospects with such a motivational message that they are compelled to grab their checkbooks or credit card, complete their response form, and put it in the mail as soon as they finish reading your letter. However, experience shows that at least half or more of your respondents will set your letter aside and respond at some later date. Many people won't keep your letter and outer envelope; they will just retain the response form and the return envelope (as they would for paying a bill). Therefore, it's important to reiterate some of the motivational message of your letter on the response form itself. Exhibit 10.2 shows how the Bicycle Alliance accomplished that.

The letterhead and the response form for this package also list the Bicycle Alliance's Web address. Many prospects will visit your Web site to find out more about your organization and judge its credibility. Although the majority will still join using the response form you enclosed, your Web site becomes an important source for information, affirmation of the legitimacy of your organization, and the importance of the issues you're addressing. For people who are likely to join from your Web site, make sure that the Web site has a "Join now" or "Join here" option on most or even all of its pages.

YES! I want to help guarantee all Washington cyclists access to scenic trails, bike lanes, and safe roads to ride. I want to join the "raw political power" of the Bicycle Alliance today.

Bicycle Alliance *of Washington*
www.bicyclealliance.org

☐ $25 Individual ☐ $100 Patron ☐ $500 Life
☐ $35 Family ☐ $250 Sustaining ☐ $15 Student/Senior or Living Lightly
☐ $50 Sponsor ☐ Other _____

Please charge my: ☐ Visa ☐ Mastercard # _____

Expires _____ Signature _____

Phone _____ E-mail _____

☐ My check is enclosed
☐ My gift will be matched by my employer: _____ **PA999HP**
Send/make checks payable to: The Bicycle Alliance
PO Box 2904, Seattle, WA 98111

Your contribution is tax-deductible to the full extent of the law.
The Bicycle Alliance occasionally exchanges its mailing list with organizations involved in issues we feel you may also find of interest. *If you DON'T want to have your name exchanged, please check here.* ☐

```
**.  .*****.  ****   9UT.  -DI.  98103
9R.  BLAL  & t  L N ORIG.
18  INDEN VE
TT.  WA S  )3  14
```

EXHIBIT 10.2.
Bicycle Alliance of Washington Response Form
Note that this response card reiterates the major points of the letter it accompanied.

If you want to grow, exchange your list

Your own membership list is a valuable asset to your direct mail campaign, as you can exchange it for other allied groups' mailing lists. List exchanges benefit your organization because members of affiliated organizations are likely to share an interest in your issue and be responsive. Many of the best lists (those for other niche groups like yours) are only available by exchange. Exchanging lists can also save money, since renting lists can cost between $85 and $130 for every thousand names.

Here are a few guidelines for making sure that your list exchanges are productive for you and your members:

- Do not exchange the names of anyone on your list who has asked for privacy. Make sure your database includes a "Do Not Mail" field and offer that option to all new and renewing members. (See the bottom left corner of Exhibit 10.2 for sample wording.)

- Do not exchange the name of anyone who has given you $100 or more in a single gift. This protects your most generous donors.

- Exchanges are based on raw names: the gross number of names provided before dropping any duplicates. Exchange one-for-one with "futures" or "owes" balancing out over time. Keep a log of what is owed to you and what you owe, listed by exchanging organization.

- All exchanges are for one-time use only, unless otherwise specified. This restriction also helps you make sure that you are always using the most up-to-date addresses.

- Exchange donor names for donor names (up to twenty-four months old). Inquiry or in-house prospect names probably aren't worth giving or receiving; stick with names of people who have given money.

- Before releasing your list, ask for and approve a sample of what the exchanger will be mailing.

- Block the exchanging organization from mailing to your list during two weeks either side of your special appeal mail date.

- Provide only the information the exchanger needs for mailing: name(s), address, city, state, and zip code.

- Include "seeds" in lists you exchange—that is, include yourself and a colleague on the list of names. This common practice has two benefits: you will get a sample of all mailings going to your members, and you will be able to track whether a list you provided for a one-time use has been used again.

- Never mail to more than five thousand names from any new list. If possible, test by using two thousand or three thousand names from a large list first.

Whom will you mail to?

One of the truisms of direct mail is that you can have the best letter in the universe but if you mail it to the wrong people it will flop. Finding those best lists is critical to the success of your campaign.

Begin by making a working list of where you can get names. Worksheet 10.1 will help you organize list options from most responsive to least responsive.

When identifying possible sources, consider the following types of lists:

- *In-house lists.* These are lists that you "own," because you have compiled them yourself. You do not need to ask anyone else's permission to use them, and you have relatively unlimited access to them. Virtually every direct mail campaign should include two standard in-house lists: *lapsed members* (previous members who have been through your complete renewal cycle and not rejoined) and *in-house prospects* (people who have come into contact with your organization through an inquiry, special event, or some other avenue, but are not yet members; see Chapter Eight).

- *Closely allied groups and campaigns.* Building on the knowledge that joiners join, your next best source of prospects will come from organizations with members who have similar interests or concerns to yours. For the Bicycle Alliance, these fell into two categories: other bicycle organizations and other Washington advocacy organizations (see Worksheet 10.2 on p. 178). The Alliance was able to exchange lists with Adventure Cycling Association, League of American Bicyclists, and Rails-to-Trails Conservancy, all national groups with a high number of bicyclists among their members. In order to find more responsive names from Washington state, the Alliance exchanged names with statewide organizations that also were active in the state legislature, including 1000 Friends of Washington, Friends of Columbia Gorge, Northwest Ecosystem Alliance, and participants in a Washington Conservation Voters bicycle event.

• *Member or donor rental lists.* One category not represented on Worksheet 10.2 is a common one for most organizations: rental lists. Most large nonprofit organizations offer their lists for rent. Once you have identified a list you want to use, contact the group's membership department. Staff there will tell you if they are open to an exchange or if they only rent their list. Rentals are normally managed by a list broker. These professionals are paid on commission, at no direct cost to you. They can save you hours of tracking down details and can direct you to lists that have worked for groups similar to yours (see Resource A).

• *Magazines and catalogs.* In some cases, you may be able to identify lists of magazine subscribers or catalog customers who can be expected to be closely enough related to your mission to be effectively solicited by direct mail (for the Bicycle Alliance, this meant subscribers to *The Bicycle Paper* and purchasers from the Terry Bicycles catalogue). These response rates will usually be lower than what you can expect from lists from membership organizations. That's because, although these folks clearly make purchases through direct mail, they are not necessarily joiners.

• *Compiled lists.* Also available through list brokers are compiled lists. These names come from information gathered on customer product registrations, warranty cards for home appliances or computer products, and the like. Such registrations often collect a gold mine of demographic information, which is likely to be sold to a list broker. The list owner compiles all that information into a massive database that can be analyzed and rearranged according to specific interests. One effective use of compiled lists is for neighborhood or other geographically defined mailings (join our community center; visit our nature center). Postal address or carrier route lists are also usually available, at about two-thirds the price of compiled lists, but they usually include only addresses, not names.

• *Duplicates.* At the bottom of Worksheet 10.2 is information about a follow-up mailing to go out a couple of weeks after the first mailing to the "Dupes from this Mailing." This list is made up of the households that appear on more than one of the lists you own, exchange for, or rent for this mailing. Although when you exchange for or rent a list you only have permission to use that list once, there are

List Identification Worksheet

Use this worksheet to brainstorm possible mailing lists. Lists in category A should produce a higher response rate and average gift than those in categories B and C.

Geographic Select = _____

	List Cost/ Thousand	Total Names	Estimated Unique Names
A Lists: Your very best prospects, known givers who have had contact with your organization or are members of closely allied groups			
Lapsed Members:			
Recent (expired 6 to 18 months ago)	_____	_____	_____
Vintage (expired more than 18 months ago)	_____	_____	_____
In-House Prospects:			
_____	_____	_____	_____
_____	_____	_____	_____
_____	_____	_____	_____
_____	_____	_____	_____
Closely Allied Groups and Campaigns:			
_____	_____	_____	_____
_____	_____	_____	_____
_____	_____	_____	_____
_____	_____	_____	_____
_____	_____	_____	_____
_____	_____	_____	_____
_____	_____	_____	_____
_____	_____	_____	_____
_____	_____	_____	_____
_____	_____	_____	_____

	List Cost/ Thousand	Total Names	Estimated Unique Names
B Lists: Members or donors to other social change groups			
_____	_____	_____	_____
_____	_____	_____	_____
_____	_____	_____	_____
_____	_____	_____	_____
_____	_____	_____	_____
_____	_____	_____	_____
_____	_____	_____	_____
_____	_____	_____	_____
_____	_____	_____	_____
C Lists: Direct mail–responsive buyers (magazine subscribers, catalog customers); political donors; survey respondents; permittees; and so on			
_____	_____	_____	_____
_____	_____	_____	_____
_____	_____	_____	_____
_____	_____	_____	_____
_____	_____	_____	_____
_____	_____	_____	_____
_____	_____	_____	_____
_____	_____	_____	_____

likely to be people who show up on these outside lists who are also on your in-house prospect list or appear on more than one outside list. These folks should be even better prospects for you because you know they've made a joining decision more than once, since they appear on more than one membership list, or you know they are more active in issues related to yours, because they've indicated their level of interest more than once. This Dupes List (also called the Duplicates List, or the Multi File) is a list of those folks who appear on more than one list and thus can be mailed to more than one time. In the case of the mailing for the Bicycle Alliance, 2,731 people of the total 21,879 raw names that the mailing began with appeared on more than one list and were not already a member of the Bicycle Alliance. With another nod to The Rule of 27, these dupes were mailed the exact same package that they and about fourteen thousand other people received in the first round. That means they got two identical packages within two weeks of each other. Soon you'll see why that's worth doing.

As you go about securing your list exchanges and rentals, your working list will be trimmed and supplemented until you end up with a list like that shown in the left column of Worksheet 10.2.

Estimating your returns and costs

Another benefit of creating a spreadsheet like the one in Worksheet 10.2 is that it allows you to go through the somewhat complicated process of comparing different lists with different estimated response rates and estimated average gifts and still approximate just how much you might need to invest in this undertaking. Without this kind of estimate and advance agreement on what makes success, you run the risk of disappointing your board and executive director to such a degree that they decide never to do another direct mail campaign.

Since this campaign was the Bicycle Alliance's first test of direct mail membership recruitment, we did not have the benefit of history to use in our estimate of average response by list and average gift. In lieu of that kind of information, here are some general ranges for estimating responses by type of list:

• *Lapsed members: 1 percent–3 percent.* Lapsed members will almost always be your hottest list. Even if you have been especially aggressive in retaining your members, you should still get a minimum of a 1 percent response from lapsed members. Similarly, your lapsed members should have a strong average gift. You can probably peg this to about 10 percent higher than the average gift that you're receiving from members now (see Worksheet 3.1, "Membership Benchmarks," in Chapter Three). Average gift may change, depending on the amount you are requesting as your basic membership fee. Sometimes—but not always—a discount membership offer reduces the average gift.

• *In-house prospects: 0.5 percent–1.4 percent.* Your in-house lists are a less predictable source of returns because their source of acquisition ranges substantially. People who spent money with you (attendees at your local auction, purchasers of services or publications) may return as much as a 1.0 to 1.4 percent response. If, however, these names are less engaged (petition signers, attendees at a rally), your response rate will probably be more in the range of 0.5 percent to 0.8 percent. The average gift will probably be close to your current member average.

• *Exchanged lists: 0.6 percent–1.3 percent.* By exchanging your list with allied organizations, you not only save the cost of the list-rental fee, you also gain access to audiences that are more likely to give because they are so closely aligned with your issues. Moreover, these people often give a higher average gift, in part because they are usually solicited less frequently than those people on rental lists. For these lists, you can usually expect a response of 0.6 percent to 1.3 percent and an average gift of 80 to 100 percent of your existing members' average gift.

• *Rented member or donor lists: 0.5 percent–0.9 percent.* Rental lists are usually less responsive than exchange lists because their larger size, made possible by aggressive recruiting, includes a greater percentage of less dedicated members than the smaller organizations you exchange with. In addition, national organizations usually delete names of anyone who has given $50 or more. Finally, because these lists are available for rent, the prospects are contacted more often to join organizations like yours, diluting your message among many. Nevertheless, rental lists can provide an invaluable source of prospects for your new-member campaign, especially if you want to reach an area with relatively low population or need to target a specific small or rural location. Estimate responses to rental lists at 0.5 to 0.9 percent, with average gifts of 20 percent less than your basic membership dues request. The larger the rental list, usually the lower the response.

• *Publication subscribers and catalog buyers: 0.3 percent–0.7 percent.* Subscribers and catalog customers are usually less responsive still. Estimate these at 0.3 to 0.7 percent response, with an average gift similar to those for the rental lists mentioned in the previous paragraph. The reason it's worth using these kinds of lists is to allow your message to get out to as many prospects as possible.

By incorporating these estimates and choosing a specific response rate and average gift based on your intuition or sense of affinity for the list itself, you can project what level of revenue you can expect from this campaign. Estimate these responses conservatively. It's always better to underestimate your success than to overestimate it.

Prospect Mailing Estimates

This worksheet is prepared before a campaign to identify desired mailing lists, estimate their response, and project the campaign's net loss or gain. For example, this mailing would be considered a success if it required an investment of $2,352 to recruit 166 new members.

Bicycle Alliance of Washington
September Prospect Mailing—Estimates
To Be Mailed 10/12/99, Follow-up 10/27/99

Package A: "The Raw Political Power . . ."

Code	List	Number of Names	Number Mailed	Cost/ Thousand	Number Returns	Percent Response	Total Dollars	Average Gift	Net Income	Net per Member
PA999LM	*Lapsed members 1996—1998	398	384	$360	4	1.20%	$128	$32.00	($10)	($2.56)
PA999HP	*In-house prospects	3,896	2,878	$360	28	1.00%	$784	$28.00	($252)	($9.00)
PA999WA	*1000 Friends of Washington	827	718	$360	6	0.90%	$174	$29.00	($84)	($14.08)
PA999AC	*Adventure Cycling Association	1,004	756	$360	8	1.10%	$240	$30.00	($32)	($4.02)
PA999BP	Bicycle Paper subscribers	4,506	3,286	$360	29	0.90%	$870	$30.00	($313)	($10.79)
PA999LS	*East Lake Sammamish	1,549	991	$360	9	1.00%	$270	$30.00	($87)	($9.64)
PA999CG	*Friends of Columbia Gorge	494	466	$360	4	0.90%	$120	$30.00	($48)	($11.94)
PA999AB	*League of American Bicyclists	1,482	813	$360	8	1.00%	$224	$28.00	($69)	($8.59)

Code	Name									
PA999NW	*Northwest Ecosystem Alliance	1,741	1,537	$360	13	0.90%	$364	$28.00	($189)	($14.56)
PA999RT	Rails-to-Trails Conservancy	1,866	1,353	$360	13	1.00%	$338	$26.00	($149)	($11.47)
PA999RE	Bicycle Co-Op	2,251	1,964	$450	13	0.70%	$390	$30.00	($494)	($37.98)
PA999TB	*Terry Bicycles	1,464	1,189	$360	9	0.80%	$270	$30.00	($158)	($17.56)
PA999WV	*WCV Bike Ride	401	281	$360	1	0.70%	$30	$30.00	($71)	($71.16)
First Mailing Total		21,879	16,616	$371	145	0.87%	$4,202	$28.98	($1,957)	($13.49)
Follow-up Mailing—10/27/99										
PA999ZZ	Dupes from this mailing		2,731	$360	21	0.80%	$588	$28.00	($395)	($18.82)
Campaign Total		21,879	19,347	$369	166	0.86%	$4,790	$28.86	($2,352)	($14.17)

Income	**$4,790**
Cost	**$7,142**
Net	**($2,352)**

*Lists for Bike Alliance to secure

The remaining factor to be incorporated into this spreadsheet is the cost per thousand for your mailing. Again, if you do not have reliable historical numbers, you'll have to estimate this as closely as possible. Worksheet 10.3 itemizes the specific costs of the Bicycle Alliance's campaign. Since these costs are from Autumn 1999, add about 20–30 percent to approximate 2003 rates. As a working number, you should be safe with a figure of $450–500 per thousand, depending on the number of names and lists you are using and the tests you are conducting, with an added cost of $100 to $120 per thousand names mailed for any lists you're going to be renting. Economies of scale allow larger mailings to trim these costs a bit.

Looking back at the "Campaign Total" line on Worksheet 10.2, you see that we estimated a response rate for this first Bicycle Alliance direct mail campaign of 0.86 percent overall, with an average gift of $28.86. This estimate resulted in total projected revenue of $4,790, with a total estimated cost of $7,142. This means we estimated that it would take an investment of $14.17 to get each new member. That's $14.17 *more* than the amount we expected people to donate as their membership dues. Multiplied by the 166 expected donors, the net cost of the campaign would be $2,352. Given how important it was for the Bicycle Alliance to grow, they expected to spend money to attract new members, then later recoup that investment with additional gifts from special appeals, renewals, and political activity. (This practice is similar to the for-profit world, where profits are usually made on repeat customers, not first-time or one-time clients.)

The actual numbers

Worksheet 10.4 shows the results of the Bicycle Alliance's first campaign.

Look again at the bottom line: overall, they recruited 442 new members, who contributed just under $15,400, with an awesome 2.28 percent response rate and $34.82 average gift. As a result, even though the cost per thousand was higher than we originally estimated because of an unexpected list charge, the net return per member was a positive $15.94, compared to the estimated $14.17 loss.

Note that actual response rates range from a low of 0.85 percent from *Bicycle Paper* subscribers to a high of 9.11 percent from lapsed members. Similarly, average gift amounts ranged from $24.64 to $44.17, and two lists had a rental charge. The best indicator of response by list is the net amount spent or earned per member gained, found in the "Net/Member" column. This column provides an easy comparison of how lists are performing by factoring in cost (with or without a rental list charge), average gift, and percent response by each list. It's also valuable to consider this information in the context of earlier projections. For example, the bicycle co-op list actually did better than we projected initially. It's only in the context of how magnificently the other lists did that this response seems lackluster.

Estimating the Costs of a Direct Mail Campaign

This worksheet itemizes the direct costs of the Bicycle Alliance's initial prospecting mailing. Add 20–30 percent to estimate 2003 costs.

Bicycle Alliance of Washington
October Prospecting Mailing
Mailed 10/12/99, Follow-up 10/27/99, Total 19,347

Package A: "The Raw Political Power . . ."
Updated 1/6/00

Vendor/Item	Number Used	Cost/ Thousand	Total Cost
PRINTING/PROCESSING (number printed)			
#10 carrier envelopes—BAEA (21K)	20,000	$46.77	$935.40
#6 3/4 return envelopes—BABRE (21K)	20,000	$24.09	$481.80
Letter sets—BALA (20K)	20,000	$64.98	$1,299.60
Response forms—BARA (20K)	20,000	$22.70	$454.00
Second set-up for redoing logo + layout			$181.00
Sales tax			$356.38
Printing Subtotal (19,347 mailed)		**$191.67**	**$3,708.18**
Data processing—Data Direct		$52.93	$1,024.05
Mail services—MailHandlers		$37.27	$721.15
Postage		$97.42	$1,884.81
Printing/Processing Subtotal		**$379.00**	**$7,338.19**
LIST RENTAL			
Bicycle Paper—directly invoiced	3,286	$228.00	$750.00
Bicycle Co-Op	1,964	$134.00	$262.55
List Subtotal			**$1,012.55**
TOTAL COSTS		**$432.00**	**$8,350.74**

Actual Costs and Returns of a Prospect Mailing

This worksheet reflects which lists the Bicycle Alliance actually mailed to and the response for each list. This is the "after" view that corresponds to Worksheet 10.2's "before" estimate.

Bicycle Alliance of Washington
October Prospect Mailing Actual Returns
Mailed 10/12/99, Follow-up 10/28/99, Total 19,347

Package A: "The Raw Political Power . . ."

Code	List	Number of Names	Number Mailed	Cost/ Thousand	Number Returns	Percent Response	Total Dollars	Average Gift	Net Income	Net per Member
PA0999LM	Lapsed members 1996–1998	398	384	$379	35	9.11%	$1,490	$42.57	$1,344	$38.41
PA0999HP	In-house prospects	3,896	2,878	$379	86	2.99%	$3,385	$39.36	$2,294	$26.68
PA0999WA	1000 Friends of Washington	827	718	$379	9	1.25%	$320	$35.56	$48	$5.32
PA0999AC	Adventure Cycling Association	1,004	756	$379	38	5.03%	$1,345	$35.39	$1,058	$27.85
PA0999BP	Bicycle Paper subscribers	4,506	3,286	$607	28	0.85%	$690	$24.64	($1,305)	($46.59)
PA0999LS	East Lake Sammanish	1,549	991	$379	26	2.62%	$820	$31.54	$444	$17.09
PA0999CG	Friends of Columbia Gorge	494	466	$379	6	1.29%	$235	$39.17	$58	$9.73
PA0999AB	League of American Bicyclists	1,482	813	$379	29	3.57%	$1,025	$35.34	$717	$24.72

Code	Name									
PA0999NW	Northwest Ecosystem Alliance	1,741	1,537	$379	27	1.76%	$825	$30.56	$242	$8.98
PA0999RT	Rails-to-Trails Conservancy	1,866	1,353	$379	61	4.51%	$1,829	$29.98	$1,316	$21.58
PA0999RE	Bicycle Co-Op	2,251	1,964	$513	19	0.97%	$560	$29.47	($448)	($23.55)
PA0999TB	Terry Bicycles	1,464	1,189	$379	18	1.51%	$795	$44.17	$344	$19.13
PA0999WV	WCV Bike Ride	401	281	$379	4	1.42%	$100	$25.00	($6)	($1.62)
First Mailing Total		**21,879**	**16,616**	**$440**	**386**	**2.32%**	**$13,419**	**$34.76**	**$6,109**	**$15.83**
Follow-up Mailing—10/28/99										
PA1099ZZ	Dupes		2,731	$379	56	2.05%	$1,970	$35.18	$935	$16.70
Campaign Total		**21,879**	**19,347**	**$431**	**442**	**2.28%**	**$15,389**	**$34.82**	**$7,044**	**$15.94**

Income	$15,389
Cost	$8,345
Net	$7,044
Projected Net	($2,352)
Difference	$9,396

Results through 1/18/00
Costs finalized 1/6/00

The results also reaffirm the power of mailing the duplicates. These 2,731 prospects were already included among the 16,616 that were mailed on October 12. They were sent the identical package sixteen days later. (To save money, these packages were labeled, assembled, and prepared for the post office at the same time as the master mailing, so this group undoubtedly included some people who had already responded to the first mailing.) The average response from these prospects—many of whom may have responded to the earlier mailing before they received the second piece—was almost as high as the average for the entire mailing. Better yet, the Bicycle Alliance office received no complaints from these double-mailed prospects, once more affirming the wisdom of The Rule of 27.

Certainly this campaign enjoyed stellar, high-above-average returns. Since then, we have conducted mailings of this package six more times. Although none of the six subsequent mailings have enjoyed quite the same level of success as this first campaign (in part because the hottest prospects responded to previous mailings), responses have continued to be strong and steady, nearly tripling the size of the Bicycle Alliance's membership in less than three years. It would have been virtually impossible for the organization to have this kind of growth with such efficiencies of staff investment without using direct mail.

Two examples of successful direct mail campaigns

The following two exhibits show different approaches to designing a direct mail campaign—both of them successful.

A great community campaign

Exhibit 10.3 illustrates a case in which a grassroots community group made a big impact and raised big money with direct mail.

The outside of this self-mailer by the Methow Valley Recycling Project features a photo of a car filled with materials to be recycled, a woman who looks like she could be your neighbor, and a teaser most everyone receiving the mailing can relate to: "If only it were easier to recycle."

The mailer then opens up to four panels of text and pictures. The first offers hope with the title "Recycling is about to get easier!" and a letter from a Steering Committee volunteer. Specific facts and sticky stats reinforce the need for the recycling center. A classic fundraising thermometer shows how much has been raised to date, how much is still needed, and what the reader's contributions will buy. The bottom panel is the donor form and mail-back envelope.

Consultant Susie Stephens shared these details about this most-successful campaign:

Will you throw that aluminum can away or put it in a box
with the growing pile of cans, bottles, and newspapers?

If only it were easier to recycle...

**Goal:
$250,000**

$37,000 will add drop off boxes
We need to raise **$68,000** to open in the fall
$12,500 Grants being pursued
$132,500 raised from Public Donations, Department of Ecology, Horizons Foundation and Wentachee Foundation Grant

Plus an
$8,000
Okanogan County
grant match of
in-kind and land

Costs to Open The Recycling Center

We have raised $132,500 ⟶
to build the building and operate for six months; and we've
secured the baler needed to make commercial quality bales

We have a pending grant for $12,500

To open the Recycling Center this fall, we need to pay the
balance of the bailer cost, buy a fork lift and supplies, and put
down some asphalt to keep the dust down. **$68,000**

Public drop boxes in Twisp, Winthrop and at Liberty Bell High
School will make recycling convenient. $37,000

Total Project $250,000

Sale of recycleables after the first 6 months will support a part-time manager.

Yes, I want to support the Methow Valley Recycling Center!

*All contributions are welcome. Donations of $1000 or greater will be listed as **Project Partners** on our literature.*

I will contribute/pledge $_____ to the Methow Valley Recycling Project

Name _____

Address _____

Phone (optional) _____

❑ credit card   Visa/Mastercard # _____   Exp. date __/__

❑ I'm interested in volunteering for the recycling center.

May we list your name or business name on fund-raising materials?   ❑ Yes ❑ No

If yes, exactly how? _____

Sponsoring adminstrator: **Okanogan County Electric Co-op,** *Fund-raising partner:* **Methow Conservancy**

Send tax-deductible contribution to: Methow Conservancy Recycling Fund,
                                  PO Box 71, Winthrop, WA 98862   **Thank you!**

Project Partners to Date: Cascade Concrete Products Inc., Ann George & Paul Brown, Horizons
Foundation, Hank & Judy Konrad, Les Schwab Tires, Methow Valley Community Center, Methow
Conservancy, Methow Valley Inn, Methow Valley Sanitation Service, Methow Valley School District,
Moccasin Lake Foundation, Okanogan County, Okanogan County Electric Cooperative, Inc., Town of
Twisp, and the US Forest Service

EXHIBIT 10.3.
Methow Valley Recycling Project Self-Mailer

This self-mailer combined local issues and pictures people could relate to with specific dollar goals and a
matching gift to create a successful and versatile piece.

- Total cost of the mailing (printing, mail house, postage) was $2,200 for seven thousand pieces. That does not include my time designing the mailing nor the cost of the list rentals. We sent to three hundred postal patrons and three thousand property owners from the county assessor's list. We are saving the remaining pieces to distribute at our upcoming event and to leave in stacks at local merchants around the valley.
- Income after three weeks was $19,960 for a 3 percent return so far, with an average donation of $118.00.
- The thank-you card advertises a fundraising event. We plan to hand out the mailer to everyone who enters the event. At the intermission we'll do an enthusiastic plea for dollars. There will be large containers on the way out for people to deposit their money-filled envelopes in.
- The thank-you postcard is easy for volunteers to send. Some of the committee members stop in the office every few days to personally sign a stack of notes I prepare.

The power of a personal story

The wonderful package for Make-A-Wish Foundation of Canada shown in Exhibit 10.4 illustrates how effective a passionate personal story can be in explaining the importance of your organization's work.

Consultant Harvey McKinnon began work on this project by interviewing the father of a Make-A-Wish recipient named Carlie, as well as Make-A-Wish staff and volunteers. "By interviewing people, you get fabulous stories," he told me. "I knew Carlie's story was going to work, because I wept while writing the copy, everyone in our office and at the Make-A-Wish office wept when they read the letter, and so did Carlie's parents.".

The package immediately reinforced the importance of the individual receiving it with the following statement on the back of the envelope: "INSIDE: How people like *you* helped turn Carlie's simple wish into a powerful miracle."

Note the letter's use of large type, short paragraphs, and abundant white space. Spread across two sheets of paper, Harvey's copy is bright and easy to read and leaves space for two great snapshots of Carlie. Harvey says, "It's worth spending the money to use an extra page to make sure people can read it."

This campaign's initial launch brought in about a 2 percent response, about twice as much as a "good" return for Canadian direct mail. At this writing, the mailing is out a second time and already returning a 1.7 percent response.

Your campaign calendar

Worksheet 10.5 lists the steps in putting together your first (or next) direct mail campaign. It's important to allow enough time to put your first direct mail prospecting campaign together. It will take a goodly amount of time to develop a new piece and put in place the vendor relationships and other systems that you will use for future campaigns. As indicated on the calendar, it is difficult to do all this in less than about three months. Your target mail date is shown as week "0" on the chart, with each week's tasks leading up to that goal shown in "minus" weeks below.

Reading from the bottom up, the first items focus on past history, project strategy, budgeting, and copywriting. Future campaigns, when you will be simply adapting your past materials with a few text updates and perhaps a test of pricing or premium, can be accomplished in as little as eight weeks and perhaps six weeks if you are very diligent. For your first campaign, however, you will need longer. If you end up finishing early, your mail shop can still deliver your mailing to the post office on the date you want it to be out the door. Chances are, however, that in the last few weeks before your mail date, even this ample schedule will seem like a tight fit.

Timing your mailing

People often think there is an ideal time to send out a prospecting mailing. My ideal time is, "As soon as you can." There are few horrible times to mail your recruitment campaigns, although you might want to avoid April (too close to tax day in the United States), the two or three weeks before primary or general elections, the last half of December, and days just before major holidays. For every caution, there is an exception. Many groups avoid mailing in August, yet this was the strongest month for Rails-to-Trails Conservancy's early campaigns; perhaps that was because few others were mailing at that time and folks were outside enjoying the resources the organization was working to protect. The most important date is now: start planning.

Test, test, test

It's a good idea to test something with every mailing. Since direct mail works best when it is an integral, on-going part of your membership program rather than a one-shot project, you'll have a chance to run several tests over time, gradually honing your package to be the best. Consider testing a "letterhead" style of envelope against something with a teaser or graphics. For little or no additional cost, your mail shop can often meter your mail (even for bulk-rate postage) as it seals the envelope; this treatment enhances the sense of personalization of your package. Try testing an introductory rate or discount membership offer. This can be especially

MAKE·A·WISH®

Make-A-Wish Foundation® of Canada
2239 Oak Street, Vancouver, BC V6H 3W6
1-888-822-WISH   www.makeawish.ca

Dear Friend,

    There is absolutely nothing worse than watching your three-year-old child die.

    And there is nothing better than stealing her back from heaven.

    My daughter Carlie came back from certain death thanks to people like you.

    I hope you'll give me one minute of your time because I'm not a fundraiser, I'm a parent. And when I tell you my story I think you'll realize that you can make miracles happen . . .

    My daughter Carlie was a perfectly healthy child. Then one day she got a bad fever. We took her to the hospital only to discover every parent's nightmare. Carlie had cancer.

    We started the treatment, and we prayed.

    Then, when Carlie was near the end of 10 months of chemotherapy, her grandmother gave us a wonderful surprise. She

please read on

...A-Wish Foundation and asked that

...e got her dream wish (she wished
... with pneumonia and influenza.

...0% chance to live. Then it got

...e had lost 98% of her lung
... body. She was paralyzed.

...live through the weekend.
...rrible it was to hear this

...y morning they were
...een told to say goodbye
...t.

...d lost half her body

...to a plane to fly to
...wim with dolphins.

...had the strength to
...very was amazing.

...nvinced that

next page please

EXHIBIT 10.4.
Make-A-Wish Foundation Recruitment Package

This prospecting package shows how effective a passionate personal story can be.

Carlie came back from certain deat͏͏ ... dream wish.

When you're as sick as Carlie
get you out of bed is a <u>dream</u> — so
for.

Today, 3 years later, Carlie i͏

You know, I volunteered to v͏
of the luckiest people on earth.

My dying child was given li͏

And I believe it's because s͏
she came back from heaven to g͏

I'm hoping today that you͏
who are very ill. Please send a͏
today, so that a child's dream w͏

I know we were lucky. I l͏
chance to live long lives. But ͏
wish fulfilled.

And as a parent who al͏
you will be making a wonderf͏

Knowing that your pre͏
something you hold on to for͏
fulfilled wish wherever they͏
with your grieving.

And you know, when y͏

---

also help dozens of people who love that child. Their wish is to make a very ill child's dream wish come true. Their other wish is to experience a miracle like the one that happened to Carlie.

Please, while you have my letter in your hand, fill out your reply form and mail it back with your gift. By doing so, you fulfill a very ill child's dream.

You may even bring a child back from heaven.

Yours sincerely,

Russell Lewis
Carlie's Dad and
Make-A-Wish Volunteer

P.S. When you decide to help a child with a life-threatening illness, please consider joining the *Wish Angels* club — it's the best way you can make a child's dream come true.

Thank you!

EXHIBIT 10.4. (continued)

☑ **YES,** I'll give a child like Carlie that special wish. Here's my gift of:

❏ $25   ❏ $50   ❏ $100   ❏ Other $_____

❏ $250   ❏ $1000   ❏ $6518 (average cost for a wish)

27/20 M xx(U)

'iss ͏ ͏bin͏
͏ ͏H ͏ ͏rea
La͏ ͏, Q͏ ͏J ͏

Email _____   Phone No. _____

I prefer to give by: ❏ Cheque ❏ Visa ❏ MasterCard
Please make cheques payable to Make-A-Wish Foundation of Canada.

Card No. _____   Expiry _____/_____

Signature _____

Become a Wish Angel!
❏ I want to become a monthly **Wish Angel** and help Make-A-Wish Foundation grant children's wishes all year long. I authorize Make-A-Wish Foundation of Canada to receive the following amount from my account on the 15th of each month. (For banking purposes, a sample cheque marked "VOID" is enclosed.)

❏ $10   ❏ $15   ❏ $25   ❏ Other $_____

SIGNATURE _____

❏ I prefer to make my monthly gift by credit card. (Please complete credit card information above.)

My guarantee: I understand I can change or cancel my pledge at any time. And, I will receive a full tax credit at the end of the calendar year.

MAKE·Ⓐ·WISH.

Make-A-Wish Foundation®
of Canada
2239 Oak Street
Vancouver, BC V6H 3W6
1-888-822-WISH
www.makeawish.ca

Thank you!

Charitable Registration
89526 9173 RR0001

Direct Mail Prospecting Campaign Calendar

Give yourself ample time to develop and distribute your first campaign package. Planning begins at the bottom of the calendar.

Tasks/Timing	Week	1st Quarter	2nd Quarter	3rd Quarter	4th Quarter
Theme: _____ _____					
Mail Date: _____ ☐ Postage check deposited	0				
Labeling and inserting	–1				
Printing to mail shop	–1.5				
Merge/purge approved ☐ Data sent to mail shop	–2				
Lists to data processing ☐ Source codes assigned	–3				
Final art to printer ☐ Quantities confirmed	–3				
First draft art completed	–4				
Final copy approved	–5				
Second draft comments returned	–5				
Design concepts due	–6				
Second draft circulated	–6				
Second draft written	–6				

Tasks/Timing	Week	1st Quarter	2nd Quarter	3rd Quarter	4th Quarter
First draft comments returned	−7				
Meet with designer re: concept	−7				
First draft circulated	−7				
First draft written	−8				
List orders placed	−8				
Copywriting research	−9				

Revenues/costs projected:
☐ Testing/quantities set
☐ Offer confirmed
☐ Format confirmed
☐ Vendors identified:
  ☐ Designer
  ☐ Copywriter/editor/ buddy
  ☐ Printer
  ☐ Data processing
  ☐ Mail shop
  ☐ List broker
☐ Lists selected
	−9				

Strategic issues addressed	−10				
Past campaign data updated	−11				

helpful for new campaigns; by lowering the financial barrier, you increase the probability of a spontaneous response. For example, in October 2001 Montana Wilderness Association tested a $20 offer against their basic $35 offer. The $35 basic offer returned 1.75 percent and an average gift of $38.29. The $20 offer received a 2.26 percent response, 25 percent better, and an average gift of $35.37, a drop of just eight percent.

For decades, direct mail has been an effective, reliable tool for recruiting new members and publicizing an organization. Although competition has reduced response a bit over the years, direct mail remains one of the most powerful membership techniques. With the help of competent vendors—data processor, printer, and mail shop—you can establish a productive, comprehensive prospecting program for your organization.

CHAPTER 11

Electronic and Community Networking

As discussed in Chapter Seven, there are myriad methods for recruiting new members to your organization. As you've discovered by reading this far, few techniques operate independently: thank-you notes invite members to bring a friend to a concert, welcome packets request referrals to other potential members, author readings recruit charter members, one-to-one campaigns recruit friends and colleagues using e-mail.

Earlier chapters have touched on a few ways to put special events, e-mail, and your Web site to work recruiting new members for you; this chapter highlights some additional ways groups like yours have made the most of electronic and community networking.

Two principles of successful special event planning

Selecting the right special event for your group combines your organizational culture, your geography (often local groups have more options than national groups), your expertise and interests, and the enthusiasm of your volunteers. It is almost impossible to come close to breaking even financially on a special event without hundreds of hours of dedicated volunteer time. Fortunately, there are

I am greatly indebted to Gary MacFadden and Harvey McKinnon for their assistance with the section on membership and the Web.

many people who enjoy planning and coordinating such parties and may be happy to help with yours.

There are several helpful books about the details of creating special events. Here are two tips to add to their wisdom:

• *Whenever possible, approach special events on an annual, ongoing basis.* Few events make money their first year. By anticipating a multi-year cycle, you can build on your experience and increase your systems, your expertise, and your fans.

• *Build a succession system into the event committee.* For example, early in its planning, the steering committee for the Miami Valley [Ohio] Regional Bicycle Council's annual Thunder Road Bike-a-Thon established a leadership progression from Site Director to Company Rider Chair to Event Chair. This three-year transition helped busy volunteers become familiar with all aspects of the event before they took over as chair. It also limited each volunteer's time commitment to three years and helped make it easier to recruit volunteers for leadership positions.

Building membership recruitment into an existing special event

Chapter One mentioned, and your membership survey probably confirmed, that one of the most valuable benefits your organization provides your members is the chance to be part of a community. Special events are a great way to reaffirm and celebrate that community—and bring in new members with the promise of fun.

Most existing special events can include a membership-building component. Here are some examples:

• Include "buy a membership" as an item in your live auction and use it to recruit an unlimited number of new and renewing members. Add the opportunity to support your advocacy program by buying a week, day, or hour of your lobbyist's time; this is another item where every bidder wins.

• Offer a member discount on registration to conferences, after-school programs, or other services you provide. This offer reminds participants that you are a membership organization and the savings will encourage some to join up.

• Make sure your outing leaders have remit envelopes and the encouragement to ask for membership. If participants need to sign an insurance waiver, use the information on these waivers for collecting prospect names.

• Is one of your board members or key volunteers opening a new business? Offer to "staff" an open house in return for visibility about your organization— and follow up on the attendance list, perhaps with a letter on the company's letterhead.

Membership is a free dinner ticket

Exhibit 11.1 features Ridgway-Ouray Community Council's tantalizing and successful dinner-for-your-membership invitation. Western Colorado Congress development director Amy McBride shared their story:

> Our group in Ouray County (population 3,200) had gotten a pretty good reputation for holding fun spaghetti dinner fundraisers with entertaining slide show presentations from various community members. We generally had 150 people attend, we charged $6 for non-members, $5 for members, and netted $500. We never made much money but we decided that they were "community-building activities."
>
> For a recent dinner, we succeeded in booking John Fielder, a very well-known nature photographer, to give the slide show, and we decided to combine the dinner with a direct mailing for membership. I convinced the group to raise the price of the dinner to $10 for non-members and $7 for members. We made the decision to mail to the whole county (2,500 addresses) and, since we couldn't easily get names and addresses, we did a general boxholder mailing ("Postal Patron"). We advertised "JOIN NOW & Receive 2 Free Tickets to John Fielder (Slide Show & Spaghetti dinner)" on the outside of the envelope. Member Lee Ann Davis wrote a witty letter about how there's no such thing as a free lunch and that the catch for the free dinner tickets was to join the Ridgway-Ouray Community Council. We went on to describe all the good things the group had done in the county and why people should join.
>
> We got fifty replies to the mailing before the dinner and 450 people came to the dinner. We had to turn people away because there wasn't enough room. We got another twenty-five memberships at the dinner, and John Fielder helped by plugging the group. We also got great coverage in the local paper, as the dinner had a larger attendance than anyone could recall. It was also a great "time sensitive" membership drive tactic. We got more responses in a shorter period of time than from any mailing I've done.
>
> Our total cost for the 2,500-piece mailing was $1,200 and we brought in seventy-five memberships for a total of $2,800. We also netted more than $3,000 at the dinner! Ridgway-Ouray Community Council increased its membership by 50 percent and now has nearly 10 percent of the county as members, which significantly increases its political clout.

Celebrate anniversaries

Special dates, such as the twenty-fifth anniversary of your founding, the tenth anniversary of a special law your group got passed, or the five-hundredth participant in one of your signature programs, can offer a great excuse for a special event. Plan them far enough ahead and you can generate considerable media attention and member enthusiasm.

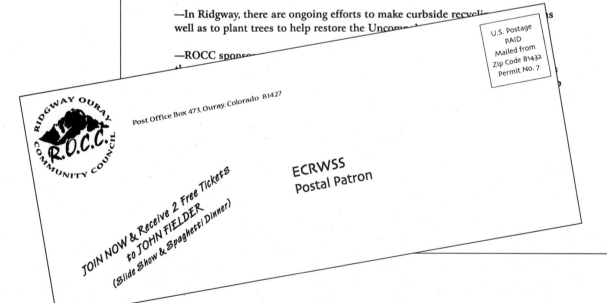

Post Office Box 473, Ouray, Colorado 81427

Dear Neighbor,

OK, OK, it is safe to say that there is no free lunch, or in this case, dinner. However, there are great opportunities, and we believe this is one. By accepting our spaghetti dinner invitation, all we ask is that you become a member of ROCC, the Ridgway-Ouray Community Council.

We happen to live in one of the most spectacular places on Earth. Not many people have the opportunity to literally live in a postcard. The San Juan Mountain Range, along with the elk, deer, bald eagle and bighorn sheep, fill this valley with life. However, the entire West is exploding with growth. Colorado's population increased a staggering 30 percent in the last decade. Although there is still one traffic light in the county, these issues are rippling out to us. There is still beauty here, and there is also much to do.

Here are some of the things we have been up to.

—Our DarkSky committee is protecting our pristine night skies by working with Ouray County to enact a Light Pollution Ordinance.

—ROCC's Forest Committee has also been working with the US Forest Service on their new forest plan to preserve wildlife habitat. We have also been working to protect the solitude and splendor of the Dallas Trail from off-road vehicles in the Forest Services' new Travel Management Plan.

—In Ridgway, there are ongoing efforts to make curbside recycling as well as to plant trees to help restore the Uncom

—ROCC spons

U.S. Postage
PAID
Mailed from
Zip Code 81432
Permit No. 7

Post Office Box 473, Ouray, Colorado 81427

JOIN NOW & Receive 2 Free Tickets
to JOHN FIELDER
(Slide Show & Spaghetti Dinner)

ECRWSS
Postal Patron

EXHIBIT 11.1.
Ridgway-Ouray Community Council Dinner Invitation

This creative yet inexpensive package tripled event attendance and boosted Ridgway-Ouray Community Council's membership to 10 percent of the county.

Our next community event is the spaghetti dinner, Saturday, February 16th, 6:00 p.m., at the Ouray Community Center. In addition to dozens of homemade spaghetti sauces and desserts, you will be able to feast on the sumptious photography of nationally-renowned nature photographer John Fielder. John will be showing slides and telling stories about *Colorado: 1870-2000*, Colorado's best-selling book ever. The book features Fielder's photography as well as the images of early west photographer William Henry Jackson. Standing exactly where Jackson stood and pointing his camera in precisely the same direction, John Fielder has rephotographed Jackson's Colorado images to capture the often startling changes that have occurred over the last century.

If you join ROCC soon (hint hint) you will receive free admission to the John Fielder Spaghetti Dinner, as well as discounts on upcoming events, including Western Colorado Congress' 22nd annual meeting in Grand Junction on September 21st, featuring political commentator and author Molly Ivins. So come to a great event, meet great people, eat a lot of food and be our guest. Use your free tickets as an opportunity to join a group committed to preserving the beauty and wildness of Ouray County. Use the membership form and enclosed envelope to join.

We hope to see you there!

Join Ridgway-Ouray Community Council (ROCC) today!

__ $30 individual   __ $18 individual -- limited income   __ $60 Friend or Affiliate
__ $48 family   __ $29 family -- limited income   __ other: $_____

Membership in ROCC includes membership in the Western Colorado Congress.

☐ My check made payable to WCC is enclosed.

Please bill my ☐ Visa ☐ MasterCard *(signature)* _____

Acct. No. __ __ __ __ __ __ __ __ __ __ __ __ · __ __ __ __   Exp. Date: __/__

Send to: Western Colorado Congress,
P.O. Box 472, Montrose, CO 81402; (970) 249-1978

Name_____

Address_____

_____

Phone_____

E-mail_____

Area(s) of interest: _____

EXHIBIT 11.1. (continued)

Consider incorporating membership and fundraising goals into the celebration. Set up a special commemorative fund named for the anniversary and use your special appeal to recruit contributions for related programs, a rainy-day fund, down payment on an office, or the launch of a new initiative. Hold an awards dinner and invite non-members to join at founding-day prices. Use the anniversary as the deadline for your board and staff get-a-member campaign (described in Chapter Nine) and invite new members to your celebration.

Recruit table captains or sponsors

Whatever your special event, chances are it will raise more money, attract more members, run more smoothly, and be more fun if you use table captains. Also sometimes called sponsors, table captains are members who agree to support your event by recruiting enough friends to fill a table, team, or other attendance goal.

Table captains or sponsors are often listed in the invitation, providing them with recognition and associating your event with this cadre of movers and shakers (or just fun folks). Table captains will invariably attract a number of attendees—and potential new members—whom you probably could not have found any other way. Table captains can also help in other important ways, as itemized in an effective e-mail from executive director Lisa Stone to her table captains just before The Northwest Women's Law Center Gala Dinner (see facing page).

Membership recruitment in cyberspace

It's hard to believe, but the World Wide Web and e-mail have only been around for twenty years—and you can count their real mainstream growth in a third of that time. In the late 1990s, the dot-com revolution tried to convince us that a paperless society was on the way. Although cybercommunications have brought many new and exciting opportunities to membership development and fundraising, they offer an adjunct to the other techniques described in this *Toolkit,* not a replacement.

There are a growing number of books, Web sites, and trainings available on how to design the best nonprofit Web site. This field is changing so quickly, and we are learning and proving new methods so fast, that those resources will be much more comprehensive than anything I can provide here.

Instead, this section focuses on some specific, proven, minimally technical ways you can apply the marvels of cyberspace to building your membership.

E-mail: a personal note flashed on your member's computer

As with other membership recruitment techniques, e-mail has both benefits and drawbacks. The benefits include the following:

E-Mail to Table Captains for Gala Dinner

From: Lisa Stone

Sent: Monday, April 23, 2001 10:20 AM

Subject: The Northwest Women's Law Center Gala Dinner will be fabulous!

Thank you so much for agreeing to act as a table captain at the Gala Dinner on Wednesday. We're looking forward to a great event—can't wait to hear what Ann Richards has to say! I just wanted to remind you of a couple of things that sometimes get lost as we approach the actual event, but that make the difference between a successful and a so-so Gala Dinner. First, please thank your guests for joining us. We know everyone is very busy, and we're touched and pleased that people take the time to join us at our annual celebration.

Second, over the years we've had guests observe (okay, "complain" is closer to the truth) that it's difficult to hear the speakers over the table talk. We know this is tricky, as we want people to enjoy themselves and this is often one of the few times they get to see friends outside of work. Nonetheless, we ask that you help us remind folks to give courteous attention to the person at the podium, so others can enjoy the program.

Third, we very much appreciate your help in facilitating the "pitch." Those of you who work on events know this, but it's often a shock to others to learn that the Law Center makes no money on the ticket price. Tax laws dictate what amount of the ticket price is deductible, but that bears no relation to any "profit" the Law Center makes. With a speaker the caliber of Ms. Richards, we sometimes even lose money on the admission price, so the pitch for money is very important to the success of the event.

All we ask is that when Audrey Haberman, who will be making the pitch this year, begins to speak, you pull out your checkbook and write a check for any amount you feel comfortable with. Studies show (yes, people study this) that modeling the act of making a gift induces others to follow suit. Please also make sure each guest has a NWLC donation envelope. Then place your check in one of those small NWLC envelopes, and place everyone's completed NWLC envelope in the large white envelope on the table. Thank your guests again, and settle back to hear Ms. Richards wow us. (Yes, we take MasterCard and VISA: there's space on the inside of the envelope to write the credit card #.)

Finally, you should know that we make it a practice not to argue with folks the night of the event about whether they've paid for the Dinner or not. If they tell us they have, we smile and send them in. We do go back later and figure out who has paid and who hasn't, and if there is a discrepancy, we may be asking you, as the table captain, to help resolve it. But it's rare that there is a problem.

I'll be circulating much of the evening, as will Kelli Maguire, who organizes all our events. If you have questions or concerns, please track one of us down and we'll do our best to resolve the problem.

Thanks again for your contribution to making this Gala Dinner a fun and successful evening. We couldn't do it without you!

Lisa

- **Speed.** The recipient of your e-mail has access to it usually the day you send it, if not within the hour. This gives you the opportunity to get late-breaking news out, make last-minute discount offers, or announce unexpected openings at special events in a matter of minutes rather than weeks.
- **Personalization.** Membership database programs can personalize e-mails with members' name, town, and other information. Also, you can increase readership by using your organization's extension on your e-mail address (olivia@canterburycoop.org), so members can easily identify who the message is from.
- **Cost-effectiveness.** E-mail messages are perhaps the least expensive of all the membership techniques. They offer the ability to reach hundreds, even thousands of members, with little more investment than the time it takes to write the message.

In order to optimize its use and be realistic about response expectations, it is important to keep in mind the following limitations of e-mail:

- **Workplace addresses.** Although this drawback is gradually decreasing, the vast majority of e-mail messages are still received at work addresses and during work hours. As discussed earlier, the mindset of the working person is vastly different from that person's attitude and attention at home. Few people can easily shift to "personal giving mode" at work.
- **Message brevity.** E-mail messages often show up in small print on small screens. That makes them harder to read. Because messages are delivered through a variety of Internet service providers, any formatting you apply to your message to make it more readable may be lost in the delivery. All this adds up to the need to be brief and succinct with e-mail messages, ideally keeping them to no more than three or four paragraphs—about one screen-full.
- **Competition.** Jupiter Research, which analyzes Web use for business, states, "In 2001, U.S. consumers received over 140 billion spam e-mails—6.2 [unsolicited] e-mails per day" ("Marketing and Branding Forecast: Online Advertising and E-Mail Marketing Through 2007," Sept. 2002). In 2000, Jupiter Research estimated that the average on-line user received an average of 447 impressions per day! Cyberspace is getting as crowded as every other medium.
- **Transience.** E-mail messages pop up, then can disappear at the touch of a delete key; the recipient does not even need to walk it over to the recycle bin. Your message must communicate in a flash, or you will lose out.

Keeping these challenges and opportunities in mind, here are some tips on how to make e-mail and the World Wide Web work for your membership program.

E-newsletters

More and more organizations are using regular e-mail newsletters to keep their members informed. Many of these began as activist tools to inform supporters of when and how to place timely phone calls, faxes, or e-mails to policymakers on specific issues.

If your group already distributes an e-newsletter, consider working with the editor to include membership news, updates, and asks. Adding a membership function to an existing communication like an e-newsletter is much more efficient than creating a new vehicle. Furthermore, your e-newsletter already has visibility and readership within your organization; build on that success.

When Julie Huck, development and membership director for Adventure Cycling Association, included the following announcement in their biweekly e-newsletter *Bike Bits,* she recruited thirteen new life members at their Web site for a total of $6,175. The hyperlink at the end of the message connected readers directly to a membership form.

LIFE MEMBERSHIP ALERT

The cost of an individual life membership is about to go up to $750, but there's still time to get in at the old rate of $475. You can pay in a lump sum or with a credit card payment plan (initial charge of $150, then three quarterly payments of $110 each). Joint life member rates for two individuals living at the same address will increase to $1,000 from $650, but again you can still get in at the old rate, payable either as a lump sum or with a credit card payment plan (initial charge of $200, then three quarterly payments of $152 each). The increase goes into effect Jan. 1, 2002, so you'll need to act soon to never receive another renewal notice.

http://www.adventurecycling.org/members/life.cfm

Julie also attracts nearly two thousand new members annually through the Association's Web site. Occasional contests ("Join now and get a chance to win this touring bike") and other special offers, along with members-only access to downloadable copies of the organization's magazine archives, keep the membership aspects of the Web site fresh and appealing. Adventure Cycling Association was an early adopter of using the World Wide Web and their communications reflect the comfort level their staff and membership have with cyberspace. For more ideas, check out their Web site at www.adventurecycling.org.

Grist Magazine (www.gristmagazine.com) is a free daily on-line environmental publication. The magazine publishes environmental news, investigation, analysis, and opinion, spiked with a sense of humor and designed to motivate readers to take action on behalf of the environment. In May and June 2002, Grist issued a fundraising appeal to its readership. Using personal e-mail messages to friends and colleagues, a three-piece dedicated e-mail campaign, and announcements leading each day's e-mail news, Grist raised more than $90,000 in less than a month from more than two thousand donors (this dollar figure includes a matching gift). Most donations were given through Groundspring.org, but Grist's cyber-friendly audience also included two hundred folks who sent checks by mail. (Not everyone is comfortable giving on-line.)

Editor Chip Giller estimates that the campaign cost about forty hours of his time, plus eight hours of other staff time. Volunteer advisers helped by donating a couple hundred hours of their time to establish the on-line donation system. Groundspring.org also charged a nominal fee to set up the system.

What would Chip do differently? He would avoid launching the project on a holiday (Memorial Day), write the ask copy a month in advance, use testimony from readers, and test more. He stresses the importance of taking good care of volunteers; the campaign wouldn't have been successful without their help. One of the announcements that led to Grist Magazine's success is shown at the top of this page.

Viral mail

Another powerful use of e-mail is "viral mail": asking your members to send along your message to others who might also be interested in your work. By making sure your e-communications are lively, informative, and engaging—and by encouraging your members to forward your missive to others in their address book—you expand your visibility and access to hundreds, if not thousands, of others. Be sure to include a reference to your Web site in the message so those new prospects can reach you directly as well.

Grist Magazine has recruited more than sixty thousand subscribers, in no small part by taking advantage of cyberspace's equivalent of word-of-mouth communication.

MoveOn.org recruited hundreds of thousands of activists for peace and raised more than $6 million in donations to anti-Iraq-war candidates in the fall 2002 elections thanks to their viral mail campaign. Since then, MoveOn's ranks have grown into the millions. The message shown on pages 204–206, summarizing their projects, illustrates how powerful e-mail newsletters can be.

Viral mail was also a powerful giving tool following the September 11, 2001, tragedy: friends shared giving information by e-mail nationwide and most Internet service providers (including AOL and Yahoo) provided special giving links for their members. Combined with free announcements and endorsements in virtually every newspaper in the country (and on almost every radio and television station), the American Red Cross raised $54 million in on-line donations in the ten days following the event.

Some useful tips for maximizing your on-line communications and increasing your on-line donations (courtesy of Harvey McKinnon) are given on page 207.

Keep in mind, however, that despite this incredible outpouring of generosity, on-line giving accounted for less than 1 percent of all donations during 2001, according to *Giving USA 2002*. E-mail and your Web sites are helpful tools for membership, but they work best in combination with a comprehensive membership plan that uses a variety of techniques.

MoveOn's E-Mail Newsletter

Subj: Reporting the truth about war.
Date: 3/26/03 10:34:37 PM Eastern Standard Time
From: moveon-help@list.moveon.org (Eli Pariser, MoveOn.org)

Dear MoveOn member,

Our country is at war, and many of us continue to feel grief and anger that this terrible conflict is being fought on our behalf. It's a hard time.

It's also a critical time for us to stay involved. As we report below, together we've had some amazing successes over the last month, both domestically and in opposition to this war. We need to keep this momentum building. As a next step, please consider joining MoveOn's Media Corps—a group of committed online activists who will keep the media accountable. Help make sure that our news media report the war the way it happens, not the way the Bush Administration wishes it would happen.

You can sign up now at:

   http://www.moveon.org/mediacorps/

. . . .

One exciting internal development is the growth of MoveOn.org itself. In July 2002, we had a little over 480,000 folks on our domestic list, with another 390,000 MoveOn members in other countries around the world. Today, less than eight months later, there are over 1,300,000 of us in the United States alone. (Think of it this way—one out of every 216 Americans is a MoveOn member.) With our 750,000 international members, we're over two million strong.

It's not just that there are a lot of us, of course. We're also getting things done. In reverse chronological order, here are some of our events and campaigns since the beginning of March:

(*) TUESDAY, MARCH 25TH: Big win on tax fairness

Almost 10,000 phone calls from MoveOn members helped Democrats win with a razor-thin majority in the Senate, cutting the Bush tax cut by half. The AFL-CIO helped make these calls possible by providing a toll-free phone line to Capitol Hill.

(*) SATURDAY, MARCH 22ND: Hundreds of thousands march in NYC

MoveOn members and many others peacefully marched in one of the largest domestic anti-war events in the last thirty years. Organizers put the crowd at over a quarter of a million folks—and this wasn't even a nationally promoted march.

(*) FRIDAY, MARCH 21ST: Raised over $500,000 for Oxfam

Over 6,000 MoveOn members chipped in over half a million dollars in a matter of days to help support desperately needed humanitarian aid work in Iraq. If you haven't yet given, your contribution would still be put to very good use. Go to:

http://www.moveon.org/oxfam/

(*) WEDNESDAY, MARCH 19TH: Launch of Citizens' Declaration

Our Citizens' Declaration urged folks to pledge a continued commitment to opposing the Bush war policy and to resolving conflict through international institutions. The response was tremendous—by now, over 550,000 signers from virtually every country in the world have signed.

We still encourage folks to sign up—you can do so now at:

http://www.moveon.org/declaration/

The Citizens' Declaration was also highlighted as the centerpiece of a Washington Post editorial. "The sentiments in that statement could be endorsed by much of the American foreign policy establishment," wrote Robert Kuttner, the author. You can read the whole editorial at:

http://www.washingtonpost.com/wp-dyn/articles/A8220-2003Mar21.html

(*) WEDNESDAY, MARCH 19TH: We win Senate vote on ANWR

Here's what Peter Schurman, MoveOn's executive director, wrote to the members from key states who participated in this fight:

"The Senate voted 52-48 today to protect the Arctic National Wildlife Refuge from oil drilling, by removing from the budget bill a provision that would have permitted drilling there. More than 2,000 MoveOn members helped make this possible by calling key Senators since yesterday. It may have made all the difference: two of the swing votes on whom we focused most attention, Senators Norm Coleman (R-MN) and Mark Pryor (D-AR), both voted to protect the Refuge. They made up the margin of victory today."

(*) MONDAY, MARCH 17TH: Thousands of lights in windows

Following on our global candlelight vigil, we asked folks to put a light in their window every night:

"It could be a Christmas string or candle, a light bulb, or a lantern. It's an easy way to keep the light of reason and hope burning, to let others know that they are not alone, and to show the way home to the young men and women who are on their way to Iraq."

By now, over 96,000 of us in over 200 countries have registered that we're keeping the light burning.

(*) SUNDAY, March 16TH: Over 6,700 vigils in 141 countries

. . . .

For some amazing pictures of vigils around the world, go to:

http://www.moveon.org/vigil/

(*) MONDAY, MARCH 10TH: U.N. emergency petition delivered

In less than a week, MoveOn members in the United States and around the world gathered over a million petition signatures to deliver to the members of the U.N. Security Council. Our message was simple: "The U.N. Security Council should back tough inspections, not war." Along with actors Jessica Lange,

Steve Buscemi, and Ethan Hawke, we delivered the petition in a press conference at the U.N. And it appears that we had an impact—the United States and Britain abandoned their push for a second resolution because they could not get the necessary votes.

The final count on our emergency petition was 1,030,775.

(*)THURSDAY, MARCH 6TH: Dems filibuster Estrada

With the support of more than 40,000 phone calls from MoveOn members, the Democrats are now taking a stand against a far-right judiciary. A filibuster against Miguel Estrada, a stealth right-wing nominee, has held for six weeks now, and survived three attempts to end it. Senate Democrats are learning the power of unity, proving to themselves that they can prevent the right wing from taking even greater control over our lives. This filibuster has stiffened Democrats' resolve across the board, enabling other victories as well.

For a tactical report on our domestic work from Peter Schurman, go to:

http://www.moveon.org/otherside.html

We'll keep on working—there's a lot to do, both domestically and internationally. For now, take a moment to thank yourself for being a part of this tsunami of action. We really are changing the country and the world.

With great appreciation from all of us,

—The MoveOn Team
Carrie, Eli, Joan, Peter, Wes, and Zack
March 26th, 2003

P.S. We do this work with only four paid staff; the folks on our list pay for our operating expenses and salaries. If you'd like to chip in, you can contribute by credit card or check at:

http://www.moveon.org/support.html

P.P.S. If you're looking for other ways to help out, think again about the Media Corps. You can sign up right now at:

http://www.moveon.org/mediacorps/

_____

This is a message from MoveOn.org. To remove yourself from this list, please visit our subscription management page at:

http://moveon.org/s?i=1271-1319105-P1_bHqXk1SfrZwVYjfMvlQ

E-Mail and Web Site Donating Tips

Harvey McKinnon, President, Harvey McKinnon & Associates

Popular wisdom says that when people who are e-mail activists become donors, they are more likely to become better activists. They will be more responsive to urgent calls for action or requests to take initiative on different issues. Similarly, when donors take urgent actions, they become better donors. So it's a symbiotic relationship, and it's very important for campaigners to know that, far from alienating people, you bring them closer to the mission of the organization by inviting them to give financially.

Here are some tips that have been successful for progressive organizations.

1. If you animate your "join now" or "donate now" button on your Web site (for example, have it blink or move to make it more noticeable), you can increase the number of visitors who click on the button and give a gift by 300–400 percent.

2. Having a "join now" or "donate now" button on every single Web site page dramatically increases the number of people who make gifts because they don't have to go through many screens to find out how to join.

3. On your Web site, you can ask members to provide their friends' names so that they too can become activists. A national wildlife protection organization tested asking for ten referrals and discovered that this request reduced response. They found that asking for three names is the optimal number.

4. The best way to retain Web members once you acquire them is through a combination of e-mail and direct mail.

5. With e-mail gift requests, you should never send people to your home page. Instead, give people a direct link to your donation page so they don't get distracted or frustrated by other information.

6. By using a specific URL for a campaign, you get three to five times more people taking action and joining your organization compared with a referral to your standard donation or "join us" page.

7. If people get an instant thank you for their gift, it doesn't work as well as thanking them twenty-four hours later. The logic behind this is that people know an instant thank you is probably generated by a machine, whereas a twenty-four-hour delay makes it feel more like the thank you could be from a human being.

   It's also very important to reinforce a Web donor thank you with a postal thank you. This increases the likelihood that the donor will make future gifts.

8. Should you choose to do an on-line newsletter, it should be sent approximately every second week, but you should try and arrange it so that it doesn't arrive on the same day each week. This gives the newsletters a bit more spontaneity.

PART FOUR

Strategic Planning for Future Growth

Now that you have a solid understanding of the basics of membership development, this section suggests some opportunities for expansion, as well as examples for pulling all the pieces together. Chapter Twelve introduces monthly giving, major donor programs, and bequests, three important techniques for upgrading members to long-term sustainers of your organization.

Chapter Thirteen provides three examples of complete membership plans, illustrating how other groups have integrated the various techniques outlined throughout this *Toolkit* into a manageable, program-related system for sustaining and building support.

Chapter Fourteen briefly reviews several regulatory issues important to keeping your membership program legal. If your organization is dependent on legislative change—at the local, state, or national level—to accomplish its goals, this chapter gives you further information on your rights to lobby and on the option of establishing a sister group to help carry out your lobbying efforts.

CHAPTER 12

Upgrading Your Members

So far we have covered recruiting new members; putting in place reliable, productive systems for thanking them, renewing them, and distributing special appeals; and integrating your messages so that your membership materials, your newsletter, and your Web site all reflect your most compelling messages and resonate with your member survey responses. But you need a lot more funds in order for your group to do its good work. It's time to talk about upgrading those wonderful members you have.

Once again, I suggest you take a look at what others have written about ways to convince your members to give much more and more often (see Resource A). These resources can guide you further as you expand and build your program. In the interest of helping you get started, here are some suggestions for manageable ways to tackle these invaluable next steps in membership development.

Seven great reasons to start a monthly giving program

A monthly giving program invites your members to donate to your organization each month. The member gives your group permission to charge a standard contribution to their credit card or arrange for an electronic funds transfer (EFT) directly from their checking account. There are many reasons for your organization to start a monthly giving program. Here are the top seven:

My gratitude goes to Harvey McKinnon, who coauthored the section on reasons to start a monthly giving program in this chapter and provided Exhibit 12.1, which is also available at his Web site.

1. ***You will dramatically increase your annual income.*** Typically, a donor who contributes two $25 gifts per year, for a total of $50, will sign up for monthly giving at $10 or more per month. That's at least $120 per year, or nearly two-and-a-half times the donor's previous total annual giving. In seven years, your $10-a-month donor will give you $840.

2. ***You will build a better relationship with your donors.*** Monthly giving programs can help draw donors closer to your organization. They become among the best people to attend special events, and they're the people most likely to leave your organization money in their wills.

3. ***Donors will stay with your organization longer.*** From long-term value studies, I've learned that monthly donors are going to be with you, on average, for five to ten years, especially if they give via electronic funds transfer. Many will give until they die.

4. ***Monthly giving revenue is predictable.*** You are guaranteed a minimum level of income every month. This money will cover overhead costs and help cash flow. These are especially big advantages for smaller nonprofits. Exhibit 12.1 estimates the annual and cumulative return on fifty monthly donors over ten years.

5. ***You'll lower your fundraising costs.*** You don't *have to* send monthly donors renewal notices if they are giving through their credit card or by EFT. Every organization Harvey McKinnon & Associates has worked with has lowered its administrative costs and increased its income through monthly giving programs.

6. ***Your income will continue to grow over time.*** A $15 monthly donor gives $180 a year, or $1,260 over a seven-year period. But upgrading can increase that amount. For example, in a recent mailing for one of Harvey McKinnon & Associates' clients, 33 percent of the donors on the file increased their gifts by an average of $5 per month, or $60 a year. That's $60 a year extra for every upgrading donor!

7. ***Monthly giving is convenient.*** It's easy for you and it's easy for the donor.

Monthly donations almost always come from either a credit card charge that your organization processes on the same day each month or a transfer directly from your member's checking account, similar to an automatic mortgage or car loan payment. A bank or an electronic funds transfer service can set up these transactions for you. An EFT service provider offers reports and analysis that are unavailable from most banks. Since your members probably change their checking accounts less frequently than their credit cards (and the latter require periodic expiration date updates), there is an advantage to your group to encourage EFT over credit card payments. However, because members are often reluctant to share checking account information, credit cards are fast becoming the monthly giving option of choice.

To begin your monthly donor program, you need just one member who values this convenient, consistent, hassle-free way to support your organization. Consider launching the program by recruiting board and staff members to participate. Once

	Number in Program	Percent Fulfillment	Average Monthly Gift	Cumulative Dollars	Cumulative Cost	Cumulative Profit
Year 1	50	80%	$12.36	$5,933	$1,000	$4,933
Year 2	40	80%	$14.00	$11,309	$1,600	$9,709
Year 3	32	80%	$15.00	$15,917	$2,122	$13,805
Year 4	29	90%	$16.00	$20,893	$2,601	$18,292
Year 5	26	90%	$17.00	$25,652	$3,068	$22,584
Year 6	23	90%	$18.00	$30,187	$3,511	$26,676
Year 7	21	90%	$20.00	$34,722	$3,931	$30,791
Year 8	19	90%	$22.00	$39,212	$4,328	$34,884
Year 9	17	90%	$24.00	$43,620	$4,702	$38,918
Year 10	15	90%	$25.00	$47,752	$5,054	$42,698

EXHIBIT 12.1.
Long-Term Value of Fifty Monthly Donors

This chart shows how beginning with fifty monthly donors will yield substantial profit over ten years, even with some attrition.

Source: Copyright © 2001 by Harvey McKinnon & Associates. www.harveymckinnon.com

you have worked through any bugs, such as remembering to process credit card charges on the same day every month, it is easy to expand the program by adding the monthly giving option to your renewal and special appeal response forms. Alaska Wilderness League recruited thirty-five monthly donors, and more than $500 in contributions each month, simply by including the option on the response forms of two special appeals. Exhibit 12.2 shows how Make-A-Wish Foundation promotes their "Wish Angels" monthly giving program on their special appeal response form.

Eventually, consider expanding your program by dedicating one of your special appeals to your monthly donor program. For more ideas on taking your monthly donor program to the next level, see Harvey McKinnon's book, *Hidden Gold* (see Resource A).

Bequests: leaving a legacy

Planned giving is the term used to refer to the variety of tools available for making a gift from an estate. The most common legacy gifts are bequests, simple statements

Make-A-Wish Foundation®
of Canada
2239 Oak Street
Vancouver, BC V6H 3W6
604 739-WISH (9474)
604 739-9422 fax
888 822-WISH toll free
nationaloffice@makeawish.ca
www.makeawish.ca

Mr. Joe Sample
2239 Oak Street
Vancouver, BC
V6H 3W6

☑ **YES, I want to make a child's wish come true!**
Here's my gift of:

☐ $25.00   ☐ Other $_____

Phone No. _____   Email _____

I prefer to give by:

☐ Cheque *(made payable to: Make-A-Wish Foundation of Canada)*

☐ Visa   ☐ MasterCard

Card No._____ Expiry ____/____

Signature _____

Please fill out this form and enclose it in the postage paid envelope provided.
Please make any changes to your name or address above.

Become a *Wish Angel!*

☐ I'd like to become a monthly *Wish Angel* and help the Make-A-Wish Foundation
   grant children's wishes all year long. I'd like to make a monthly contribution of:

☐ **$10**   ☐ **$15**   ☐ **$25**   ☐ Other $_____

☐ I authorize the Make-A-Wish Foundation of Canada to receive the above amount from my
   account on the 15th of each month. For banking purposes, a cheque marked "VOID" is
   enclosed.

Signature: _____

☐ I prefer to make my monthly gift by credit card. (Please complete information above.)

My guarantee: I understand I can change or cancel my pledge at any time. And, I will receive a full
tax credit at the end of the calendar year.

Thank you!
Charitable Registration # 89526 9173 RR0001

A1

 *Share the Power of a Wish*ₛₘ

EXHIBIT 12.2.

Make-A-Wish Foundation's Promotion of Their Monthly Giving Program

The Make-A-Wish Foundation of Canada highlights its monthly Wish Angel program by boxing the option on its response form.

in a will that designate a specific amount or percentage of a member's estate as a gift to a group. For that reason, it makes the most sense for you to focus your planned giving efforts on bequests. These are also the simplest planned giving option to promote with your members; anyone who can use and benefit from the more complex options, such as charitable remainder and other types of trusts, will probably be using a financial adviser to aid their giving plans.

Perhaps ironically, planned gifts are difficult for a group to plan for. Since there doesn't seem to be a "season" for writing or updating wills, it is to your advantage to keep the concept of remembering your organization before your members as often as possible. The fact that a disproportionate share of bequests come from entry-level donors (regular members) rather than major donors provides a good reason to inform members regularly about this option. (People with limited assets usually need them during their lifetime, so cannot give large amounts until after they are gone.)

Regularly include in your newsletter some sample wording that members could use to remember your organization in their will. (Consult a legal adviser to confirm the best statement, including the legally correct organizational name and address to use.) Another way to raise the subject is to feature an interview or a statement from someone who has already remembered your group in their will. Idaho Conservation League incorporates both the appropriate language for a bequest and a quotation from a donor who has put the group in his will in their Legacy Gifts brochure, shown in Exhibit 12.3.

In many communities, a chapter of the national planned giving support group Leave a Legacy can be a great source for ideas, materials, clip art, and other suggestions.

One of the reasons legacy gifts are difficult to plan for is that only about one-third of people who place a group in their will actually tell the group in advance. Since you don't know who is planning to leave you money, keep those legacy reminders out there and those thank-you letters current and you will see bequest gifts down the road.

Beginning your major donor program

When it comes to next steps in member cultivation, there are few programs as promising or as daunting as major donor efforts. Fortunately, there are scores of books and articles about how to create a fabulous major donor program (see Resource A).

To help you take the next step—building on the practice in asking that your board and staff got in their get-a-member campaign in Chapter Nine—I share with you here Sarah Forslund's inspiring e-mailed report about her first major donor campaign as outreach director of Green Corps, an organization that trains environmental organizers (see p. 217).

Legacy Gift options

Bequests

Pass on your passion for Idaho through a bequest of money, securities, or personal property. Bequests are as simple as including the following language in your will:

Unconditional bequest:

"I hereby bequeath to the Idaho Conservation League, a nonprofit charitable conservation organization with headquarters at 710 N. 6th Street, Boise, Idaho, the sum of $_____ to be used for the Idaho Conservation League Endowment Trust Fund."

Conditional bequest:

"I hereby bequeath to the Idaho Conservation League, a nonprofit charitable conservation organization with headquarters at 710 N. 6th Street, Boise, Idaho, the sum of $_____ to be used for the specific purpose of_____, however, if in any event the specific purpose should no longer be necessary or appropriate, I give the Board of Directors the authority to use the sum of money however it deems best."

Residue bequest:

"I hereby bequeath to the Idaho Conservation League, a nonprofit charitable conservation organization with headquarters at 710 N. 6th Street, Boise, Idaho, after specific bequests have been fulfilled, all of the rest and remainder portions of my estate and property, real and personal, to be placed in the Idaho Conservation League Endowment Trust Fund."

To bequeath securities and personal property, simply substitute in place of "the sum of $_____" in your will, both 1) the name of the securities or of the personal property, and 2) the number of shares or other descriptors (i.e., real estate address, artist's name, serial numbers, etc.). Appreciated securities bring even greater benefits by dramatically reducing the capital gains taxes to you or your estate.

For information on planned giving options that include income for life, please contact us about Charitable Remainder Trusts and Charitable Gift Annuities.

Keith Axline, Board Member Emeritus

"Pat and I have included the Idaho Conservation League in our will because of our love for Idaho and our desire for our children and grandchildren to enjoy our beautiful lands in the future."

EXHIBIT 12.3.
Excerpt from Idaho Conservation League's Legacy Gifts Brochure

The most important action you can take to promote legacy gift options is to include in your newsletter some specific language for your members to use to remember you in their will. Idaho Conservation League expanded on this approach with a brochure, adding an endorsing quotation from a member.

Results of a First Major Donor Campaign

I thought this might interest you. I just got back from NY, NJ, & MA where I was doing major donor visits. Here are my results. As background, I mailed letters to $50+ Green Corps members requesting a meeting, followed up by phone to schedule a visit and meet with people in person to ask for a larger gift. Note that everyone I met with had been giving to Green Corps for six to eight years, so they were a loyal bunch to begin with. —Sarah

———————

Central staff,
Following is an analysis of my major donor work in MA, NY, and NJ over the last two weeks. . . . Obviously, this only represents one cycle of donor work, so future rates will vary.

Completes:	40	(40 percent)
Yes to visit:	16	(40 percent)
Visits held:	11	(69 percent)
# of pledges:	11	(100 percent)
$ pledged:		$8,574
Average contribution:		$779

Explanation of numbers:

1. My completes rate [number of people actually contacted] is lower because I mistakenly requested too many names. I started with 89 names for a two-week cycle. Plus, I was only doing meetings for 5 days, so my schedule couldn't accommodate that many names.

2. Because of my travel schedule, I did my calling one week earlier than planned, which I think resulted in the lower visits-held rate.

3. I pushed the Green Guardian [monthly giving] program to lock people into a higher contribution rate indefinitely. The preceding totals reflect the annual pledge of donors (that is, a $50 per month pledge is reflected as $600 in the preceding total). 4 of 11 donors signed up for Green Guardian.

Lessons:

1. With a 100 percent pledge rate, clearly our membership is ripe for major donor work. I don't think I am particularly gifted at this work; I think any of our central staff could have had the same success. While our membership is limited, we should obviously be maximizing our membership while we can.

2. The combined membership income (largest gifts) from the 11 donors increased 10-fold from $822 (phone and mail) to $8,574 (visit). Clearly, whenever possible we should be meeting with people in person.

3. I continue to believe that, for Green Corps, it makes sense to sign people up for Green Guardian and meet with them less frequently. Since our members are spread out and in fewer numbers, we don't have the capacity to meet with them every year.

Observations about our membership (clearly a small focus group):

- 9 out of 11 donors were women
- 7 out of 11 donors were married, most were dual-income families
- 9 out of 11 were Caucasian
- 9 out of 11 were between the ages of 35 and 50
- 5 out of 11 donors give to no other environmental group but Green Corps (and have limited knowledge of environmental issues)

Pledges:

1—$3,500
1—$2,500
2—$600
1—$400
1—$240
3—$200
1—$84
1—$50

If and when we expand our major donor work, we should invest in professionally produced pledge cards, business cards, folders, and gift charts.

It's really amazing how meeting in person with a donor has such a dramatic result in their giving. Go ahead and share this info with others. Other stories have certainly been an inspiration to me, and I would be honored to share my success with others.

Sarah

CHAPTER 13

Creating Your Membership Plan

Congratulations! Not only have you been willing to take on responsibility for your organization's membership program, you've made it through a dozen chapters of details and worksheets to get to this point. The next step is pulling all these pieces together into a practical, manageable plan. This chapter includes some guidelines for developing your plan as well as some examples of how others have put together plans that work.

1. Assemble your resource documents

The best way to start your planning process is to assemble the background information and other materials that can serve as building blocks in developing your plan. If you have been doing the exercises and using the worksheets provided so far, you have already prepared most of that information. Here's the list:

- ☐ Your elevator statement (see Chapter Two)
- ☐ Summary analysis of your member survey (See Chapter Two)
- ☐ Membership Benchmarks (Worksheet 3.1)
- ☐ Renewal and Special Appeal Mailing Calendar (Worksheet 4.2)
- ☐ Renewal Rate Calculation Worksheet (Worksheet 4.3)
- ☐ Renewal Planning Calendar (Worksheet 4.4)

- [ ] Annual Special Appeal Planner (Worksheet 5.2)
- [ ] Matching Audience to Technique Worksheet (Worksheet 7.1)
- [ ] In-House Prospect Processing Procedure (Worksheet 8.2)
- [ ] Board and Staff Get-A-Member Campaign Worksheet (Worksheet 9.1)
- [ ] Direct Mail Prospecting Campaign Calendar (Worksheet 10.5)
- [ ] Response history for past prospecting campaigns (if available)
- [ ] Special events history and future plans
- [ ] List of current monthly donors and total monthly donations

These materials can also serve as a helpful set of appendixes to include with your plan, both to document where your organization is today and to provide a solid context for updating the plan in the future. This assemblage will also underscore to your higher-ups, if necessary, the amount of work you have put into developing your membership program and plan and the legitimacy of your recommendations.

2. Set your strategy and goals

The next step is to determine the strategy and assumptions that will direct your membership plan. These are best arrived at by agreement with your colleagues and leadership. Your strategy will be based in large part on your organization's strategic plan, especially the identification of priority audiences and timeline. The more specific you and your team can be in defining these parameters, the more sure you will be that your membership plan will complement your group's overall goals.

These strategic conversations can be challenging for two reasons: most groups lack a historic context for discussing membership in this way, and some of your program strategies may be unformed or in flux. Worksheet 13.1 on goal setting may help set a framework for these discussions and decisions.

Ultimately, it will be helpful to agree to goals or objectives to guide your membership plan. These statements can be straightforward (for example, "In year one, we will focus on putting our internal systems in order" or "Our goal is to maintain our current size and focus recruitment on families with young children") or they can be more complex (for example, "In order to assure passage of an important bill in the 2005 state legislature, our goal is to double our membership in the next two years, with special attention to residents of rural counties").

The latter statement comes under the category of a BHAG: Big Hairy Audacious Goal. BHAGs come in all shapes and sizes and can be both exciting and terrifying. BHAGs are exciting because of the extraordinary energy and opportunity they can create. The enthusiasm that blooms from a BHAG can bring your organization unprecedented attention and support and open unexpected doors. If you can achieve your BHAG, you will have brought your organization to an important and impressive next level of success and effectiveness. (Foundations often love BHAGs as projects to fund.)

However, BHAGs also require and demand extraordinary commitment from your entire team to make them possible. They often devour time (yours and others') and usually money as well. Failure can devastate the participants—and significantly deflate your credibility and reputation.

Membership BHAGs fail when they are developed without a knowledgeable appreciation of what is involved in managing and expanding membership. However, you now have the tools to create reliable projections, anticipate pitfalls, and develop a plan with a reasonable chance of success. When adopting your own exciting (and scary) BHAG, make sure to include regular checks on your progress and establish procedures for defining interim milestones to help gauge your success throughout the journey.

3. Estimate time and staffing needs

A major determinant of success for any membership plan is having the needed level of people-power. Begin by identifying what you are doing now in your membership program, who is actually doing the work, and how much time they are spending. Use Worksheet 13.2 to determine your quarterly membership staffing needs for your current program. Use this information as your baseline; unless you can stop doing something you have on your plate today, anything new or different that you include in your membership plan will add to your staffing needs. Also, be sure to note how many members you are serving today with this level of paid or volunteer staffing. Then you can make at least some rough projections regarding the workload you will be adding for each increment of new members.

To make a comprehensive evaluation of your staffing needs today and what you may need in the future, count both volunteer and staff time and include non-membership people who perform membership duties, such as your organization's bookkeeper, information services person, or special events chair. In addition, include your mail shop or other vendors or consultants who provide services that you or your team would have to perform otherwise. Such "adjunct personnel" can be especially useful as you look to expand your membership or adopt new recruitment techniques. For example, as mentioned in Chapter Five, hiring a mail shop to manage your mailings can free up your in-house staff and volunteers for higher-level responsibilities that will bring in more money. Many groups also work with an outside consultant and vendors such as a data-processing service, list broker, and print broker to assist with their direct mail recruitment programs. These

Membership Goal-Setting Worksheet

This worksheet helps you collect background information on which to base realistic goals. Setting goals for your membership program allows you and your staff and board colleagues to specify how your membership activities can best complement your program priorities. Goal setting also provides focus for your work by making sure that everyone agrees on what constitutes success.

Date: _____ Number of Active Members: _____ Number of Lapsed Members: _____

In the next three to five years, our organization plans to accomplish:

Members are necessary to the success of our overall program because:

Our program provides the following benefits to members; our program fulfills the following individual needs of our members:

As we progress with our strategic plan, the role and need for members will evolve in the following ways:

200__:

200__:

200__:

During the past three years, our organization has grown/lost membership:

200__: Net number of members (+/–): _____   Percent change (+/–): _____%

200__: Net number of members (+/–): _____   Percent change (+/–): _____%

200__: Net number of members (+/–): _____   Percent change (+/–): _____%

Our organization needs more members because:

We are willing to commit the following resources (for example, money, training, staff and volunteer time) to our membership efforts:

200__:

200__:

200__:

Our current membership goals and objectives are:

Quarterly Membership Staffing Needs

This worksheet helps you quantify how many hours your membership team devotes to your program. The "Now Needed" column is for tasks that are a priority but are not now getting done. Use the other columns to estimate time needed for additional activities—such as another special appeal or renewal round—based on how much time it is taking to get things done now. The person responsible for accomplishing a specific task (as identified in the "Staffer" column) could be an employee, a volunteer, a consultant, or a service provider. You can also use this worksheet to identify work overloads or opportunities to assign responsibilities more efficiently.

Quarterly Membership Staffing Needs	Now		Now Needed					
	Staffer	Hours/ Quarter	Staffer	Hours/ Quarter	Staffer	Hours/ Quarter	Staffer	Hours/ Quarter
Special Appeals								
Strategy, planning, and logistics								
Copywriting and design								
List/data selection								
Production and mailing								
Data entry and thank yous								
Other								
Renewals								
Strategy, planning, and logistics								
Copywriting and design								
List/data selection								
Production and mailing								
Data entry and thank yous								
Other								

Quarterly Membership Staffing Needs	Now		Now Needed					
	Staffer	Hours/ Quarter	Staffer	Hours/ Quarter	Staffer	Hours/ Quarter	Staffer	Hours/ Quarter
Recruitment/ Prospecting								
Strategy, planning, and logistics								
Copywriting and design								
List/data selection								
Production and mailing								
Data entry and thank yous								
Other								
Inquiry Follow-up								
Special Events								
Cyber Work								
Staff Meetings, etc.								
Data Management								
Program Coordination								
Training								
Supervision								
Other								
Total								

consultants and vendors give you access to expertise that you don't need full-time on your staff, at least not right away.

Another important element to include in your staffing needs calculations is time for training, learning, and orientation. It always takes more time than you hope—and, too frequently, more time than you anticipate—to bring a new program on line. For that reason, adopt no more than one or at most two major new techniques or programs each year, such as direct mail prospecting, a new special event, a get-a-member campaign, field or telephone canvass, and the like. This will give you the chance to learn the ropes, establish a routine, and thoroughly incorporate these new systems into your work before jumping into something else.

If, because of your BHAG, you must launch new programs more quickly, include extra time for learning and frustration, line up a consultant or expert to help you, and make sure you can call in temporary personnel (for data entry, for example) when you need them.

4. Find the capital

Many of the on-going in-house techniques described in this *Toolkit* (such as improvements to your renewal systems, adding special appeals, and managing inquiries) will make more money for your group than they will cost to administer. However, new-member recruitment almost always costs you real cash as well as time to put in place. You can often raise this capital from grants, gifts, or loans.

• *Grants.* Increasingly, foundations are funding "capacity-building" programs on the realization that, if the groups they are supporting are to be able to continue to flourish after a program grant is completed, those groups will have to create independent, ongoing funding programs of their own. Building your membership (and from that your major donor and bequest programs) is one of the best projects for such a grant. If you receive a foundation grant for program work, talk to your program officer about the possibility of a capacity-building grant to build your membership program. Use the plan you are developing here along with its supporting materials to explain your goals and strategy and as the basis for preparing your grant proposal.

• *Gifts.* Some groups have had luck identifying a member or group of members willing to underwrite the membership program with a significant donation. This could take the form of a matching gift ("Join now and a generous donor will match your membership donation dollar for dollar") or an outright contribution. Alaska Wilderness League's board was so insistent upon adopting an extra-aggressive BHAG that they committed themselves to donate or raise $40,000 (in addition to an existing foundation grant) to capitalize their membership growth.

• **Loans.** Most businesses depend on loans at one time or another to fuel their expansion; your nonprofit can use the same tactic. Some foundations offer loans, also called program-related investments. In fact, with foundations currently reducing their gift-giving because of the declining stock market, a loan might be easier to secure than a grant. Some technical assistance groups such as the Environmental Support Center have revolving loan funds they make available to nonprofits in their field, often offering below-market-rate loans for entrepreneurial ventures. A generous board member or major donor also may be willing to provide your group with a low-interest loan. If you do negotiate such a loan, be sure to document the conditions well, have a lawyer review the wording, and always make your loan payments on time.

Sample membership plans

The following examples show how your colleagues in various organizations have approached their membership plans. The first (pp. 229–231) is from Alaska Marine Conservation Council, a small statewide organization. The second (pp. 232–237) is from a mid-sized, established statewide organization, which I'll call "The Alliance," since they do not wish their name to be used. And the third is from the Alaska Wilderness League, a national organization that just made the leap into membership in 2000.

Alaska Marine Conservation Council and The Alliance each use a narrative outline to develop and document their plan. By following the categories itemized in these plans, you can build a similar plan for your group.

The Alliance's plan includes nearly a dozen objectives and almost as many recruitment techniques. This plan builds on the organization's forty-year history and the five years of experience its membership director has with the group. Although all these techniques were included in a long-range membership plan drafted four years earlier, new programs were added incrementally to ensure support and success.

Alaska Wilderness League's membership plan, shown in Worksheet 13.3 (pp. 238–241), was developed in response to a request for a proposal from a foundation. The foundation first gave the League a planning grant of $25,000 to assess its membership program. In doing so, the League adopted a BHAG of growing from four hundred to ten thousand members in three years to create a national constituency to oppose drilling in the Arctic National Wildlife Refuge. The plan was capitalized by generous grants from the same foundation as well as additional gifts from and raised by the organization's board of directors. These spreadsheets show the calculations used in developing that plan. The final document included more than sixty pages of background and back-up materials, similar to those you have developed throughout this *Toolkit*. This spreadsheet approach helps the group estimate both revenues and costs by quarter, while providing a snapshot of work requirements during each quarter.

Pulling all the information you have collected into a plan such as one of these will help your membership program grow and your organization flourish. After making your initial plan, regularly update your projections with actual results and amend your plan as appropriate. Note that all three of the plans shown in this chapter are just that: plans. Actual returns and accomplishments differed from these projections—some significantly, some only slightly.

Alaska Marine Conservation Council
Membership Plan—Draft October 11, 2001

MEMBERSHIP GOALS FOR FY 2002:

- Increase total membership by 25 percent

- Increase renewal rate to 55 percent

- Conduct survey

- Improve membership benefits and communications

- Improve Web site for greater public exposure and memberships/on-line contributions

- Increase contributions from members in addition to annual dues

- Administration and operations

OBJECTIVES AND PLAN TO REACH GOALS:

Increase total membership by 25 percent.

Prior to launching the membership project in 1998, AMCC had approximately 380 members. Since kicking off the membership project, AMCC's membership has increased to 500 plus in both 1999 and 2000. As of October 2001, our total membership is roughly 800. Anticipating a 25 percent net increase by December 2002 would mean an additional 200 members, for a total of 1,000. To achieve this net increase, assuming 45 percent attrition, our total new member recruitment must equal 560.

While increasing total membership, continue to maintain strong coastal resident and fishermen membership base.

Plan to achieve results:

1. Direct Mail. Attain average 2 percent response on direct mail solicitations.

- Bi-annual mailings – March and September

  Target audiences include Exxon Valdez Oil Spill [EVOS] Plaintiffs, commercial fish permit holders, observers, United Fishermen of Alaska, Anchorage- and coastal-based conservation supporters, and current prospects reaching a total audience of 3,000.

  Note: Exxon Valdez Oil Spill plaintiff list to target larger, long-term gifts from settlement toward our endowment.

  Result = 60 new members

  Cost of reaching 3,000 prospects = $2,500

- Optional mailings:

  - Second mailing to non-member EVOS plaintiffs in November reaching 1,100 prospects while anticipating a 2 percent return.

    Result = 22 new members

    Additional cost = $1,200

- Prospect mailing to "500 Alaskans" campaign participants in conjunction with the Rationalization workplan reaching 400 non-members who have signed our petitions and expressed a commitment to our cause. Expect a 5 percent response rate.

   Result = 20 new members

   Additional cost = $500

   Note: Optional mailings based on final approval of 2002 budget

2. Conduct Outreach & Three Community Membership Drives annually

   - Conduct $1 get-a-member campaign during outreach
   - Attend community fairs and events
   - Explore giving opportunities with fishing charters/sport fishing license holders/eco-tourism groups, cruise ship passengers
   - Create opportunities for coastal community residents to get involved through petitions, letters to editor, etc.
   - Create "membership packet" for program/outreach staff to grow membership (includes a remittance envelope)

   Result = 200 new members

3. Lapsed Members

   Target members who have expired and not renewed within the last 18 months and prior.

   Result = 30 lapsed members will have returned and considered "new"

4. Offer complimentary membership to all raffle ticket buyers

   Result = 175 new members

5. Convert newsletter subscribers and complimentary members to active status

   Currently have 708 newsletter subscribers and 16 complimentary memberships, expect 5 percent to convert

   Result = 35 will subscribe to newsletter by joining AMCC

6. Conduct a member-get-a-member campaign

   Involve board/staff in recruiting by creating teams and incentive program.

   Result = 30 new members

7. Offer "Submarine Club" to non-joiners

   Offer anonymous membership for individuals and tribal organizations that do not want recognition

Increase Renewal Rate to 55 percent

Currently renewal rate is approximately 40 percent. With the increased renewal efforts and successful phone canvas, we can anticipate an increased renewal rate of 55 percent.

Plans to improve retention rate through the following activities:

1. Send 5 renewal notices.

2. Personalize 3rd renewal letter with board/outreach staff signature and follow-up with phone call.

3. Consider offering low-cost premium with renewal.

4. Conduct phone canvas after 5th renewal notice with assistance from staff and board.

5. After 5th notice without response individual will be moved into lapsed member (LM) category and considered a hot prospect.

Result = 440 renewing members

Conduct survey

In addition to the "list enhancement project" offered by League of Conservation Voters, we will survey members to obtain feedback, track programmatic concerns/priorities and demographics.

Improve membership benefits and communications

- Produce 3 issues of *Sea Change,* AMCC's newsletter

- Produce 6 member bulletins per year (includes Fish Speak)

- Produce 6 action alerts per year

- Produce outstanding Annual Report

Improve web site for greater public exposure and memberships/on-line contributions

- Create credit card giving opportunities

Increase contributions from members in addition to annual dues

- Conduct 3 special appeals per year

- Initiate monthly giving program

- Create major donor program

- Continue to support Alaska Community Share and offer payroll deduction giving options

- Explore matching gift opportunities & endowment giving options

Administration and Operations

- Refine database

- Develop "membership procedure manual"

- Outline staffing responsibilities

- Contract with membership consultant and seek funding opportunities

- Develop membership budget and funding plan

- Seek training opportunities for staff members

FY 2002 The Alliance Membership Development Plan—Draft 2/8/01

Our group is well on its way to expanding its membership to new levels, thanks to very strong growth in FY 2001. We continue to set ambitious goals, keeping in mind that these high levels may not be sustainable over the long run. The following plan encompasses a mix of the traditional forms of development, such as direct mail, along with the continuation of the personalized membership outreach campaign, exploration of the new medium of the Internet, and efforts to improve benefits and communications to existing members. An additional positive development in FY 2001 has been the raised consciousness of the entire staff about the need for a large, well-informed membership not only for financial support but for more effective advocacy. Staff primarily responsible for completion of this plan include the Membership & Marketing Director, Membership Coordinator, and Development Assistant, along with assistance from the Outreach Director.

MEMBERSHIP GOALS FOR FY 2002

(in no particular order of importance)

1. Increase total membership by 15 percent.

2. Maintain renewal rate of 76 percent.

3. Expand membership campaign.

4. Conduct survey of members and non-members to benchmark current membership program.

5. Improve membership benefits and communications.

6. Improve web site for greater public exposure and memberships/contributions online.

7. Develop public relations campaign to increase name recognition and exposure.

8. Increase contributions from members in addition to dues.

9. Expand Annual Meeting participation and include educational events.

10. Produce four issues of the newsletter.

11. Produce outstanding Annual Report.

OBJECTIVES AND PLAN

1. Increase total membership by 15 percent.

Assuming a total membership of 5,100 by March 31, 2001, this objective would represent a net increase of 867 members—20 percent—in FY '01. Several factors point to caution for FY '02, including an anticipated slow down in Board member recruitment in the second year of the campaign. Thus, anticipating a 15 percent net increase by March 31, 2002 would mean an additional 765 members, for a total of 5,865. To achieve this net increase, assuming 25 percent attrition, our total new member recruitment must equal 2,040.

To obtain these results, we will use a combination of traditional direct mail, targeted recruitment of qualified prospects (activists, complimentary members, lapsed members), a personalized membership outreach campaign, and increased public relations activity.

a. DIRECT MAIL—Attain average 0.8 percent response on direct mail solicitations.

    i. Three mailings—May, Oct/Nov, Feb/Mar—averaging 34,000 pieces each, reaching total of 100,000 prospects.

    ii. Incorporate more testing of packages, premiums, copywriters. Expand list research to increase number/type of mailing lists tested and avoid list fatigue.

    iii. Continue to develop/refine control package (e.g., our legislative niche and an emotional appeal re: protecting our state's special places). Test various issue-oriented pieces.

    iv. Identify well-known personalities to contribute quotes or letters about our group.

    RESULT = 800 new members

b. RECRUIT ACTIVISTS

    i. Mail twice to entire list – June with legislative follow-up; November looking ahead to new legislative session.

    ii. Work with Outreach team to develop policy for recruiting new people to membership before adding them as activists. Consider mailing newsletter only to those activists who have special interest areas checked off.

    iii. Mail to recent additions every 3–4 months (June, Sept, Dec, Mar).

    RESULT = 35 new members

c. CONVERT 25 percent of complimentary members to paying dues. Track and follow-up on staff or Board contacts and proposed "termination" dates. Recruit with personal letter, follow up with reminder letter, then phone call, then drop from list.

    RESULT = 25 new members

d. LAPSED MEMBERS. FY '01 estimate 250 lapsed members will have returned, with an average gift of $33. With greater recruitment efforts, our goal is to increase this number to 300 for FY '02.

    i. Develop consistent and effective program for recruiting lapsed members and retaining those about to lapse.

    ii. Develop specific, targeted letter/package to mail to lapsed members identifying them as former members and providing specific benefits to entice them back. With address updates conducted in Feb. 2000, incorporate longer-lapsed members into this mailing. Target mail date: September.

iii. Conduct telemarketing through professional vendor in November. Explore other opportunities for telemarketing through vendor or volunteers.

iv. Include lapsed members (1 year?) in Annual Fund mailings; response added as dues payment.

RESULT = 300 returning members @ $29.53 avg. gift = $8,861

2. Maintain renewal rate of 76 percent.

As of this writing, it appears the renewal rate for FY '01 will be an outstanding 79 percent (based on third quarter returns). The average gift of general member renewals is $33. The addition of the 5th notice has clearly increased this rate by 2 percent; we can anticipate a total of 53 members being renewed on the 5th letter, adding over $2,000 in membership dues (at a higher average gift of $41.70). Further, by the end of January, we successfully upgraded 45 members to the Landmark level, transferring $5,250 to the major gifts line.

For FY '02, we will continue to improve our retention and upgrades through the following activities:

a. Evaluate and refine renewal letters and 1st-4th notices. Continue 5th personal letter.

b. Evaluate impact of lower introductory rate on subsequent renewals. Consider special renewal letter to soften impact of change in dues.

c. Staff telephone expiring members at the end of every month to urge to renew and survey reasons for not renewing.

d. Explore effective promotion of automatic monthly payments.

e. Consider re-issuing decal or other low-cost premium with renewal.

f. Develop standardized form letters to address common questions/concerns, thus lessening staff time requirements to answer member correspondence.

RESULT = 3,770 general members x 0.76 renewing = 2,865 x $33 = $94,551 revenue

3. Expand Membership Outreach Campaign

The membership campaign was begun in FY '01 to increase membership through greater personalized outreach by Board members, staff and volunteers. Specific target goals include: a. increased absolute numbers; b. greater geographic diversity; c. greater efforts to recruit younger members, and d. more economic and ethnic diversity.

Results after the third quarter FY '01 are very strong. As of January 31, Board members have recruited 222 members (Landmark and general), 27 percent more than anticipated, and brought in $12,792 (avg. gift $57.62). Staff members have recruited 22 members for $662. Additional members have been recruited from lists of conferences, trade shows, fairs, and phone banking by Board members. Importantly, both the Board and the staff have a renewed commitment to building membership from the inside out.

The second full year of the campaign will be focused on the following activities:

a. COORDINATE BOARD MEMBERS recruiting 10 members each through one-on-one contacts, gatherings, etc.

   i. Continue to encourage top recruiters in second year of campaign. Explore options to motivate new Board members and others to meet goal.

   ii. Develop contest with incentives.

   iii. Track progress and report monthly at Board meetings.

   iv. Involve Board members in making phone calls to welcome new members (LM or general) in their area.

   RESULT = 175 new members @ $57 = $10,084

b. Develop recruitment materials, fact sheets, promotional items to assist Board efforts.

c. SURVEY new members and renewals to track progress in demographic diversity goals (geographic area, age distribution, ethnicity).

d. TARGETED LETTERS to smaller audiences with affinity to our group's issues:

   i. Summer property owners – using property tax records from coastal towns, mail to out-of-state owners who love our state (target: May); consider expanding to inland camp owners later in year

   ii. Organic Farmers & Gardeners Association, People's Alliance – letter addressing our work on toxics issues (discuss schedule with program staff)

   iii. Registered fishing guides – mail to list of 3500 guides; discuss and coordinate timing around June conference

   iv. Explore other lists (Friends of Bay, hospitals, Medical Association, town conservation commissions, voter lists)

   v. Consider targeted low-cost premium, e.g., include hazardous waste brochure in toxic letter, clean air brochure to clean air folks, etc.

   RESULT = 100 new members @ $29 avg. = $2,900

e. EXHIBIT AT FAIRS and other statewide events (Kayaking expo, Common Ground Fair, Earth Day event, Sportsman's show, others). Ensure that membership is prominent part of exhibit, with tote bag giveaway.

   RESULT = 35 new members @ $25 avg. = $875

f. MEMBER-GET-A-MEMBER CAMPAIGN to involve more people in recruiting. This project could vary in intensity from all-out with extensive promotion and tracking, to simple and low-effort. More intense effort could involve contracting with consultant to run the campaign, using advertising, etc. which is currently not budgeted for.

   i. Establish an incentive contest/prize. Suggest rafting trip donated by involved/activist guide or corporation. To be determined no later than April.

   ii. Distribute one membership brochure to all members in special, targeted mailing asking that they recruit. Allow them to request additional brochures and help from our office.

iii. Update membership through newsletter, special mailings, etc. to generate excitement.

RESULT = 50 new members @ $25 avg. = $1,250

g. Continue to seek out volunteer to focus entirely on recruitment. This would be a long-time member or former Board member who may volunteer 1–3 days per month to focus entirely on recruitment in targeted area (geographic or other).

h. Coordinate with Outreach to recruit members from Environmental Action Teams.

   i. Target membership building using a variety of screens (e.g., current membership, number of general environmental voters, geographic distribution, population, political significance, etc.)

   ii. Incorporate membership pitch into all group-sponsored meetings, trainings, outreach events. Engage team members in identifying others who might join.

   iii. Work with EAT leaders to ensure follow-up with phone calls, letters, etc. to encourage participants to become members, while building strength of local circle.

4. **Conduct survey of members and non-members to benchmark current membership program.**

   a. Survey members, lapsed members, activists, and prospects to identify perceived strengths/weaknesses and effective enticements to membership.

   b. Rate perceived value of benefits

   c. Evaluate reasons for not/joining, not/renewing, not/contributing, etc.

5. **Improve membership benefits and communications.**

   a. Evaluate and improve contents of New Member Welcome Kit

   b. Better identify, specify, and communicate extent of benefits offered

   c. Evaluate use of tangible benefit/thank you/premium to increase loyalty and attractiveness

   d. Consider adoption of position statement and/or promise to members to be included in all communications

   e. Improve consistency of design of communications material to develop brand identity

6. **Improve web site for greater public exposure and memberships/contributions online.**

   a. Improve membership section to make more accessible and enable online contributions

   b. Evaluate effective sites for online fundraising (e.g., GiveForChange.com) and determine whether to list our group on these sites.

   c. Research additional uses of web site to increase public involvement, such as online data entry, links to other action groups, etc.

7. **Develop public relations campaign to increase name recognition and exposure.**

   a. Consult with public relations expert on effective activities to support the growth of our group (public service announcements, name change, events, etc.)

b. Explore free/discount advertising opportunities in magazines and other groups' publications. Coordinate advertising in local areas with outreach/speaking/community events.

c. Ensure membership is communicated in press releases, interviews, and at all speaking engagements

d. Pursue sponsorships with friendly businesses

8. Increase contributions from members in addition to dues.

a. Increase percentage response and average gift of Annual Fund by 5 percent.

    i. Mail three solicitations on targeted issues. Develop control letter for each issue area.

    ii. Schedule mailings to be supported by newsletter.

    iii. Test avenues for increasing both rate of response and average gifts (e.g., personalized appeals in closed envelopes, pre-cancelled stamp, target only previous AF givers, etc.)

    iv. Consider including activists, lapsed members, prospects in mailings.

b. Continue to support workplace giving through participation in United Way board and committee work

9. Expand Annual Meeting participation and include educational events.

a. Coordinate with advocacy team re: workshops, speakers, etc.

b. Invite lapsed and prospect members, activists, members of other environmental organizations, general public(??) for recruitment tool. Determine member benefit (discount, etc.) to encourage participation.

10. Produce four issues of newsletter.

a. Develop editorial calendar; improve writing/editorial/production process (develop style guidelines, including word lengths).

b. Coordinate coverage of issues with topics of annual fund, direct mail, and membership outreach activities.

c. Include human interest stories to make organization more accessible. Include information on joining activist network in every other issue.

11. Produce outstanding Annual Report

Determine theme, outline and draft articles in August; review cycle in September; design, print, mail by October 30.

Alaska Wilderness League Membership Plan

This pair of worksheets shows the revenues, expenses, and timing of Alaska Wilderness League's plan to grow from 200 members in 2000 to 13,000 members by the end of 2002. By projecting campaigns, costs, and income quarterly, staff and board were able to anticipate investment needs and track their success. To develop your own such plan, use the Excel version of this worksheet (available on-line at www.josseybass.com/go/ellisrobinson).

Alaska Wilderness League
Membership Plan—YR 2001: Challenge Plan

		2000	First Quarter	Second Quarter	Third Quarter	Fourth Quarter	2001 Total
Major Recruitment Campaigns			3/5/2001	5/21/2001	8/13/2001	11/7/2001	
A	# Mailed		80,000	150,000	250,000	250,000	730,000
B	% Response		1.00%	0.90%	0.80%	0.80%	0.88%
C	Avg Gift		$30	$29	$28	$28	$28.48
D	Cost/k		$430	$450	$460	$460	$455
E	Design/Copy/Prod. Mgmt		$4,000	$1,500	$1,500	$1,800	$8,800
F	Fulfillment (@ $2.00 ea.)		$1,600	$2,700	$4,000	$4,000	$12,300
G	Total Expenses		$40,000	$71,700	$120,500	$120,800	$353,000
H	Total Revenue		$24,000	$39,150	$56,000	$56,000	$175,150
I	**New Members**		**800**	**1,350**	**2,000**	**2,000**	**6,150**
Renewals				4/30/2001	7/30/2001	10/30/2001	
J	# Mailed			100	50	50	200
K	% Renewal rate			75%	75%	75%	75%
L	Average Gift			$45	$45	$45	$45.00
M	Fulfillment (@ $1/renewal)			$75	$38	$38	$150
N	P/P/M Expenses			$650	$75	$75	$800
O	Revenue			$3,375	$1,688	$1,688	$6,750
P	**Renewed Members**			**75**	**38**	**38**	**150**
Special Appeals/Date					9-Aug	8-Nov	
Q	# Mailed				2,625	5,063	7,688
R	% Response				7.00%	8.50%	7.75%
S	Average Gift				$35	$45	$42.01
T	Fulfillment (@ $1/resp.)				$184	$430	$614.06
U	P/P/M Expenses				$1,500	$2,700	$4,200
V	**Revenue**				**$6,431**	**$19,364**	**$25,795**

	2000	First Quarter	Second Quarter	Third Quarter	Fourth Quarter	2001 Total
Special Pros. Campaigns		BoD		Mini Mlg.		
W Est. New Members		100		100		200
X Expenses		$250		$3,000		$3,250
Y Average Gift		$45		$35		
Z Revenue		$4,500		$3,500		$8,000
New Members—Other Sources						
aa Web & On-Line		20	100	200	300	620
bb Revenue @ $30		$500	$2,500	$5,000	$7,500	$15,500
cc Inquiries & Slideshow		50	80	150	200	480
dd Revenue @ $30		$1,500	$2,400	$4,500	$6,000	$14,400
Education and Member Services						
ee Newsletter		$885	$1,638	$2,856	$4,100	$9,479
ff Other Publications		$6,000		$1,100		$7,100
gg Website		$5,500	$1,500	$750	$4,000	$11,750
hh Training & Database		$2,000	$700	$200	$4,200	$7,100
ii Other Expenses		$15,300	$14,500	$4,500	$4,500	$38,800
jj Consultants		$6,600	$3,300	$3,300	$3,300	$16,500
kk Staffing		$9,500	$9,500	$9,500	$9,500	$38,000
ll **Est. Total Expenses**		$81,635	$112,263	$151,503	$157,643	$503,043
mm **New/Renew This Quarter**		970	1,605	2,488	2,538	7,600
nn **Members (Cumul.)**	200	1,170	2,675	5,113	7,600	7,600
oo Membership Revenue		$30,500	$47,425	$77,119	$90,552	$245,595
pp Major Donor Upgrades (2%@$150)		$2,910	$4,815	$7,463	$7,613	$22,800
qq Foundation		$25,000	$30,000	$60,000	$25,000	$140,000
rr Other Sources		$25,000	$35,000	$10,000	$30,000	$100,000
ss **Est. Total Revenues**		$83,410	$117,240	$154,581	$153,164	$508,395
tt **Quarterly Cash Flow (e-b)**		$1,775	$4,978	$3,079	($4,479)	
uu **Cash Flow Cumulative**		$1,775	$6,753	$9,831	$5,353	$5,353

Alaska Wilderness League
Membership Plan—YR 2002: Challenge Plan

		2001	First Quarter	Second Quarter	Third Quarter	Fourth Quarter	2002 Total
Major Recruitment Campaigns			Feb.	May		Oct.	
A	# Mailed		300,000	300,000		300,000	900,000
B	% Response		0.75%	0.75%		0.75%	0.75%
C	Avg Gift		$28	$28		$28	$28.00
D	Cost/k		$460	$465		$470	$465
E	Design/Copy/Prod. Mgmt		$4,000	$1,700		$2,500	$8,200
F	Fulfillment (@ $1.20 ea.)		$4,500	$4,500		$4,500	$13,500
G	Total Expenses		$146,500	$145,700		$148,000	$440,200
H	Total Revenue		$63,000	$63,000		$63,000	$189,000
I	**New Members**		**2,250**	**2,250**		**2,250**	**6,750**
Renewals							
J	# Mailed		970	1,605	2,488	2,358	7,601
K	% Renewal rate		60%	55%	58%	60%	58%
L	Average Gift		$45	$42	$42	$42	$42.39
M	Fulfillment @ $1		$582	$883	$1,443	$1,523	$4,431
N	P/P/M Expenses		$2,183	$3,611	$5,598	$5,711	$17,102
O	Revenue		$26,190	$37,076	$60,608	$63,958	$187,831
P	**Renewed Members**		**582**	**883**	**1443**	**1523**	**4,431**
Special Appeals/Date			Jan.	Mar.	Aug.	Nov.	
Q	# Mailed		6,630	8,357	9,502	8,957	33,446
R	% Response		7.00%	7.00%	7.00%	8.50%	7.38%
S	Average Gift		$35	$35	$40	$45	$39.42
T	Fulfillment @ $1		$464	$585	$665	$761	$2,475.54
U	P/P/M Expenses		$4,641	$5,850	$6,651	$6,270	$23,412
V	**Revenue**		**$16,244**	**$20,475**	**$26,605**	**$34,260**	**$97,583**
Special Pros. Campaigns							
W	Est. New Members						0
X	Expenses		$1,000	$1,000	$1,000	$1,000	$4,000
Y	Average Gift						$0
Z	Revenue		$0	$0	$0	$0	$0

	2001	First Quarter	Second Quarter	Third Quarter	Fourth Quarter	2002 Total
New Members—Other Sources						
aa Web & On-Line		300	300	350	350	1,300
bb Revenue @ $30		$9,000	$9,000	$10,500	$10,500	$39,000
cc Inquiries & Slideshow		200	200	200	200	800
dd Revenue @ $30		$6,000	$6,000	$6,000	$6,000	$24,000
Education and Member Services						
ee Newsletter		$8,173	$9,593	$9,246	$10,496	$37,508
ff Other Publications			$6,600	$1,300		$7,900
gg Website		$1,000	$1,000	$1,000	$1,000	$4,000
hh Training & Database & Eqt.		$3,000	$7,000	$1,000	$500	$11,500
ii Other Expenses		$4,500	$33,500	$4,500	$4,500	$47,800
jj Consultants		$3,600	$3,600	$3,600	$3,600	$14,400
kk Staffing		$10,500	$13,500	$13,500	$13,500	$51,000
ll **Est. Total Expenses**		**$190,643**	**$236,922**	**$49,504**	**$201,360**	**$678,429**
mm **New/Renew This Quarter**		**3,332**	**3,633**	**1,993**	**4,323**	**13,281**
nn **Members (Cumul.)**	**7,600**	**9,962**	**11,990**	**11,495**	**13,280**	**13,280**
oo Membership Revenue		$120,434	$135,550	$103,713	$177,717	$537,414
pp Major Donor Upgrades (3%@$150)		$14,994	$16,347	$8,969	$19,453	$59,763
qq Foundation		$55,000	$65,000			$120,000
rr Other Sources		$5,000	$20,000			$25,000
ss **Est. Total Revenues**		**$195,428**	**$236,898**	**$112,681**	**$197,170**	**$742,176**
tt **Quarterly Cash Flow (e-b)**		**$4,785**	**($24)**	**$63,178**	**($4,190)**	
uu **Cash Flow Cumulative**		**$4,785**	**$4,760**	**$67,938**	**$63,748**	**$63,748**

CHAPTER 14

Staying Legal

At points throughout this *Toolkit,* we've talked about how to be accountable to your members. This chapter covers how to be accountable to the various government entities that take interest in your membership program—and how to do so in ways that provide the greatest benefit to your group. The references listed in this chapter relate to the United States. If you operate in another country, these categories should alert you to the kinds of regulations you may have to consider there.

Your rights to lobby

As you have probably deduced by now, I believe that advocating for social change is an important and valuable responsibility of your nonprofit organization. The government agrees—up to a point; within some limits, you are allowed to lobby elected officials and still qualify under the Internal Revenue Service Code as a 501(c)(3) tax-exempt charitable organization.

First, it's important to understand what lobbying is and what it is not. As far as the IRS is concerned, lobbying involves only direct contact with elected officials or other activities specifically intended to influence legislation. Lobbying is not talking to agency officials, writing to the president, seeking to change or update regulations, or taking court action. Lobbying just involves trying to get bills passed into law. And you can do such lobbying as long as it does not involve what the IRS calls a "significant" amount of time and money.

The information in this chapter is provided only to alert you to your opportunities and obligations. Please contact an attorney or financial adviser for up-to-the-minute information on how these policies and regulations can affect your organization.

If you anticipate that your group will be involved in extensive lobbying activities, or if your lobbying might be controversial and visible, consider making an election under IRS Code Section 501(h) to be subject to specific dollar limitations on lobbying expenditures. This will allow you to spend up to 20 percent of your resources on lobbying and, perhaps more important, give you some protection against frivolous accusations and time-consuming responses to complaints by your opposition. Even if you do not make this election, your group can still seek to influence legislation; the problem is that what the IRS considers a "significant" expenditure of time and money is not clearly defined.

Filing for Section 501(h) is not a particularly difficult process, but it does require some paperwork. For a thorough examination of the process and to see whether your group should file for election or not, refer to the workshops, publications, and Web site of the Alliance for Justice at http://www.afj.org/. OMB-Watch's Web site, npaction.org, is another online resource for nonprofit advocacy. If you are lobbying your state legislature or county or city commission, be sure to check out any state or local filing requirements as well. Check with your secretary of state or clerk of council.

501(c)(4)s, PACs, and 527s

In addition to limitations on lobbying, being designated as 501(c)(3) tax-exempt, charitable organization by the Internal Revenue Service also prevents your group from endorsing political candidates or getting involved directly in electoral campaigns.

In order to allow involvement in the electoral process, some groups create sister organizations that are allowed to raise funds for candidates or otherwise influence elections; such organizations can be a strategic asset to your group. These entities can be organized under IRS Code Section 501(c)(4) or as political action committees (also known as PACs) or as 527s (a relatively new designation). With campaign finance reform a regular topic of congressional attention, the abilities and responsibilities of these kinds of entities are continually changing. Alliance for Justice and OMBWatch provide thorough, practical information about potential sister organization structures as well.

Charitable solicitation registration

Most states require that any charity that solicits its residents for contributions register, usually with the secretary of state. For purposes of this requirement (in most states), solicitation means seeking new members or donors. It usually does not apply to asking your existing members for an additional contribution.

First, you need to register with your home state as a charitable organization. If you are local or statewide in your scope and do not anticipate actively recruiting new members outside your state, then you do not have to register anywhere else. (At this writing, the fact that people from out of state may find your Web site and join up from there is not usually considered solicitation. Nor is it solicitation if you then send these out-of-state members your special appeals.)

If your organization is multistate or national in scope and will be actively recruiting members from other states, you should register with those states as well. Fortunately, more than thirty states accept the Unified Registration Statement, a standard form that saves you time and frustration by allowing you to compile the required financial information and other data once and copy it for all participants. (Some states also require supplemental information.) The Unified Registration Statement is managed by the Multi-State Filer Project, which has a complete and helpful Web site at www.nonprofits.org/library/gov/urs. This Web site also lists which states charge for registration, if they require a bond, if you have to include notification that you are registered on your materials, and other information. The site will also tell you which states exempt small groups, religious organizations, and colleges and universities.

Your group is supposed to register *before* you actually mail or otherwise deliver a solicitation into a state, but it is always better to register late than not at all. Because registration costs can build up, however, you might want to check out the costs and requirements before you target a state for activity. For example, some states require that not only does the charitable group have to register, its fundraising counsel must also register and put up a bond. Some groups have decided that the benefits of recruiting members in that state are not worth the costs of this triple annual registration fee.

If you are going to tackle registration in more than a couple of states, consider these pointers from Andrew Davis, membership director of Alaska Wilderness League:

> The system we set up here [for registering using the Unified Registration Statement (URS)] seems to work pretty well, but there's always room for improvement. You do have to issue separate checks for each state that has the requirement, and many of the forms/letters will need to be notarized. Follow all the requirements very carefully too! In most cases, if components are missing or incomplete, they won't even look at your materials and will send them back. Extra diligence at the beginning saves headaches later for sure.
>
> I set up a spreadsheet with criteria to remind me of URS expiration dates, previous correspondence, requirements, contact information, etc. It makes life much easier and will help keep you in compliance.
>
> You should be able to find registered agents on line. If you go to google.com and type "[your state] registered agent" you'll likely find someone willing to help

you out. Usually, it's a lawyer in some small office somewhere that does it on the side for anywhere from $25 to $100 a year. All they are is a go-between for your organization and the state attorney general's office. Unless there's a complaint, they really don't do anything other than sign you up; you still have to take care of all the compliance stuff.

It's a good idea to make a file for each state you're registering with because there will always be correspondence specific to them. Keep a copy of *everything* you send *and* receive. I keep mine in date order. Helps with proof of compliance, fee payment, etc. I also make copies of the checks or jot down the check number and keep it in the file.

Complying with SOP 98–2

SOP 98–2 is The American Institute of Certified Public Accountants' Statement of Position entitled, "Accounting for Costs of Activities of Not-for-Profit Organizations, and State and Local Governmental Entities That Include Fundraising." It went into effect on December 15, 1998, as part of Generally Accepted Accounting Principles (GAAP).

SOP 98–2 offers your organization some specific ways to credit some of the costs of your direct mail campaigns and other fundraising efforts to the program or education part of your budget rather than entirely to fundraising. This can be a real asset to a group that is implementing an aggressive new member recruitment plan—or even enough direct mail that it shows up as a significant portion of your budget. By following SOP 98–2, you can account for some of your direct mail and perhaps other fundraising expenses—including costs for statements of support, petitions, or other calls to action—as program costs. This practice can ultimately reduce the percentage of your budget that appears as administration and fundraising costs.

SOP 98–2 does require some pre-planning and intentionality. You can find information on this and other topics at the Online Compendium of Federal and State Regulations for U.S. Nonprofit Organizations at www.muridae.com/nporegulation/.

Resources

This section expands on several of the tips and suggestions described in the *Toolkit*. Resource A recommends publications, periodicals, service providers, and Web sites that colleagues and I have found particularly helpful and reliable.

Consider sharing Resource B, a recommended protocol for managing membership records and finances, with your treasurer, accounting team, and data entry personnel to help establish a reliable system of checks and balances between your membership and financial records.

The source code protocol outlined in Resource C suggests a system for tracking your recruitment, renewal, and special appeal efforts so that you can reliably evaluate their success and effectiveness. The forms in Resource D help streamline this documentation.

With humble acknowledgment that dozens of excellent books have already been written on writing mail appeals, I offer the checklist in Resource E as a brief refresher for your reference. The "Quick Check" there is a handy tool for reviewing your recruitment, special appeal, and renewal letters before they go to print.

For More Information

Looking for more information on one of the topics in this book? This listing is a compendium of suggestions from colleagues and clients, as well as my favorite references. The list below includes books, periodicals, vendors, consultants, Web sites, and more. Those marked with an asterisk (★) received multiple recommendations or are my personal favorite in the category. If you are looking for more information on a topic not specifically identified, check out the "General Fundraising" section.

Branding and marketing

★*Chuck Pettis,* BrandSolutions, 8222 Overlake Drive W., Medina, WA 98039. Tel: 425-637-8777. Fax: 425-637-8778. E-mail: cpettis@brand.com.

Chuck Pettis is president of BrandSolutions, Inc. (www.brand.com), a leading brand consulting and market research firm that helps companies and organizations create, implement, and manage their brand identity. Branding considers the perceptions, feelings, culture, status, and values of your members and other constituents—and how they affect the way those constituents respond to and value your group. Branding is about genuinely connecting with your members and other target audiences so they better understand what you do and adopt your brand identity as part of their self-identity. BrandSolutions' clients include Microsoft, Nokia, and Hewlett-Packard, as well as several of the nonprofit organizations referenced in this Toolkit. When not working on branding, Chuck can be found at Earth Sanctuary (www.earthsanctuary.org), a nature reserve and meditation parkland on Whidbey Island near Seattle.

*Developing Your Case for Support, Timothy L. Seiler, 2001. 192 pages. $28. Jossey-Bass, 10475 Crosspoint Blvd., Indianapolis, IN 46256. Tel: 800-956-7739. Web site: www.josseybass.com.

This book will help you and your team confirm the specifics of your organization's case statement. One colleague explains, "We needed to define who we were and why we needed memberships in our Case for Support before making the effort to grow our membership."

*Guerrilla Marketing: Secrets for Making Big Profits from Your Small Business, 3rd ed., Jay Conrad Levinson, 1998. 388 pages. $14. Houghton Mifflin Company, 222 Berkeley Street, Boston, MA 02116. Tel: 617-351-5000. Web site: http://www.hmco.com/trade/.

This is the source for The Rule of 27. Although written for for-profit businesses, the theories, examples, and techniques can be easily adapted to most nonprofits. See also The Guerrilla Marketing Handbook *and other books in the Guerrilla Marketing Series.*

*Positioning: The Battle for Your Mind, 2nd ed., Al Ries and Jack Trout, 2000. 213 pages. $10.95. The McGraw-Hill Companies, 2 Penn Plaza, New York, NY 10121. Web site: http://books.mcgraw-hill.com/.

This classic has been updated to include current statistics and examples. It's a quick, sobering read with helpful suggestions about how to rise above the noise in today's marketplace.

Data Smog: Surviving the Information Glut, David Shenk, 1998. 213 pages. $14. HarperCollins Publishers, 10 East 53rd Street, New York, NY 10022. Tel: 212-207-7000.

What is the impact of those 3,000 marketing messages we are each receiving each day? Here's the source for analysis of information overload and how to counteract it.

TechnoBrands: How to Create and Use Brand Identity to Market, Advertise and Sell Technology Products, Chuck Pettis, 1995. 222 pages. $26.95. AMACOM, a division of American Management Association, 135 W. 50th Street, New York, NY 10020.

If you are intrigued with the organizational brand identity concepts introduced in Chapter One, this book will provide more background, examples, and exercises.

United States Zip Code Atlas, 2002. 174 pages. $29.95. American Map Corporation, 46-35 54th Road, Maspeth, NY 11378-9864. Tel: 800-432-6277.

This handy reference includes maps and charts that show U.S. zip codes by municipality and by region within each state. It also supplies 2000 U.S. Census demographic information by household, providing a handy way to compare a statewide organization's representation by region. This is a great research tool, as well as a helpful aid to selecting geographic areas for direct mail recruitment campaigns.

The Wilder Nonprofit Field Guide to Conducting Successful Focus Groups, Judith Sharken Simon, 1999. 70 pages. $15. Amherst H. Wilder Foundation Publishing Center, 919 Lafond Avenue, Saint Paul, MN 55104. Tel: 800-274-6024. Web site: www.wilder.org.

> *Focus groups can help you explore the nuances of your members' and prospects' opinions and priorities. They can be a great follow-up to your membership survey. But the process can be expensive. This handy workbook guides you through planning, conducting, and evaluating focus groups.*

Zoomerang. Web site: www.zoomerang.com.

> *Zoomerang is a Web-based service for conducting and analyzing membership (and other) surveys. An advantage of Zoomerang is that it allows your survey respondents to enter all their own data, saving you data-entry costs. However, respondents are limited to people whom you have e-mail addresses for and who are willing to log on to Zoomerang's Web site to complete the survey. There is a modest fee.*

Database management

★Data Direct, 66 N. First Street, San Jose, CA 95113. Tel: 408-350-9900. Fax: 408-350-9909. Contact Bob Moore, President, via e-mail at bob@edatadirect.com.

> *I have worked with nearly a dozen data processing companies, and I highly recommend that you save yourself a passel of headaches and work with the talented folks at Data Direct. They are experts at managing the complicated list procedures discussed in Chapter Ten and can also handle updating your list with National Change of Address and other tasks.*

ebase. Visit www.ebase.org to download a test program.

> *ebase is community-built and community-supported software, created by nonprofits for nonprofits. The software is currently free, but you will need to buy a copy of FileMaker software to allow full functioning and customization. At this writing, a year of tech support costs $45. ebase technical support is based on the community model: users work together to help each other learn the in's and out's of ebase membership database software and to extend its functionality.*

Direct mail recruitment and copywriting

★The Complete Book of Model Fund-Raising Letters, Roland E. Kuniholm, 1995. 400 pages. $48. Aspen Publishers, Inc., 200 Orchard Ridge Drive, Gaithersburg, MD 20878. Web site: www.aspenpublishers.com.

This book includes more than 350 model letters, one of which is bound to provide some inspiration for your next renewal, special appeal, or prospecting campaign.

★How to Write Successful Fundraising Letters, 2nd ed., Mal Warwick, 2001. 320 pages. $27.95. Jossey-Bass, 10475 Crosspoint Blvd., Indianapolis, IN 46256. Tel: 800-956-7739. Web site: www.josseybass.com.

This step-by-step guide to writing fundraising letters became a classic in its first printing. This second edition is even more powerful. Mal Warwick also offers consulting services and letter rewrites. His newsletter and Web site are listed next.

★Marketry, 320 - 120th Avenue N.E., Suite 202, Bellevue, WA 98005. Tel: 425-451-1262. Web site: www.marketry.com. Contact the owners, Greg and Norm Swent.

Marketry is the list broker I work with. Their staff are creative, helpful, and responsive.

The Conservation Coalition. Contact Ken Kerber at 603-876-3324 or ccmailbox@earthlink.net.

The Conservation Coalition makes direct mail fundraising more cost-effective for state and regional conservation groups. Each group's mailing is completely customized, but costs are reduced by sharing list rentals and printing, design and mail shop services. Consulting on list selection, copy, designs, offers, lists, and overall strategy is included. Three mailing windows (winter, spring, and fall) are offered annually, allowing for mail dates throughout the year.

General fundraising

BOOKS

★Fundraising for Social Change, 4th ed., Kim Klein, 2000. 416 pages. $35. Chardon Press, an imprint of Jossey-Bass, 10475 Crosspoint Blvd., Indianapolis, IN 46256. Tel: 800-956-7739. Web site: www.josseybass.com.

This is the best all-around manual on fundraising, especially for smaller advocacy groups. Kim's entertaining, practical writing style makes it fun to read, too.

★Fundraising for the Long Haul, Kim Klein, 2000. 161 pages. $20. Chardon Press, an imprint of Jossey-Bass, 10475 Crosspoint Blvd., Indianapolis, IN 46256. Tel: 800-956-7739. Web site: www.josseybass.com.

This is the sequel to Fundraising for Social Change, *especially designed for organizations that have a history of at least five years and are looking to be around for a lot longer. This is another standard that you will refer to again and again.*

Achieving Excellence in Fund Raising, 2nd ed., Hank Rosso, 2003. 576 pages. $40. Jossey-Bass, 10475 Crosspoint Blvd., Indianapolis, IN 46256. Tel: 800-956-7739. Web site: www.josseybass.com.

Raise More Money, Kim Klein and Stephanie Roth, editors, 2001. 200 pages. $28. Chardon Press, an imprint of Jossey-Bass, 10475 Crosspoint Blvd., Indianapolis, IN 46256. Tel: 800-956-7739. Web site: www.josseybass.com.

This book features the best articles from Grassroots Fundraising Journal.

Giving USA: The Annual Report on Philanthropy, a publication of the AAFRC Trust for Philanthropy, researched and written by the Center on Philanthropy at Indiana University, 10293 North Meridian Street, Suite 175, Indianapolis, IN 46290. Tel: 317-816-1613. Web site: www.aafrc.org. Updated annually. $65.

This 200-plus page report is the best comprehensive source for statistics and trends in philanthropic giving in the United States. Many of the statistics in Chapter One are based on the research in Giving USA 2002: The Annual Report on Philanthropy *for the Year 2001.*

PERIODICALS

★*Grassroots Fundraising Journal.* Web site: www.grassrootsfundraising.org.

The Grassroots Fundraising Journal *helps nonprofit organizations learn how to raise more money to support their important work. Published bimonthly, it offers practical, how-to instruction on fundraising strategies such as direct mail, special events, major gift campaigns, and phone-a-thons, as well as tools to help build a board of directors that is willing to raise money, choose a database to track donors, manage your time effectively, and ultimately develop a successful fundraising program. Copublisher Kim Klein is a nationally known fundraiser, trainer, and author who specializes in training organizations that are working for social justice and have budgets of less than one million dollars.*

★*Mal Warwick's Newsletter: Successful Direct Mail, Telephone and Online Fundraising™.* Web site: http://www.malwarwick.com/subscribe.html.

Every two months, Mal Warwick's Newsletter *offers you ideas you can take to the bank: money-saving tips, no-nonsense analysis of fundraising, mail samples galore, plus advice from top pros. The Web site often offers a free issue.*

The Chronicle of Philanthropy, 1255 23rd Street N.W., Suite 700, Washington, DC 20037. Tel: 202-466-1200. Web site: www.philanthropy.com.

The Chronicle of Philanthropy *is the newspaper of the nonprofit world, published for charity leaders, fundraisers, grantmakers, and other people involved in the philanthropic enterprise. In print, it is published biweekly. A subscription includes full access to the Web site and news updates by e-mail at no extra charge. An on-line-only subscription is also available.*

Keeping you legal

Alliance for Justice. Web site: http://www.afj.org/.

> *Alliance for Justice has been working since 1979 to promote a fair and independent judiciary and strengthen public interest advocacy. The Alliance offers workshops, publications, and an informative Web site.*

IRS Insubstantial Benefit Limit. Web site: http://www.irs.gov/pub/irs–irbs/irb02–46.pdf.

> *This is the amount you can spend on premiums and other membership benefits without requiring the member to deduct the value from their gift. At this writing, the amount is $8.00. The Web site www.irs.gov provides several other publications on nonprofit fiscal requirements.*

OMBWatch. Web site: http://www.ombwatch.org.

> *OMBWatch focuses on the Office of Management and Budget, including the processes that the OMB oversees. OMBWatch now concentrates on five main areas: budget and government performance issues; regulatory and government accountability; information for democracy and community; nonprofit advocacy and other cross-cutting nonprofit issues; and nonprofit policy and technology. Visit their Web site to sign up for their e-newsletter or read news updates.*

NPAction. Web site: www.npaction.org.

> *NPAction, a project of OMBWatch, provides an on-line resource center for nonprofit groups, with information about rules governing policy participation, examples of successful and unsuccessful efforts, key resources and people, and other resource materials.*

Unified Registration Statement. Web site: www.nonprofits.org/library/gov/urs.

> *The Unified Registration Statement (URS) allows you to use the same form to register to make charitable solicitations in more than thirty states. URS is managed by the Multi-State Filer Project. It has a very complete and helpful Web site, which lists information such as which states charge for registration, which states require a bond, and which states require notification that you are registered on your materials.*

Major donors

The Seven Faces of Philanthropy: A New Approach to Cultivating Major Donors, Russ Alan Prince and Karen Maru File, 2001. 240 pages. $23. Jossey-Bass, 10475 Crosspoint Blvd., Indianapolis, IN 46256. Tel: 800-956-7739, Web site: www.josseybass.com.

> *See also the "General Fundraising" resources listed earlier.*

Membership

Membership Development: An Action Plan for Results, Patricia Rich and Dana Hines, 2002. 315 pages. $64.95. Aspen Publishers, Inc., 200 Orchard Ridge Drive, Suite 200, Gaithersburg, MD 20878. Tel: 800-638-8437. Web site: www.aspenpublishers.com.

Monthly giving

★Hidden Gold: How Monthly Giving Will Build Donor Loyalty, Boost Your Organization's Income, and Increase Financial Stability, Harvey McKinnon, 1999. 208 pages. $39.95. Bonus Books, Inc., 160 E. Illinois Street, Chicago, IL 60611. Tel: 312-467-0580. Web site: www.bonus-books.com.

★Harvey McKinnon & Associates, 218-2211 W. 4th Avenue, Vancouver, BC, Canada V6K 4S2. Tel: 604-732-4351. Web site: www.harveymckinnon.com.

For more than twenty years, Harvey McKinnon has launched, managed, inspired, advised, or evaluated monthly giving programs for hundreds of nonprofit organizations in Canada, the United States, Australia, and the United Kingdom. Harvey McKinnon & Associates also offers direct mail consulting services.

Name changes

The NameStormers, 2811 Declaration Circle, Lago Vista, TX 78645. Tel: 512-267-1814. Fax: 512-267-9723. Web site: www.namestormers.com. Contact Mike Carr, Director, via e-mail at mike@namestormers.com.

The NameStormers works with nonprofits and other companies around the world to develop names for products, organizations, and programs. They are fast, responsive, and much more affordable than most.

Planned giving

LEAVE A LEGACY®. Web site: http://www.leavealegacy.org/.

This is a community-based program that helps people learn about charitable giving through a will or from an estate. LEAVE A LEGACY® does not solicit gifts for any particular organization. Instead, the program is a cooperative effort by all types of nonprofit groups, including social service and arts organizations, churches, hospitals, educational institutions, and other philanthropic groups. Their Web site provides many useful statistics and materials.

National Committee on Planned Giving®, 233 McCrea Street, Suite 400, Indianapolis, IN 46225. Tel: 317-269-6274. Fax: 317-269-6276. Web site: http://www.ncpg.org/.

The National Committee on Planned Giving® is the professional association for people whose work includes developing, marketing, and administering charitable planned gifts, including fundraisers for nonprofit institutions and consultants and donor advisers working in for-profit settings.

Printing

★McCallum Print Group, 4700 9th Avenue N.W., Seattle, WA 98107. Tel: 800-676-6716. Fax: 206-782-3628. Contact Sal Canino via e-mail at sal@mccallumprintgroup.com.

McCallum Print Group is a full-service printing company that manufactures envelopes in just about any size and shape imaginable, among many other printing services. Contact them if you are looking for affordable remit envelopes printed on 100% recycled paper. McCallum has printed my clients' direct mail packages for years. They also offer a turnkey program with a partner mail shop to get your prospecting campaign in the mail.

Recommended Protocol for Managing Membership Records and Finances

Your database can be a treasure trove of useful information about your members and your campaigns, if you establish a standard system for retaining personal and giving records. Also, the best way to double-check the accuracy of your membership records is to reconcile your data entry with your accounting deposit. This section recommends data to be collected and a procedure for assuring the financial accountability of your membership database.

Incoming mail processing

Each day when the mail arrives separate out member contributions (new memberships, renewals, special appeal responses, and so forth) from other mail and process as follows:

1. Open each envelope and stamp the date on the membership form or other hard copy.

2. Match the amount on the check with the amount noted on the hard copy. If they are equal, circle and initial the number listed on the hard copy. If they differ, write the actual amount of the check on the hard copy, circle, and initial.

3. Endorse the back of the check for deposit only. Prepare credit card payments for processing and attach the documentation to the hard copy form.

4. Create batches of thirty pieces or less. Put credit card payments in their own batch, separate from checks. Bind each batch with a batch slip showing the date received, a unique batch designator (letter A, B, or C), and the number of pieces in the batch. Record date, batch designator, and number of pieces on your master deposit log.

Next, for each batch, proceed as follows:

1. Separate the hard copy (form) from the payment (check or credit card receipt), making two stacks. Run an adding machine total on each stack. Once these totals match, write the batch letter and deposit date on each tape and attach it with a rubber band to the appropriate stack (hard copy or checks/credit card). Note this total in your master deposit log.

2. Prepare the bank deposit by batch:

   a. Write the batch number on the deposit slip

   b. Complete the deposit slip and make a copy

   c. Attach the adding machine tape to your copy of the deposit slip

   d. Deliver the deposit to the bank on the date listed on the batch

   Note: If possible, send each member a thank-you note on or before the date you deposit their donation (as Kim Klein says, "Thank before you bank"). This may mean that your deposit is not made on the date the contributions are received. In that case, note the change in date on the bank deposit copy, the master deposit log, and the batch slip accompanying the hard copies. If your system requires you to complete your data entry before generating thank-you notes, plan to make your deposit the day after you complete your data entry for the batch and use that date for your membership records. To ensure accountability, all dates should match the deposit date.

3. Prepare the hard copies for data entry by binding the hard copies with the adding machine tape and batch slip, changing the date if necessary to match the deposit.

Data processing

For each record, take the following steps to prepare the materials for data processing:

1. Check for duplicates. For each gift, check to see if the member is already included in the database, either as a previous donor or member or as a

prospect. Look for matches by both name and household address. If there is a match, write the member ID number on the hard copy. Check to see if the new form includes any updates to the member's address, phone, or other information.

2. If there is not a match, create a new donor record.

Each individual donor or member should have a unique master record that holds the basic background information on the member. For each new member, fill in the basic fields of the member record, including the following:

- *ID number.* This is a number uniquely identifying each discrete entity that has donated to or contacted your organization (each individual or household, and perhaps each contributing foundation, corporation, or organization, depending on your system). If your data entry program does not automatically assign a sequential ID number, begin this batch with one number higher than your last record. Write this number on the first hard copy of the first batch.

- *Greeting or salutation.* In the interest of promoting the "family and friends" feeling of your organization, this field should include the donor's first name (unless, of course, someone requests otherwise). By using first names, you also minimize gender mix-ups (for example, is Chris a man or a woman?). For couples, use "[first name] & [first name]." When the first name is unavailable, this field reads "Mr. [last name]," "Ms. [last name]," "Dr. [last name]," or "Mr. & Mrs. [last name]."

- *First name.* Include the donor's first name as he or she listed it on the response form. For example, if the member joined as Jim White, this field reads "Jim" even if the check reads "James." If the member uses initials only, include them in this field. If there are two people with the same last name, list both first names, separated by an ampersand: "Susan & Rob." If there are two people with different last names, include the full name of the first person, an ampersand, and the first name of the second person: "Joe Smith & Susan" (Jones), unless your database can accommodate two different names as a couples record.

- *Initial.* If the member includes a middle initial in his or her name, log that here, followed by a period.

- *Last name.* Use this field for the member's last name only, or the last name of the second person in a couple, if last names are different.

- *Suffix.* If the member uses a trailing title, such as Ph.D., AIA, or M.D., include it here, exactly as written on the response form. In the case of couples, list the first name of the person with the suffix last, to clarify the link.

- *Address.* Enter the street address or post office box of the member. Use approved postal abbreviations such as Rd., Dr., Ave. List apartment or suite numbers by using the pound key: "#A3." Some databases allow for two address lines. In that case, use the second line only when the address requires two lines, as in "Waverly Apartments" on the first address line and "246 Main St." on the second address line.

- *City.* This is the name of the municipality designated by the address.

- *State or province.* Use the official two-capital-letter postal designator.

- *Zip code.* Include all alphanumeric digits available in the postal or zip code.

- *Telephone number.* Include area code with the member's telephone number. If possible, include both day and evening phones and indicate any preference for calls.

- *E-mail address* (if available).

- *Origination code.* This code should identify the mailing, article, event, or other contact device that first brought you in touch with this member (or prospect). This information will help you evaluate your outreach efforts in the future, to determine which activities attract the most generous and loyal members. If this is a new record, the origination code will be the same as that registered on the hard copy.

- *Date joined.* Use the deposit date of the first membership contribution the donor ever gave.

- *Expiration date.* Use the date the current membership expires. For a new record, the expiration date is one year from the date the membership contribution was deposited. For a renewal, advance the expiration date by one year, as long as the gift is received no later than five months after the current expiration date (or the time you determined in Chapter Four). If the current expiration date is more than five months old, update the new expiration date to eleven months from the deposit date of this new joining gift.

- *Type of donor.* Use a code in this field to indicate whether the donor or prospect is an individual, business or organization, or foundation.

- *Place of work.* This information is especially helpful if you want to qualify for corporate matching gifts. Some databases include a "company" field in the basic address setup, but you should not use the company field for this information, since you do not want the member's workplace to appear in their home address.

- *Special instructions.* Use this field to note any special member requests or instructions. Create a system of symbols (called flags) for "do not telephone," "do not trade name," "only one appeal annually," and other special requests.

- *Notes and special interests.* This field can include additional annotations about the member, such as staff contact, volunteer involvement, or brief meeting notes. To avoid overloading this section, consider developing a flag or special field for characteristics you would like to document for most or many of your members.

- *Hierarchy of access.* Your membership database is a source of valuable and private information about your members. In the interests of integrating your membership and program efforts, it will be helpful to most if not all of your staff to know who your members are and how to contact them. However, it is not necessary or prudent for all staffers to have access to all information (especially financial data) or to be able to amend member information. Work with your database manager to establish a hierarchy of passwords to make sure that your team members cannot change financial or other crucial information without appropriate authorization but still have access to the information they need.

Documenting a transaction

Each individual membership financial transaction (joining, renewing, special appeal, event participation, publication purchase, and so forth) requires its own transaction record. This assures accuracy between your accounting system and your membership records. It also guarantees reliable information about the effectiveness of each recruitment campaign, renewal mailing, and special appeal.

A specific donor may have any number of transaction records during his or her association with your group. Each transaction record is discrete and separate from the donor record, yet is linked to the donor record. Each transaction record should include the following information:

- *ID number* is the same number you used earlier to call up the record in the master member file. This number links this transaction to the specific donor. It is probably entered automatically by your database system.

- *Transaction date* is the same as the deposit date (the date stamped on the covering batch slip).

- *Batch designator* is the letter of this batch (A, B, C, and so forth), as written on the hard copy.

- *Source code* is the unique source code associated with the recruitment device used to attract this contribution. This code is normally imprinted on the hard copy form, usually near the address block. If no code is printed, refer to the Master Source Code Log (see Resource C), and write the appropriate code in the lower right corner of the form. If no code has been established for this item, create one, write it on the hard copy, and add it to the log.

- *Donation amount* is the actual amount of money (check, cash, or credit card payment) received for this transaction. This number should be circled and initialed on the hard copy.

- *Donation type* refers to the category of gift. Usually this is determined by the type of ask: new member, renewal, special appeal, or publication or other purchase. In some cases, however, a special appeal or other additional contribution may be considered a renewal or new-member gift (see Chapters Three and Four).

Balancing

The final steps involve balancing the deposits. By performing this reconciliation, you ensure that your data entry is accurate and matches your accounting records.

1. Once you have finished the preceding process for the first record, repeat it for the rest of the batch.

2. Once you have completed the entire batch of records, write the range of newly assigned ID numbers on the covering batch slip.

3. Balance your entries. Query the database to total all transactions for this deposit date and batch designator. If this total matches the total on the adding machine tape attached to your batch, congratulations! Your data entry is error free. If not, check back through the transactions to find the entry error.

4. When the batch balances, file the hard copy chronologically for future reference.

Source Code Protocol for Members and Contributors

As the competition for donor dollars continues to grow, building and retaining member loyalty becomes increasingly more important. The more you know about your members—in the aggregate as well as individually—the more effectively you can address their concerns. Being responsive to your membership reinforces their belief that your organization has their best interests in focus and influences their willingness to continue to contribute to your efforts.

For many organizations, the most direct contact with members comes through mailings: special appeals, renewals, newsletters, action alerts, and other communications. New members learn about the organization from your prospecting campaigns as well as through media visibility, word-of-mouth, and special events. Data on how your members found you can provide a wealth of information about member (and prospect) interests, giving patterns, and concerns. All of this information can be retained in your giving history files, much of it in the source code. An effective source code protocol is designed to fulfill the following functions:

- Establish a consistent method for retaining information about each member's interests and giving habits
- Determine the effectiveness of specific fundraising campaigns
- Develop and track a "profile" of your members, that is, those characteristics common to most members

- Assure continuity of database management and recordkeeping
- Anticipate the success of future campaigns

The master donor record

First, each entity (person, business, or foundation) that sends you money (solicited or unsolicited; joining or donating; buying a publication or attending a special event) or contacts your organization in any other way should be logged in your membership database. Consider including your in-house prospect list in the same database as well. This helps avoid duplication while it retains information about how you first "met" your donors and prospects. Resource B suggests what information should be included in each membership record.

Giving history

Most individual contributors will make several donations over time. Each donation has the potential to tell you a little more about that donor: what issues he or she cares about most, the most likely time they will give, whether they respond to premiums, whether they attend special events, and more. Therefore, each individual master donor record includes a giving history file. This file collects data on the amount, date, and source of every financial transaction with the donor. Again, see Resource B for details.

The source code

The source code identifies the specific communication (prospecting mailing, renewal notice, special appeal, news article, staff presentation, and so on) that encouraged the donor to make his or her contribution. Each communication from your organization that can be expected to result in twenty or more donations should be assigned a source code in advance. Assigning codes in advance allows you to place the source codes directly on your printed forms, assuring accurate recording upon their return.

Optimally, this source code is eight alpha-numeric characters, always listed in a standard order, that permit you to sort on each position as needed. The source code for each significant event, mailing, or media notice is unique. Every contribution received in response to the same communication receives the same source code in members' giving history files. Then, the success of a mailing or other communications effort can be judged, in part, by compiling the number and amount of contributions logged with that source code.

The meaning of the source code is based on the logic outlined here. The numbers 1–8 indicate the positions in the eight-character code, from left to right.

1 Type of media or communication.

2 Individual communication identifier.

3&4 Month the communication was distributed.

5&6 Last digits of the year the communication was distributed.

7&8 Two-digit code indicating the list, publication, or organization contacted.

Each of the digits in positions 1, 2, 7, and 8 can be any one of thirty-four different characters: the numbers 0–9 or the letters of the alphabet, other than I or O. (This avoids possible confusion between the letter I and the number 1, and the letter O and the number 0.)

You should identify an "Official Keeper of the Master Source Code List." This person can then develop and record specific source codes to be assigned and imprinted on all in-house mailings and communications before distribution. A well-maintained and current Master Source Code List will assure your ability to evaluate and analyze your donor database accurately for years to come, in spite of any future staff turnover or absences. Suggestions for specific codes are listed here.

1: TYPE OF MEDIA OR COMMUNICATION

A   New-member/donor recruitment mailing

E   Special Event

L   Newsletter

M   Magazine article or advertisement

N   Newspaper article or advertisement

P   Presentation or speaking engagement

R   Renewal mailing

S   Special appeal mailing

T   Telemarketing

U   Unknown

2: UNIQUE APPEAL DESIGNATOR

1   First renewal notice

2   Second renewal notice

3   Third renewal notice

4   Fourth renewal notice

A First special appeal of the year, using letter A

B Second special appeal of the year

C Third special appeal of the year

D Fourth special appeal of the year

E Editorial on topic X

1 Prospecting package version #1

2 Prospecting package version #2

N Newspaper column

S In-house newsletter

0 No need for further definition

3&4: MONTH OF DISTRIBUTION

This does not change, even if the actual donation is received after this month.

01 January

02 February

03 March

04 April

05 May

06 June

07 July

08 August

09 September

10 October

11 November

12 December

5&6: YEAR OF DISTRIBUTION

97 1997

98 1998

99 1999

00 2000

01 2001

02 2002

03 2003

04 2004

05 2005

06 2006

07 2007

7&8: LIST OR AUDIENCE RECEIVING THE COMMUNICATION

This list will expand as you increase your mailings and other communications activities. The key is to assign a unique two-digit code to each specific audience. Avoid using the letters I or O in all codes, to eliminate confusion with the numbers 1 and 0.

AM Active members

HF In-house prospects (house file)

A3 2003 Auction attendees

LM Lapsed members

NC Nature Conservancy members

PS Petition Signers

2X Duplicates that appeared at least twice in your merge/purge (see Chapter Ten)

EXAMPLES

A10501NC Gifts received from a recruitment/acquisition mailing (A), using prospecting package version #1 (1), mailed in May (05) 2001 (01), to Nature Conservancy members (NC).

R20203AM Donations received from the second renewal mailing (R2), sent in February (02) 2003 (03) to active members (AM).

Membership Activities Report Form and Tracking Patterns

A helpful adjunct to your source code protocol is a hard-copy reference of what exactly the source code refers to. You can accomplish this easily by keeping your membership history in a designated three-ring binder or file. Complete a Membership Activities Report for each of your renewal, special appeal, and recruitment campaigns, as well as other significant fundraising programs. Note the information requested and identify the exact costs as the invoices arrive. Track the returns periodically: two weeks from mail date, four weeks, six weeks, eight weeks, and sixteen weeks. (In most cases, at least 95 percent of your responses will be received within sixteen weeks.) The Excel worksheet at www.josseybass.com/go/ellisrobinson includes a function for tracking this information on a chart. Eventually, you will begin to see a pattern of response to your campaigns, which in turn will help you know when you have a real winner that you may want to mail again as soon as possible.

Membership Activities Report

Project: _____

Description: _____

List	Source Code	Quantity
_____	_____	_____
_____	_____	_____
_____	_____	_____
_____	_____	_____
_____	_____	_____
_____	_____	_____
_____	_____	_____
_____	_____	_____

Date Mailed: _____   TOTAL MAILED: _____

COSTS:

Printing: _____

Processing: _____

Postage: _____

Lists: _____

Other: _____

TOTAL COST: _____

REVENUES:

	Date	Number Returned	Total Dollars	Average Gift
2 weeks	_____	_____	_____	_____
4 weeks	_____	_____	_____	_____
6 weeks	_____	_____	_____	_____
8 weeks	_____	_____	_____	_____
16 weeks	_____	_____	_____	_____
TOTAL:	_____	_____	_____	_____

NOTES: Completed by: _____

Copywriting Tips

Although Resource A recommends several sources on copywriting, no book on membership would be complete without some copywriting tips and suggestions. This resource outlines the research and thought processes I use to help tackle a significant writing project. The "Quick Check" section at the end is a handy summary as well as a list for double-checking your work before it goes to press.

Copywriting process

1. Answer the following strategic questions:

   - *Who* are you talking to? Create an image of the person you are writing this letter to. Use "you" and "I."

   - *When* will this letter be mailed? What are the external messages and activities that could influence its reception, both positive and negative? How can you make it timely? Timing themes may reflect the season, current media coverage, or major program events such as an election or the opening of the state legislature.

   - What is the primary *message* of your letter? What are the key benefits of this message to your reader?

   - Where is the *heart and emotion* in this appeal? How does the issue affect your reader's life? What will be the impact on children and future generations?

   - What is the *urgency* of this communication? Why do you need the reader to respond now?

- What is the *culture* of your organization? What *tone* best reflects that culture? How do you want the reader to feel about the organization by the end of the letter?

- What *action* do you want the reader to take by the end of the letter?

- What is the *review process* for completing this letter?

- *Who is involved* (keep the number small) and how long will it take (calendar!)?

2. Gather the following references:

   - Elevator statement (see Chapter One)

   - Results of latest membership survey, especially direct quotes

   - Recent polling data, issues surveys, focus group summaries

   - Recent media coverage about your organization and your issue(s)

   - Samples from other organizations

   - Your last three newsletters, alerts, or other communications about this issue

   - Copies of your last two most-successful appeals

   - Some samples of writing that you really like—as inspiration for you

3. Develop the key points and flow of your letter:

   - *What is the problem that needs solving?* This is the needs statement. Be as specific as possible; quantify with measurables and illustrations.

   - *How does this problem affect the reader's life?* Use examples; personify.

   - *How will your organization solve this problem?*

   - *Why is your organization qualified to solve this problem?*

   - *What is the reader's or member's role in this process?*

   - *What do you want the reader to do?*

   - *Identify the time frame.* Why must the reader respond now?

   - *What will you give the reader in return?*

4. Develop the theme for your letter:

   - What is the *story* you are telling?

   - What *emotions* does your message evoke?

   - What *universal experiences* help make this problem real to your reader?

   - Does your message or issue have any valued *historical connections?*

     . . . literary references?

     . . . celebrity friends?

- What *visual images* or word pictures connect with your message—positive and negative?

  - Landscapes or physical landmarks

  - Symbols or icons

  - People the reader can relate to

  - Evidence of the problem: scenes of destruction

- What *personal anecdotes or "heroic tales"* illustrate your issue?

- Is there a *call to action* or other involvement device that can help increase the reader's connection with your message (questionnaire, letter, petition, and so on)?

- *Who* is writing this letter? Whose story is he or she (or they) telling?

- What *key words* describe the problem?

  . . . the solution?

  . . . the benefits of action to the reader?

  . . . your organization?

- *State the theme* of your letter in fifteen words or less.

5. Identify the specifics of your package:

   a. Offer

      - Front-end premium (something the prospect receives just for opening the envelope)

      - Back-end premium (something the new member receives for joining)

      - Giving categories

      - Charter or discount membership

      - Other

      - What are you testing?

        - Lists

        - Premium

        - Message

        - Design

        - Other: _____

   b. Design

      - Style: "produced" or "grassroots" or "hot off the press"?

      - Images?

- Illustrations

- Photographs

- Icons

- Maps

  c. Format

- Paper type

- Printing: one color, two-color, four-color?

- Outer (carrier) envelope: size, window, style?

- Letter

- Response device: survey form, remit envelope; size?

- Response method: business reply envelope, courtesy reply envelope, telephone, e-mail, fax?

- Enclosures?

- Personalization?

- Segmentation?

- Addressing and coding: labels, laser, ink-jet, handwriting?

- Data processing: who, how, what format?

6. Recruit your buddy.

- Enlist a colleague or someone else who understands you, your organization, and nonprofit direct mail to be your buddy for the next few weeks.

7. Begin writing.

- Reread the inspirational pieces and background you selected in Step 2.

- Draft a brief outline of your letter text.

- Put it in a drawer.

- Look at it again in twenty-four hours.

- Supplement your outline with specifics, as appropriate.

8. Write your first draft of your new prospecting letter.

9. Put your draft in a drawer and don't think about it for a day.

- Remind yourself that no one is better prepared to do this task than you. Go do something totally different and fun.

10. Reread your draft and revise as appropriate. Pay special attention to the opening paragraph. The strongest lead is often buried three or four paragraphs down.

- Review this list of tips, especially the "Quick Check" that follows, and add any missing elements. Remind yourself that this is one of the most difficult projects anyone can undertake.

11. Ask your buddy to read your draft package.

   - Review his or her thoughts together. Remind each other that this is really hard work.

12. Revise your package as appropriate and check it with your buddy. Show this new draft to your internal decision makers.

13. Follow the process agreed to in Step 1 to complete the letter and develop text for the remaining pieces:

   - Envelope

   - Response form

   - Back of response form (use to build your credentials, reinforce your message, recruit monthly donors)

14. Send the package text to your designer.

15. Deliver final art to the printer!

16. Deliver data to mail shop.

   - Deposit postage check in bulk mail account; purchase any stamps needed.

   - If you are using BREs, make sure there is money in your postage account.

   - Prepare your thank-you and acknowledgment responses.

17. Alert your data-entry and accounting staff that money will be rolling in soon!

   - Confirm procedures for logging source codes and documenting returns.

18. Make a date with your buddy to celebrate completion of this awesome new mailing!

19. Begin planning for the next mailing!

Quick check

☐ *Use the word "you"* in the first sentence or paragraph.

☐ *Minimize the use of "we" and "us"* unless referent is very clear and inclusive.

☐ *Abolish abbreviations and acronyms!* Spell out your organization's name fully and frequently. If you must shorten, shorten to a description (the League, the Alliance, the Council, and so on) instead of abbreviating.

☐ Make sure there is a ***reason to respond today*** (for example, "Elected officials will take action in the next three months," or, "Official comments are needed by July 24.")

☐ Explain how solving this problem will ***make the reader's life better.***

☐ ***Include a call to action***—to sign a petition or letter of support, complete a questionnaire, call an elected official—to encourage involvement, demonstrate the role of the member, or reinforce the programmatic or educational function of your communication.

☐ ***Be easy to find.*** List your address, phone, fax, e-mail, and Web site.

☐ ***Be specific*** about what you are asking reader to do. Ask for support early and mid-way in the letter and end with details: "Please complete the enclosed response form and return it with your donation today."

☐ ***Reaffirm your ask in closing:*** "I look forward to hearing from you soon."

☐ Return to your lead theme in the ***P.S.*** and restate the urgency and ask.

☐ ***Retell your story with captions*** if you are using photos or graphics.

☐ To assure readability, use ***serif fonts,*** at least twelve-point size, for all your letter text. Subheads and captions can be in sans serif typeface.

☐ ***Break pages mid-sentence*** to keep readers reading.

☐ ***Use bar codes*** for the addresses on return envelopes. (The post office will provide a file containing the bar-code artwork for free.)

Organizational Contacts

Hundreds of organizations generously offered their information for inclusion in this *Toolkit*. Space constrained our ability to include all the great stories in this book. Many, many, many thanks to the groups below who allowed me to share their samples, statistics, and success. For more information, please contact them directly. (And please join!)

The Access Fund, P.O. Box 17010, Boulder CO 80308, Tel: 303-545-6772, Fax: 303-545-6774, Web site: http://www.accessfund.org/

Adventure Cycling Association, P.O. Box 8308, Missoula, MT 59807, Tel: 406-721-1776, Fax: 406-721-8754, Web site: http://www.adventurecycling.org/

Alaska Marine Conservation Council, P.O. Box 101145, Anchorage, AK 99510-1145, Tel: 907-277-KELP (5357), Fax: 907-277-5975, Web site: http://www.akmarine.org/

Alaska Wilderness League, 122 C Street, N.W., Suite 240, Washington, DC 20001, Tel: 202-544-5205, Fax: 202-544-5197, Web site: http://www.alaskawild.org/

Audubon Society of Portland, 5151 N.W. Cornell Road, Portland, OR 97210, Tel: 503-292-6855, Fax: 503-292-1021, Web site: http://www.audubonportland.org/

Bicycle Alliance of Washington, P.O. Box 2904, Seattle, WA 98101, Tel: 206-224-9252, Fax: 206-224-9254, Web site: http://www.bicyclealliance.org/

National CASA, 100 W. Harrison, North Tower, Suite 500, Seattle, WA 98119, Tel: 800-628-3233, Fax: 206-270-0078, Web site: http://www.nationalcasa.org/

Chicagoland Bicycle Federation, 650 S. Clark Street #300, Chicago, IL 60605, Tel:

312-42-PEDAL (312-427-3325), Fax: 312-427-4907, Web site: http://www. chibikefed.org/

Colorado Environmental Coalition, 1536 Wynkoop Street #5C, Denver, CO 80202, Tel: 303-534-7066, Fax: 303-534-7063, Web site: http://www.ourcolorado.org/

Earth Charter of Sanibel, P.O. Box 872, Sanibel, FL 33957

Environmental Support Center, 1500 Massachusetts Avenue N.W., Suite 25, Washington, DC 20005, Tel: 202-331-9700, Fax: 202-331-8592, Web site: http://www. envsc.org/

Greater Yellowstone Coalition, 13 S. Willson, Suite 2, P.O. Box 1874, Bozeman, MT 59771, Tel: 406-586-1593, Fax: 406-586-0851, Web site: http://www. greateryellowstone.org/

Green Corps, 29 Temple Place, Boston, MA 02111, Tel: 617-426-8506, Fax: 617-292-8057, Web site: http://www.greencorps.org/

Grist Magazine, 811 First Avenue, Suite 466, Seattle, WA 98104, Tel: 206-876-2020, Fax: 253-423-6487, Web site: http://www.gristmagazine.com/

Idaho Conservation League, P.O. Box 844, Boise, ID 83701, Tel: 208-345-6933, Fax: 208-344-0344, Web site: http://www.wildidaho.org/

Idaho Rural Council, P.O. Box 118, Bliss, ID 83314, Tel: 208-352-4477, Fax: 208-352-4645, Web site: http://www.idahoruralcouncil.org/

Leave No Trace, P.O. Box 997, Boulder, CO 80306, Tel: 303-442-8222, Fax: 303-442-8217, Web site: http://www.lnt.org/

Jay Conrad Levinson, author, "Guerrilla Marketing" series of books, 170 Seaview Drive, San Rafael, CA 94901, Tel: 415-453-2162, Fax: 415-453-0899, E-mail: jayview@aol.com, Web site: www.jayconradlevinson.com

Make-A-Wish Foundation of Canada, 2239 Oak Street, Vancouver, BC V6H 3W6, Tel: 604-739-WISH (9474), Fax: 604-739-9422, Web site: www.makeawish.ca

Harvey McKinnon & Associates, 3066 Arbutus Street, Vancouver, BC, Canada V6J 3Z2, Tel: 604-732-4351, Fax: 604-732-4877, Web site: http://www.harveymckinnon. com/

Methow Valley Recycling Project, c/o The Methow Conservancy, P.O. Box 71, Winthrop, WA 98862, Tel: 509-996-2870, Web site: http://www.methowconservancy. org/recycle/

Miami Valley Regional Bicycle Council, now **Bike Miami Valley,** P.O. Box 246, Dayton, OH 45402, Tel: 937-463-2707, Fax: 937-224-0329, Web site: http://www. bikemiamivalley.org/

Montana Wilderness Association, P.O. Box 635, Helena, MT 59624, Tel: 406-443-7350, Web site: http://www.wildmontana.org/

MoveOn.org, Web site: http://www.moveon.org/

NARAL Pro-Choice America, 1156 - 15th Street N.W., Suite 700, Washington, DC 20005, Tel: 202-973-3000, Fax: 202-973-3096, Web site: http://www.naral.org/

Natural Resources Council of Maine, 3 Wade Street, Augusta, ME 04330, Tel: 207-622-3101, Fax: 207-622-4343, Web site: http://www.maineenvironment.org/

Northwest Coalition for Alternatives to Pesticides, P.O. Box 1393, Eugene, OR 97440-1393, Tel: 541-344-5044, Fax: 541-344-6923, Web site: http://www.pesticide.org/

Northwest Ecosystem Alliance, 1208 Bay Street #201, Bellingham, WA 98225-4301, Tel: 360-671-9950, Fax: 360-671-8429, Web site: http://www.ecosystem.org/

Northwest Environment Watch, 1402 Third Ave, Suite 1127, Seattle, WA 98101, Tel: 206-447-1880, Fax: 206-447-2270, Web site: http://www.northwestwatch.org/

Northwest Women's Law Center, 3161 Elliott Avenue, Suite 101, Seattle WA 98121, Tel: 206-682-9552, Fax: 206-682-9556, Web site: http://www.nwwlc.org/

Oregon Natural Desert Association, 16 N.W. Kansas Avenue, Bend, OR 97701, Tel: 541-330-2638, Fax: 541-385-3370, Web site: http://www.onda.org

Oregon Natural Resources Council, 5825 N. Greeley, Portland, OR 97217, Tel: 503-283-6343, Fax: 503-283-0756, Web site: http://www.onrc.org/

People for Puget Sound, 911 Western Avenue, Suite 580, Seattle, WA 98104, Tel: 206-382-7007, Fax: 206-382-7006, Web site: http://www.pugetsound.org/

Chuck Pettis, President, BrandSolutions, 8222 Overlake Drive W., Medina, WA 98039, Tel: 425-637-8777, Fax: 425-637-8778, Web site: http://www.brand.com

Planned Parenthood of Southwest and Central Florida, Inc., 2055 Wood Street #110, Sarasota, FL 34237, Tel: 941-365-3913, Web site: http://www.floridachoice.org/

Rails-to-Trails Conservancy, 1100 - 17th Street N.W., 10th Floor, Washington, DC 20036, Tel: 202-331-9696, Web site: http://www.railtrails.org/

Ridgway-Ouray Community Council, c/o Western Colorado Congress, P.O. Box 472, Montrose, CO 81402, Tel: 970-626-5594 or 970-249-1978, Web site: http://www.wccongress.org/rocc.cfm

Save the Manatee Club, 500 N. Maitland Avenue, Maitland, FL 32751, Tel: 407-539-0990 or 800-432-JOIN (5646), Fax: 407-539-0871, Web site: http://www.savethemanatee.org/

Sierra Club of British Columbia, 576 Johnson Street, Victoria, BC, Canada V8W 1M3, Tel: 250-386-5255, Fax: 250-386-4453, Web site: http://bc.sierraclub.ca/

Snake River Alliance, 104 S. Capitol, P.O. Box 1731, Boise, ID 83701, Tel: 208-344-9161, Fax: 703-997-7286, Web site: http://www.snakeriveralliance.org/

1000 Friends of Oregon, 534 S.W. Third Avenue, Suite 300, Portland, OR 97204, Tel: 503-497-1000, Fax: 503-223-0073, Web site: http://www.friends.org/

TREC: Training Resources for the Environmental Community, P.O. Box 1978, Vashon, WA 98070, Tel: 206-463-7800, Fax: 206-463-7801, Web site: http://www.trecnw.org/

Washington Toxics Coalition, 4649 Sunnyside Avenue N., Suite 540, Seattle, WA 98103, Tel: 206-632-1545, Fax: 206-632-8661, Web site: http://www.watoxics.org/

Wilderness Watch, P.O. Box 9175, Missoula, MT 59807, Tel: 406-542-2048, Fax: 406-542-7714, Web site: http://www.wildernesswatch.org/

Wisconsin's Environmental Decade, now known as **Clean Wisconsin,** 122 State Street, Suite 200, Madison, WI 53703, Tel: 608-251-7020, Fax: 608-251-1655, E-mail: info@cleanwisconsin.org, Web site: http://www.wienvdecade.org/

Index

in special appeals, 79–99; for volunteer and activist membership, 32, 45. *See also* Recruitment

Auctions, "buy a membership" item in, 194

Audience(s): defining, for publications, 104; definition of term, 119; direct mail targeted to, 161, 172–176; examples of, 119; identifying and finding, 119–122; matching techniques to, 119–121; priority, membership policies for, 42–43, 45; source codes for, 267. *See also* Prospects

Audubon Society of Portland (Oregon), 58–59, 277

August, direct mail campaigns in, 187

Average annual giving: defined, 34; tracking, 34

Average gift: actual decision making returns and, 180–184, 186; estimating direct mail returns and, 176–180; in Renewal Planning Calendar, 72

Awareness-building techniques, 124–125; direct mail and, 162

B

Bar codes, envelope, 276

Believability, 10

Benefits, membership, 15–28; checklist for defining and tracking, 45; communication about, 24–28; documenting, 44–45; focusing on, in one-on-one requests, 151; new-member recruitment and, 117; premiums as, 43–44; providing, in welcome packet, 77; special event invitations as, 194, 195, 196–197; survey of, 15–23; techniques versus, 24–25; testing, 44

Bequests, 110, 213, 215, 216; resources on, 255–256

BHAGs (Big Hairy Audacious Goals), 10, 220–221, 226, 227

Bicycle Alliance of Washington, 10, 91; contact information, 277; direct mail campaign, 163–183; lapsed-member renewal letter, 62, 63

Bicycle Paper, 173

Bike Bits, 201

Black, L., 134

Board and Staff Get-a-Member Campaign worksheet, 156–157

Board members: get-a-member campaigns with, 154–159; listing, in recruitment and member materials, 110, 169; membership partnership discussion with, 11, 14, 151–154; as monthly donors, 212–213; one-on-one recruitment by, 131, 149–159; survey of, 17–18

Branding, 24–28; information resources on, 249–251

BrandSolutions, Inc., 249, 279

British Columbia, Sierra Club of, 27, 279

Budgeting, for publications, 105

Buffett, J., 143

Burwell, D., 75

Business reply envelope (BRE), 162

C

Calendar, planning: for direct mail campaigns, 186–187, 190–191; for get-a-member campaigns, 157; for newsletters, 109; for renewals, 58–59, 72–74; six-week renewal and special appeal, 58–59; for special appeals, 58–59, 94, 97–99. *See also* Timeline; Timing

Calendar-year membership renewal, 51–52

Canada, members versus donors in, 4

Canastrero, M., 62

Canvassing. *See* Field canvassing; Telephone canvassing

Capacity-building grants, 226

Capitalization, for membership recruitment plan, 226–227

Captions, 110, 276

Capturing In-House Prospects: A Checklist, 145

Carlson Foundation, 91

CASA, 27, 277

Catalog customers, as direct mail prospects, 173, 177

Celebrations, recruiting at, 195, 198

Center for Global Development, 25

Charitable solicitation registration, 244–246

Chicagoland Bicycle Federation, 143, 277–278

Chronicle of Philanthropy, The, 253

Clean Wisconsin. *See* Wisconsin's Environmental Decade

Clean-up appeal, 62

Colorado Environmental Coalition, 94, 278

Commemorative funds, 198

Commemorative premiums, 44

Common experiences, sharing, 153

Communication(s), 24–28, 101–114; copywriting tips for, 271–276; elevator statement for, 26–27, 118, 142, 153; about membership benefits, 24–28; membership program's lead in, 24; new-member recruitment and, 118, 142–143; on-line, 198–207; recruitment opportunities in, 142–143; source codes for, 265; sticky stats in, 25–26. *See also* Letters headings; Messages; Newsletters; Publications; Response packets; Welcome packets

Community, sense of, as membership motivation, 6–7

Comparisons, statistical, 26

Compiled mailing lists, 173

Complaints: responding to, 81; about too much mail, 80, 81

Complete Book of Model Fund-Raising Letters, The (Kuniholm), 251–252

Confidentiality: credit cards and, 66; of membership survey, 16, 17

Conservation Coalition, The, 252

Consistency: in member rates and benefits, 44–45; of organizational name and image, 9, 24

Consultants, 221, 226

Contact information, organizational, 137–138, 276

Contact list, staff: including, in newsletter, 110; including, in welcome packet, 76

Contact record forms, 138–139; sample, 139

Content, of publications, 104, 107–108

Contests, on-line, 201

Copywriting: buddy for, 274, 275; checklist for, 275–276; process of, 271–275; resources for, 251–252; supporting references for, 272; tips on, 271–276

Costs, membership. *See* Rates, membership

Costs, organizational, fundraising for, 97, 226–227

Costs, program, sharing information about, in special appeals letters, 90–91, 92–93

Costs, publication, 105, 111

Costs, recruitment: capitalizing, 226–227; direct mail, actual, 180–184, 186; direct mail, estimating, 176, 180, 181; e-mail, 200; with field canvassing, 130; lowering, with monthly giving programs, 212

Courtesy reply envelope (CRE), 162

Credibility: establishing, in direct mail letters, 163, 169; goal setting and, 10, 221; members as source of, 4, 5; as reason to join, 10; ways to establish, 10

Credit cards: accepting, 66, 68; electronic funds transfer versus, 212; for monthly givers' fund transfer, 211, 212

Critical mass, defining, 122

Culp, B., 62, 91, 163

Culture, membership, 107

Current active membership, defined, 33

Current members. *See* Members

Cyberspace recruitment, 198–207. *See also E-mail headings;* Web site, organizational

D

Daily Grist, 201–202

Data Direct, 144, 251

Data processing protocol, 258–261

Data Smog (Shenk), 7, 9, 250

Database, membership: access to, 261; archival data in, 144; counting individuals versus households in, 40–41; donations accounting and, 52; expiration dates in, 52; in-house prospect files in, 143–144, 264; integration of, with financial accounting system, 52, 117, 257, 261–262; list exchanges and, 161, 171–172, 173, 176; logging source codes in, 70, 143; new donor records in, 259–261, 264; new-member recruitment and, 117, 143–144; predesigned programs for, 35, 40, 251; protocol for managing, 257–262; renewals and, 52, 56; resources for starting, 40, 251; setting up, 40–41, 45, 257–262; software for, 40; thank-you letters generated from, 74; vendors for managing, 251. *See also* Source codes; Tracking

Database management resources, 251

Dates, expiration. *See* Expiration dates

Davis, A., 245–246

Deadlines: get-a-member campaign, 198; special appeal, 82, 88

December holidays, 94, 187

Decision process, prospect-to-member: decision ladder for, 8–11; steps in, 118

Demographic data: collecting, in membership survey, 16–17; comparing membership with public, 122; compiled mailing lists and, 173; sources of U.S., 122, 250

Deposits: database integration with, 52, 117, 257, 261–262; reconciling, 262

Developing Your Case for Support (Seiler), 250

Dinner invitations, 195, 196–197

Direct mail, 127–128, 161–192; advantages of, 127–128, 161–163; case study of, 163–183; costs of, actual, 180–184, 186; costs of, estimating, 176, 180, 181; defined, 127; duplicate mailings in, 173, 176, 184; elements of, 273–274, 275; e-mail, 128, 198, 200; examples of successful, campaigns, 184–186, 188–189; letter composition for, 163–168, 271–276; letter design and layout for, 168–169, 170; mailing lists for, 127, 161, 171–176; planning calendar for, 186–187, 190–191; recruitment packages in, 127, 168–171, 188–189; as recruitment technique, 127–128, 161–192; resources for, 251–252; response forms for, 170–171; response rates to, 124, 128, 176–180; returns from, actual, 180–184, 186; returns from, estimating, 176–179; strategic objectives for, 163–168; strengths of, 127–128, 161–163; testing, 187, 192; timing of, 187; weaknesses of, 128. *See also* Letters, direct mail

Direct Mail Prospecting Campaign Calendar (worksheet), 190–191

Direct response e-mail. *See* E-mail recruitment

Direct services, as membership motivation, 7

Discounts, member, 194

Display ads, 124–125

Distribution: of membership survey, 18–22; of publications and communications, 104, 106; of special appeals, 95, 96

Documentation, of member benefits, 44–45

Donation dates, renewal dates based on, 52, 55–56

Donation levels: actual direct mail returns and, 180–184, 186; below-threshold, 30–31; at commencement of membership, 33–34; entry-level, 30–31, 41–43; estimating direct mail returns and, 176–180; rate setting and, 41–43; for special appeals, communicating the impact of, 91; tracking, 33–34; upgrading, strategies for, 211–218; upgrading, with renewals, 66–68. *See also* Rates, membership

Donations: in-kind, 105; record management protocol for, 257–262; renewals based on miscellaneous, 54–56; types of, 262; to underwrite membership program, 226

Donation-year membership renewal, 52

Donors, members versus, 3–4, 51. *See also* Members

Doorbelling, or door-to-door canvassing, 130–131

Dues. *See Donation headings;* Rates, membership

Duplicates list (dupes list), 173, 176, 184

E

Earth Charter of Sanibel (ECOSanibel), 141–142, 278

ebase, 40, 74, 251

Editorial features, 124–125, 142

Educational materials: as membership benefits, 7, 44; as special appeals premiums, 94

Efficiency, of direct mail, 162–163

Elected officials: as membership prospects, 122–123; rules regarding endorsement of, 244

Election Day, 94, 97, 187
Electronic funds transfer (EFT): advantages of, 212; for monthly giving programs, 211, 212
Elevator statement, 26–27; new-member recruitment and, 118, 142, 153; one-on-one recruitment and, 153
E-mail: responding to e-inquiries with, 136–138; about special appeals, 88; "viral," 202–203; volume of, 200
E-mail recruitment, 136–137, 142–143, 198–207; benefits of, 128, 198, 200; challenges of, 128, 200; direct mail, 128, 198, 200; with e-newsletters, 200–202, 203, 204–206, 207; personalization of, 129, 200; with signatures, 142–143; thank yous in, 207; tips for, 207
E-mail surveys, 18–19
Emotional messages, for special appeals, 89–90
Empowerment, as membership motivation, 7
Envelopes, direct mail, 168, 276. *See also* Remit envelopes; Response envelopes; Return envelopes
Environmental concerns, about direct mail, 162–163
Environmental organizations, sources of population data for, 122
Environmental Support Center, 227, 278
Estimated lifetime value, 34
Estimates: of direct mail returns and costs, 176–180, 181; of membership program staffing needs, 221, 224–226
Estimating the Costs of a Direct Mail Campaign (worksheet), 181
Exchange, mailing list, 161, 171–173, 176; response rates and gift amounts with, 177
Executive leadership: input of, for audience identification, 122; one-on-one recruitment by, 131–132, 149–159. *See also* Board members; Staff
Expenditures, 81. *See also* Costs *headings*
Expertise, members as source of, 5
Expiration dates: annual, 51–52; defining membership based on, 32–33; donation-year, 52; renewal timing and, 51–60, 72–74; renewal tracking and, 72; setting, 52–56
Expired members, renewal dates for, 53–54. *See also* Lapsed members

F

Familiarity, 8–9
Fees, membership. *See* Rates, membership
Field canvassing, 130–131; advantages of, 130; challenges of, 130–131; cost and compensation issues in, 130; response rates to, 124, 130
File, K. M., 254
FileMaker Pro, 40
Financial accounting system: membership database integration with, 52, 117, 257, 261–262; SOP 98-2 and, 246
Financial stability: members as source of, 5, 30; monthly giving programs for, 211–213; strategic planning for future growth and, 209–246
First-time members: expiration date for, 52; tracking, 34. *See also* New members

Fishing communities, coastal, 4
Focus groups, 251
Follow-up: to duplicates list, 173, 176; to inquiries, 144, 146–147; one-on-one requests and, 150; to publications and communications, 104–105; to renewal letters, 60–61; to renewal phone contact, 66. *See also* Response packets; Thank yous; Welcome packets
Fonts, 276
Food bank, audiences for, 119
Forslund, S., 215, 217–218
Foundation funding: BHAGs and, 221, 227; loans from, 227; for membership or capacity-building programs, 226, 227–228
Free invitations, as membership incentives, 194, 195, 196–197
Free services, as membership benefits, 44
Friends of Columbia Gorge, 173
Fundraising. *See* Membership program; Recruitment; Renewals; Upgrading
Fundraising for Social Change (Klein), 252
Fundraising for the Long Haul (Klein), 252
Fundraising letters. *See* Letters *headings*
Future generations, special appeals and, 89–90

G

Generally Accepted Accounting Principles (GAAP), 246
Geographic distribution tracking, 35
Geographic targeting, e-mail direct mail and, 127
Get-a-member campaigns, 154–159; goal setting for, 158; measuring and crediting success in, 158–159; team captains for, 155; team participants in, 155; themes for, 155, 158; timing and duration of, 155, 198; worksheet for, 156–157
Gifts. *See* Donation *headings*
Giller, C., 202
Giving: by Americans, 118; by members versus other sources, 5; tracking membership characteristics and, 33–40. *See also* Donation *headings*
Giving history files, 264
Giving USA, 5, 118, 253
Goal setting: for get-a-member campaigns, 158; for membership plan, 220–221, 222–223; worksheet for, 222–223
Goals: big hairy audacious, 220–221; membership programs linked to, 42, 220; of publications, 104; realistic, 10; techniques versus, 24–25
Goods and services: as premiums, 43–44, 69; tax-deductibility and, 44, 45, 74. *See also* Premiums
Government officials, as membership prospects, 122–123
Grace period, to renew membership, 33, 45, 53–54
Grants, capacity-building, 226
Graphic design and layout, 106; of direct mail recruitment letter, 168–169, 170; of letters, 273–274, 275, 276
Grassroots Fundraising Journal, 40, 253
Grassroots organization, direct mail campaign of, 184–186
Greater Yellowstone Coalition, 109, 278

Trout, J., 250
Trust: direct mail and, 169; one-on-one recruitment and building on, 131, 149; renewal policies and, 61
27, Rule of. *See* Rule of 27
Typeface, for direct mail letters, 170, 276

U

UNICEF approach, 91
Unified Registration Statement (URS), 245–246, 254
Unique appeal designators, 265–266
United States: legal and regulatory issues in, 243–246; members versus donors in, 4; weaponry expenditures of, 25
United States Zip Code Atlas, 122, 250
United Way, 129
Unrestricted revenue, fundraising for, 96–97
Upgrading, of membership/donation level: with bequests, 213, 215, 216; with monthly giving program, 211–213; with renewals, 66–68
Urgency: explaining, in direct mail recruitment letters, 169; explaining, in one-on-one asks, 153; perceived, in prospects, 11
U.S. Census, 41
U.S. Census data, 122, 250
U.S. Fish and Wildlife Service, 25
U.S. Geological Survey, 25

V

Validation, members as source of, 5
Values, common, 10
"Viral" mail, 202–203
Visual images, 273
Voicemail, recruitment with, 143
Volunteers: for database system creation, 40; estimating staffing needs and, 221, 226; for hand-addressing envelopes, 129; inviting new members to become, 76; for lapsed-member phone-a-thon, 65–66; membership of, 5, 31–32, 45; for membership survey phone-a-thon, 19; recruitment by, 132
Voting power, 4

W

Walczak-Lohman, T., 46
Warwick, M., 252, 253
Washington Conservation Voters, 173
Washington Toxics Coalition, 27, 280
Web site, Jossey-Bass, blank worksheets on, 14
Web site, organizational: collecting and responding to e-inquiries from, 136–138; "join now" and "donate now" buttons on, 170, 207; recruitment with, 125, 136–138, 170, 198, 201, 207; searchable location for, 137; tips for, 207
Web-based surveys, 18–19
Welcome packets, 75–77; features to include in, 76–77; new-member recruitment and, 117; opt-out option in, 31; for prospects, 31, 45; remit envelopes in, 111; for renewals and new members, 75–77. *See also* Recruitment packages; Response packets; Thank yous
Western Colorado Congress, 195
Wilder Nonprofit Field Guide to Conducting Successful Focus Groups, The (Simon), 251
Wilderness protection organization, audiences for, 119
Wilderness Watch, 129, 280
Wisconsin's Environmental Decade (now Clean Wisconsin): contact information for, 280; remit envelope, 111–112
Wish Angels program, Make-A-Wish Foundation of Canada, 213, 214
Workplace, reaching people at home versus, 127–128, 200
www.nonprofits.org, 245, 254

Y

Yahoo, 203
Year-end giving: for operations, 96–97; power of, 94; renewals combined with, 61
Year-end special appeals, 91, 92–93, 94
Year of distribution, source codes for, 266–267
Years, membership, 51–52

Z

Zoomerang, 251

RESOURCES FOR SOCIAL CHANGE
AVAILABLE FROM JOSSEY-BASS AND CHARDON PRESS

Raise More Money
The Best of the Grassroots Fundraising Journal

Kim Klein and Stephanie Roth, Editors

"When I want to know the answer to a fundraising question, or a way to motivate and teach others, I go to some of the best fundraisers in the business—whose writing appears in this amazing collection of articles from the *Grassroots Fundraising Journal*."

—*Joan Garner, Southern Partners Fund*

Whether you are a new or seasoned fundraiser, this collection of the best articles from the *Grassroots Fundraising Journal* will provide you with new inspiration to help bring in more money for your organization. Filled with strategies and guidance, this unprecedented anthology shows you how small nonprofits can raise money from their communities and develop long-term financial stability.

Paperback $29.00   ISBN: 0-7879-6175-2

Fundraising for the Long Haul
New Companion to Fundraising for Social Change

Kim Klein

In this companion to her classic, *Fundraising for Social Change*, Kim Klein distills her 25 years of experience and wisdom to provide practical guidance for sustaining a long-term commitment to social change for organizations that are understaffed and under-resourced.

Paperback $21.00   ISBN: 0-7879-6173-6

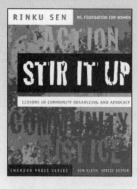

Stir It Up
Lessons in Community Organizing and Advocacy

Rinku Sen
Sponsored by the *Ms.* Foundation for Women

If social change organizations—local, regional and national—are to succeed, they must go beyond traditional grassroots organizing efforts and develop systematic, comprehensive organizing practices that will change public policy and practice.

Stir It Up, written by renowned activist and trainer Rinku Sen, identifies the key priorities and strategies that can help advance the mission of any social change group. This groundbreaking book addresses the unique challenges and opportunities the new global economy poses for activist groups and provides concrete guidance for community organizations of all orientations.

Paperback $25.00   ISBN: 0-7879-6533-2

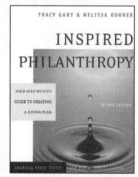

Inspired Philanthropy
Your Step-by-Step Guide to Creating a Giving Plan

SECOND EDITION

Tracy Gary and Melissa Kohner

If you want to change the world, you'll want to read *Inspired Philanthropy*. No matter how much or little you have to give, you'll learn how to create a giving plan that will make your charitable giving catalytic and align your giving with your deepest values—to help bring about the very changes you want.

Paperback $24.95   ISBN: 0-7879-6410-7

TO ORDER, CALL (800) 956-7739 OR VISIT US AT
www.josseybass.com/go/chardonpress

RESOURCES FOR SOCIAL CHANGE

AVAILABLE FROM JOSSEY-BASS AND CHARDON PRESS

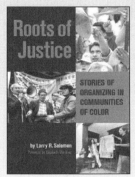

Roots of Justice
*Stories of Organizing
in Communities of Color*

Larry R. Salomon

Recaptures some of the nearly forgotten histories of communities of color. These are the stories of people who fought back against exploitation and injustice—and won. *Roots of Justice* shows how ordinary people have made extraordinary contributions to change society.

Paperback $17.00   ISBN: 0-7879-6178-7

Making Policy, Making Change
*How Communities
Are Taking Law
into Their Own Hands*

Makani N. Themba

"A much-needed life jacket for those committed to progressive social change. In a straightforward, full-blast recitation from one who knows, Makani Themba weaves powerful stories of grassroots struggles to shape and construct policy. This book is a requiem for apathy and inaction."

—*Clarence Lusane, assistant professor,
School of International Service, American University*

Paperback $20.00   ISBN: 0-7879-6179-5

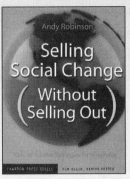

Selling Social Change (Without Selling Out)
*Earned Income Strategies
for Nonprofits*

Andy Robinson

In *Selling Social Change (Without Selling Out)*, expert fundraising trainer and consultant Andy Robinson shows nonprofit professionals how to initiate and sustain successful earned income ventures that provide financial security and advance an organization's mission. Step by step, this invaluable resource shows how to organize a team, select a venture, draft a business plan, find start-up funding, and successfully market goods and services. Robinson includes critical information on the tax implications of earned income and the pros and cons of corporate partnerships. The book also addresses when to consider outsourcing, collaborating with competitors, and raising additional funds to expand the business.

Grounded in the world of grassroots nonprofit experience, *Selling Social Change (Without Selling Out)* profiles two dozen organizations that use commerce to become more financially secure—and stay true to their fundamental values along the way.

Paperback $25.95   ISBN: 0-7879-6216-3

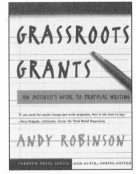

Grassroots Grants
*An Activist's Guide
to Proposal Writing*

FIRST EDITION

Andy Robinson

Andy Robinson describes just what it takes to win grants, including how grants fit into your complete fundraising program, using your grant proposal as an organizing plan, designing fundable projects, building your proposal piece by piece, and more.

Paperback $27.00   ISBN: 0-7879-6177-9

TO ORDER, CALL (800) 956-7739 OR VISIT US AT
www.josseybass.com/go/chardonpress